The Developing British Political Syste

The Developing
British Political System:
The 1990s

Edited by Ian Budge and David McKay.

third edition

 LONGMAN

London and New York

Addison Wesley Longman Limited,
Edinburgh Gate, Harlow
Essex CM20 2JE, England
and Associated Companies throughout the world.

Published in the United States of America
by Addison Wesley Longman Publishing, New York

First published 1983
Revised edition 1985
Second edition 1988
Third edition 1993
Third impression 1996

ISBN 582 090970 PPR

British Library Cataloguing-in-Publication Data
A catalogue record for this book is available from the British Library

Library of Congress Cataloging-in-Publication Data
Budge, Ian
    The developing British political system : the 1990s / Ian Budge,
David McKay.
    p.   cm.
Rev. ed. of: The Changing British political system.
    Includes bibliographical references and index.
    ISBN 0–582–09097–0
    1. Great Britain—Politics and government—20th century.   2. Great
Britain—Economic policy.   I. McKay, David H.   II. Changing British
political system.   III. Title.
JN231.B78   1993   92–34539
320.941—dc20   CIP

Set in 10/12pt Lintron Baskerville
Produced through Longman Malaysia, TCP

Contents

List of figures and tables

Preface

When we looked at our first attempt to explain contemporary British politics written in 1982 with the experience of the Callaghan and first Thatcher governments in mind, we were pleased to find so many forecasts confirmed and interpretations still valid in 1987. Political fragmentation remained the central problem for Conservatives in the late 1980s as the government tried, with mixed success, to reform the economy and impose itself on local authorities.

By late 1992, implementation problems had, if anything, become more intractable. British membership of the European Community Exchange Rate Mechanism (ERM) had limited the government's freedom to manage the economy; eventually Britain was forced to leave the ERM, thus putting the government's anti-inflationary strategy at risk; recession was once again putting pressure on public spending; and the replacement for the poll tax, the council tax, was under fire for being unfair and inefficient. At the same time the formal constitutional arrange-ments that characterize British politics – Cabinet government, party discipline in a two party system, unitary government – have changed remarkably little.

Where events have overtaken us, we have totally re-written the relevant chapters of this volume. In these areas the third edition provides an original new treatment, very up-to-the-minute in its assessment of events and personalities. Where there are continuities, or where our interpretations and forecasts have anticipated, rather than been displaced by, events, we have carefully weighed and updated what was written before. In general, we have aimed to provide a rounded assessment of the Thatcher administrations of the 1980s and an early assessment of the Major administration of the 1990s.

What we aim to provide, therefore, is a complete, new, analysis of British politics, firmly based on the experience of the last fifteen years. Where it carries on from the second edition is in its treatment of the underlying social continuities and national and international constraints on government action; above all the fragmentation of British politics and society, and the decline of the economic base.

Introduction

British society and culture have changed fundamentally since 1945. The traditional forms of social life – family, church, neighbourhood – have all lost in authority and membership while individuals – many also in previously subordinated sectors like women and youth – have gained in autonomy and independence. Inner cities have declined and the suburbs and smaller towns have grown. The economic base has changed as services have grown and manufacturing industry has declined with the centre of gravity shifting ever more firmly to London and the South-East. Both business and trade unions felt themselves increasingly under siege from national and international pressures. One can still trace the social contours of early post war Britain in the contemporary scene but it is like trying to find a buried landscape after a volcanic eruption: the whole pattern has shifted.

In sharp contrast, political institutions and practices have changed very little. Labour and Conservatives still vie for sole control of government as they have since the 1930s. Government itself still rests on control of the party majority in the House of Commons. The bureaucracy operates through a structure of autonomous Ministries and Departments which was set up, in its essentials, in the mid-nineteenth century. The Cabinet is still the major co-ordinator of government activities as it was when Bagehot first described it in 1867. Government and higher administration remain remarkably centralized with all the important decisions being taken in London. The structure of courts and police also rests on nineteenth century blueprints, while the law they administer goes back even further.

The major new institution of post-war Britain is the welfare state, a complex of boards, local authorities and hospitals delivering health-care and social support for most of the population. In its main forms this dates back to 1948, and essentially derives from ideas put forward in the 1930s. So it antedates rather than accommodates post-war social upheavals.

This lack of 'fit' between political institutions and modern changes has been viewed in two ways, depending on the national mood. Particularly in the earlier post-war period, political continuity represented a welcome element of stability in an uncertain world. It was felt that the traditional institutions had shown their strength in directing the national effort during the war, and in confronting the economic and foreign crises of the late 1940s. More recently, as unease developed about Britain's diminished position in the world, traditional political institutions and the attitudes they represent have been seen as obstacles in the way of progress, particularly economic growth. It is no coincidence that tinkering with political institutions began in the 1960s and has been continued by every government since. Perhaps the most surprising aspect of all this activity, often hailed as a major breakthrough in its time, is its negligible effect. In the early 1990s we have, with the partial exception of local government, much the same set of political institutions as before, operating in substantially the same way as they did seventy years ago.

Why is this? One explanation which we document in more detail in Chapter 1 is that the traditional structures are themselves highly resistant to change. Thus when a new Department of Economic Affairs with responsibility for a national economic plan was set up in the 1960s, it was defeated and later suppressed by the Treasury which traditionally had oversight of the area and which opposed new forms of planning.

Another explanation is that institutions set up by one party in government have often been abolished by another, which saw them as a threat. Thus the Industrial Relations Court set up by the Conservatives in 1971 was abolished by the succeeding Labour government under pressure from the trades unions. Similarly the National Enterprise Board set up by Labour governments was transformed and then formally terminated under Mrs Thatcher.

One disincentive for all governments in changing political arrangements is that they have gained power under them and may depend on them for their survival. The electoral system, for example, whereby constituency MPs can be elected if they get slightly more votes than any one of their opponents guarantees the two largest national parties, Conservative and Labour, a near monopoly on Parliamentary seats and thus the unique chance to form single-party governments with a Parliamentary majority. It is unlikely that either of these parties would of their own accord change the electoral system which produces such convenient results from their point of view. But this in turn stabilizes the traditional features of Parliamentary Cabinet government, organized through Ministries and based on alternating party majorities which is basically the same as that produced by the Second Reform Act of 1867–8.

It is against this background that the much discussed Thatcherite 'revolution' of the 1980s should be viewed. In historical perspective, it was an unusually concentrated and determined attempt to pull together and utilize all the powers of central government within the traditional framework. Far from trying to alter that framework – a single party majority dominating Parliament and supporting a Cabinet operating through the Civil Service – Thatcherism aimed at strengthening it by getting rid of institutions and influences thought to have diffused its power or challenged its authority. Consultation with unions, business and other bodies outside government was dispensed with. Challengers of governmental authority such as unions and local government were restricted by new legislation or abolished outright. Even innovations within central government, such as the Central Policy Review Staff set up to focus and co-ordinate its activities, fell victim to the Thatcherite purge as they did not form part of the traditional structure.

If the essence of Thatcherism was a re-assertion of the traditional institutions and forms of central government, what made it appear so radical to contemporaries? The answer lies in three of its aspects:

1. It was imposing a process of industrial and social change called forth to combat what was seen as British decline – not only economic decline but even more centrally moral and social decline. While the remedies were presented as a return to Victorian values – the free market, individual initiative, self-reliance and self-help – they involved quite radical reversals of post-war policies – nationalization and local government autonomy to name but two. The radical aura of these changes rubbed off on the institutional mechanisms used to implement them, even if these were quite traditional in form.
2. The implementation of these policies involved the government in conflict with many social and political groups, which was again a sharp contrast with the previous practice of consulting them – if not incorporating them into decision-making procedures.
3. To carry through the process of Thatcherite regeneration, the traditional powers of government were utilized to an almost unprecedented extent. There was nothing new in governments co-ordinating police activities, nor in using the Official Secrets Act to stop embarrassing leaks, nor in the prime minister favouring her faction in party and Cabinet, nor in using a largely supportive press to smear or undermine political opponents. What was unusual was the use of these all together over an unusually long period of eleven years, to support an exceptionally active – indeed frenetic – prime minister.

During the 1980s it seemed as if the whole of government was being re-made in a new, authoritarian, centralized mode. Mrs Thatcher's fall in December 1990 showed very clearly, however, that little had really changed in the functioning of party government in Britain.

She lost power essentially because most Conservative MPs thought they could not win the next election under her leadership. With hindsight her unchallenged predominance during the 1980s rested on her ability to win three elections in a row, helped by a relatively sustained economic upturn and the weakness of the Labour party. More spectacular political developments only masked this underlying electoral reality.

Mrs Thatcher, then, was no more nor less secure in the exercise of power than any of her predecessors. She had chosen to impart a more personal and confrontational style to politics than they had, but essentially she relied on the same political machinery and the same political support.

However, the demise of Mrs Thatcher did not signal a simple return to the *status quo ante*. Under her guidance subtle changes in the nature of policy-making in Britain did occur. To understand these fully it is necessary to go back to our previous discussion of the dynamics of British politics. Behind the facade of a highly centralized and authoritative state, unhampered by constitutional restrictions or the balance of powers, the real weakness of British governments lies in problems associated with implementing policies. It is little use getting legislation passed or policy approved by an acquiescent Parliamentary majority if it arouses the opposition of powerful social forces and cannot be applied. The Thatcher government enjoyed some highly spectacular successes over trade unions, the most obvious of the veto groups in regard to previous governments. However this was as much attributable to a temporary upsurge in export surpluses due to oil revenues, and high unemployment which put union membership at risk, as to government policies. It also engaged in running battles with opposition-controlled local governments, whose powers it curtailed and which in some cases (notably the Greater London Council and the Metropolitan Counties) it abolished.

These famous victories reinforced the image of a determined, centralizing, all-powerful government but they only aggravated its main problem. That is, as British governments do not control a local administrative apparatus of their own, they are highly dependent on other bodies for the success of direct administrative interventions in society. Above all, they need support from local government. After a decade of attacks on local government in general and on the bigger authorities in particular, they could expect only grudging compliance or overt resistance to administrative orders. Similarly, policies to change the content and style of education, or of medical care, were strongly opposed by the very teachers and doctors needed to carry through the changes – who felt betrayed and disparaged by policies imposed without consultation and often in the teeth of professional opposition.

Thatcherite social reforms of the 1980s were thus put into practice in a very piecemeal fashion. They did have the effect however of alarming the groups concerned to a degree far beyond their actual impact. Coupled with the unusual activism and personal prominence of Mrs Thatcher and the abrasive and centralizing rhetoric of her supporters, this resulted in a strong counter-reaction to her policies and even movements for major constitutional change supported by Liberals and (ambiguously) by Labour, such as Charter '88 and the Scottish Constitutional Convention.

Had the 1992 election resulted in a hung Parliament, changes in the electoral system and constitution, and in relations between the centre and regions would almost certainly have followed. The post-Thatcherite Cabinet of John Major was determined to resist any changes which threatened Conservative pre-eminence and central power. However, it still had the problem of coping with the resistance of local governments, teachers, doctors and others in areas where it wished to limit expenditure and change the content of existing policies.

Increasingly, therefore, post-Thatcher Conservatives have turned to structural change in these areas. Instead of the forceful administrative intervention which caused Thatcherism to be characterized as 'Free Market, Strong State', they have relied instead on reducing the internal cohesion of opposing groups by imposing on them, through legislation, privatization in some areas and an 'internal market' in others. Thus, instead of having a unified centrally or regionally planned health service, the various groupings within it are to be divided between purchasers of services (family doctors, area health boards) and suppliers of services (mainly hospitals). Similar changes are being introduced into education and local councils. Inside a local authority the central departments will be buyers of services while others will be suppliers in contractual relationships with them. With the 'hiving off' of various agencies of central government, an 'internal market' will also introduce business practices into the national bureaucracy.

The difference between Conservative policies of the 1980s and those of the 1990s, between classical Thatcherism and 'post-Thatcherism', lies between the Thatcher government's direct administrative interventions in society, and the Major government's indirect legislative means of enforcing free market policies. While the latter was foreshadowed by the denationalization of industry (privatization) in the 1980s it has really reached its full flowering in the 1990s.

Despite an absence of change in the central institutions of government, therefore, a major transformation is under way in the social services and local government. Such changes have reinforced the traditional aloofness of central government from other societal and economic bodies and make it even more difficult than it used to be for it to plan or co-ordinate policies.

This last point relates to the theme of this volume: the increasingly uneasy combination of a highly centralized, unitary constitutional structure and an essentially fragmented system of policy implementation. As later chapters will show, policy fragmentation persists in spite of the centralizing trends of the 1980s. Indeed, as suggested above, recent attempts to privatize and create internal markets are an acknowledgement and even acceptance that governments' powers are limited. Of course this is true in any democratic political system. But there is reason to believe that the particular pattern of state intervention that has characterized British politics over the last sixty years is unusual compared with the pattern typical of other countries. It may well be, indeed, that the pressures for change coming from European integration, Scottish, Welsh and Irish nationalism, disadvantaged groups and regions, and increasingly assertive and independent voters and consumers cannot be accommodated within the existing constitutional and institutional structure. This is a theme we will return to in our concluding chapter.

The chapters to come

These pressures for change are reflected in the new title of our book, and also shape its presentation and content. They prevent us from concentrating on the major features of current institutions in the confidence that they will remain largely as they are. Such a description would not be applicable long. What we provide instead is a self-contained and comprehensive account of contemporary British politics and of their relations with economy and society, which is as up-to-date as possible while identifying the tendencies likely to alter the present situation quite radically. We have deliberately covered important policy developments and emphasized neglected institutions such as the European Community, legal system and the police, which hardly figure at all in traditional accounts. But their importance and influence have increased markedly in the last decade, will increase further and are bound to alter the established balance.

Politics in post-war Britain are being profoundly influenced by the social and economic developments we have sketched. Chapter 1 starts, therefore, with the major economic challenges which have faced governments over the last sixty years, and their various attempts to meet them (authored by David McKay). In explaining the relative failure of these, Graham Wilson considers the internal dynamics of government and the civil service, and their relationships with societal groups, in Chapter 2. Anthony King addresses the highly topical question of cabinet coordination versus prime ministerial dominance in Chapter 3 and Melvyn Read analyses the place of Parliament in Chapter 4. Chapter 5, authored by Ivor Crewe, is devoted to the role of political parties and the crucial questions of what electors want and how they relate this to voting decisions in favour of one political party or another. This involves some consideration of political communications and the role of the media – issues examined by Kenneth Newton in Chapter 6.

Of course, central government is not the only elected authority – even less the only administrative authority – in Britain. There exists an incredibly diverse range of local and regional governments active both in servicing their constituents and in opposing central government and which Vivien Lowndes describes in Chapter 7. Another important question in the debate on government is how far Conservative attempts to impose central authority on the localities have succeeded in permanently changing relationships. European bodies also exercise authority in Britain by virtue of various treaties – most importantly those setting up the European Community. Community institutions increasingly affect life in Britain and Emil Kirchner examines their activities in Chapter 9. Both supporters and opponents of central governments have had increasing recourse to the courts, which are in many cases the only bodies left to make even interim decisions, as political disputes become more difficult to resolve. David Robertson examines their expanding powers in Chapter 8. The Conservative governments of the 1980s, faced with trade union resistance and urban disorder, placed unusual reliance on the police to ensure social and political control. As protest became more common in response to economic and social hardship, the role of police and military assumed greater significance. Usually ignored because of the traditional law-abidingness of the population, the question of the internal use of coercive forces is considered in Chapter 9. As Britain becomes increasingly enmeshed in the North Atlantic and European alliances, her international role impinges more heavily on domestic politics. In Chapter 10 David Sanders summarizes the background to this debate and presents the foreign and defence options now available. In Chapter 11 Ian Budge and David McKay draw together our conclusions on the nature of British policy-making and its prospects for overcoming current economic and social problems (which are intimately related to the ways it can adapt and change). We end with a brief assessment of the features which distinguish the new politics of the 1990s; and of the major changes which are likely to occur in this decade. In particular, are the problems of fragmentation and implementation, which we have commented on above and constantly re-emphasized in the earlier editions of this book, likely to be overcome? Or are the new trends to decentralization and institutional change likely to intensify them further? Is there any mechanism by which effective central decision-making can be combined with greater respect for the rights of individuals and minority groups?

Each chapter is based on the intimate knowledge of a specialist in his field. Yet the book is more than just a collection of separate specialist essays – it is a coherent analysis of British politics as a whole. This is due to the authors' daily association in the Department of Government at the University of Essex and their constant discussion of the problems covered in the book. As a result, the overall themes have been considered as a whole, and each chapter closely related both to the general analysis and to the other chapters. The result is an account which combines authoritative, detailed treatment of each topic with a clear overview of general developments. We hope that this avoids the weaknesses, and combines the strengths, of single-author treatments on the one hand, and collections of specialized papers on the other. If it does, this is due to the congenial atmosphere of the Essex Department, and the frequent opportunities it provides for the meeting of like (and sometimes unlike!) minds.

Obviously, the book draws on a vast range of discussions and analyses of British politics. The use we make of them is our own and we retain responsibility for any errors of interpretation or fact. Bearing in mind the need for a free-running and uncluttered discussion, we have forborne the use of footnotes and references except where discussion has relied exclusively on one source for a particular area or where sources for detailed figures are being cited. The references and bibliography list major references and make suggestions for further reading.

Chapter 1

Economic difficulties and government response 1931–1993
David McKay

We have commented on the relative absence of change in constitutional and institutional arrangements in the face of the major social transformations which have marked the post-war years. This is largely due to the fact that the two main political parties benefit from the arrangements and thus see little need to change them. They have preferred therefore to concentrate political debate and controversy not on the mechanisms of government but on the question of how far it should intervene in national life. The reforming Labour governments which largely shaped the post-war political settlement (1945–51) formulated policies of social welfare, state takeover of central industries, and land use planning, which made government at national and local level an important participant in practically every social and economic area. Although most governments up to the Thatcher administration of the 1980s accepted the broad 'social democratic consensus' dating from that period, debate raged about how far state intervention should be extended or 'pushed back' at the margin. Conservatives took the view that it should be more restricted while Labour saw the answer to social and economic problems as rendering government planning more effective.

The question of intervention gained urgency after 1960 from the fact that Britain seemed to be doing less well economically than her main international competitors – France, West Germany, Italy and, more recently, Japan. From 1960 politicians' conviction that Britain was in decline inspired them to justify their pet projects in terms of reversing this perceived trend. Labour has consistently seen a solution in more government-directed investment and planning, to ensure a rational use of resources. Increasingly, Conservatives have seen the answer in 'rolling back the state' (through denationalizing or 'privatizing' state-owned industry for example) and restoring competition and incentives through a freer market.

This chapter discusses how these positions have developed over the post-war period and how effective the various economic strategies based upon them have been in solving or exacerbating British economic problems. For a full picture we have to go back to the origins of contemporary intervention in the 1930s and during the Second World War.

British politics and government intervention 1931–93

1931–45: the rise of intervention

Contrary to usual belief, central economic management became firmly established not during the Second World War but following the world crisis of 1931. World economic dislocation exposed the weakness of the major established British industries such as steel-making, coal-mining, shipbuilding and textile manufacture; radically increased the number of unemployed to a quarter or a third of the workforce in many regions; and forced the abandonment of the Gold Standard, i.e. the link between the value of the pound and the price of gold, symbolic of the unquestioned integrity and value of the currency.

Governments of the ensuing eight years reacted to these alarming developments with a new economic strategy. Although this fell short of modern economic planning it did represent a fundamental break from the essentially liberal traditions which had dominated policies until then. The new policy was inspired by the need to protect British industry and agriculture from foreign competition. To achieve this it was necessary both to raise tariffs on imports and to encourage the reconstruction of ailing industries. A contemporary comment on the introduction of the Import Duties Bill shows how interventionist the new policy was:

[The Bill] does provide us with such a lever as has never been possessed before by any government for inducing, or if you like, forcing industry to set its house in order. I have in my mind particularly iron and steel and cotton; and my belief in the advantages of protection is not so fanatical as to close my eyes to the vital importance of a thorough reorganisation of such industries as these, if they are even to keep their heads above water in the future. (Beer, 1965, 293)

During the 1930s the government encouraged reorganization in the basic industries (mainly through the creation of private cartels), provided central marketing schemes for agricultural products (the Marketing Boards) and began a policy of regional revival (via the Special Areas Acts of 1935, 1936 and 1937). The government also pursued a low interest rate policy of monetary expansionism – although the motivations here were probably as much a desire to reduce the national debt as to fuel economic growth. However, it would be misleading to characterize the National Government as benevolent either in relation to industrial recovery or social policy. By modern standards it was neither, and on the social side cut welfare and unemployment benefits and applied means tests. But the protection of industry from foreign competition combined with reorganization was a radical change. There was no indicative planning in the sense of pointing the general direction in which economic and social change should go, and administrative innovations were few and far between (the Marketing Boards being the main exception). But a regulative framework for unsystematic, special-purpose developments was laid down, and for the first time applied to industrial protection.

Towards the end of the decade, support for more comprehensive regulation and planning was mounting steadily and manifested itself in a number of policy areas. In land use, the government legislated to control the urban sprawl which was occurring in the still prosperous Midlands and South-East. More significantly, it set up the Barlow Commission on the Distribution of the Industrial Population which in 1940 recommended a two-pronged attack on the twin problems of regional unemployment and the continuing sprawl caused by rapid population drift to London and the Midlands. Growth in the prosperous cities should be contained with rigid controls on industrial location, while industry should be given incentives to locate in the distressed North and West. These were radical proposals indeed, and clearly demanded some central co-ordinating authority if they were to be effectively implemented.

Between 1937 and 1942 a number of other commissions were initiated to provide recommendations on new towns (Reith Report), land values (Uthwatt Report), land utilization in rural areas and national parks (Dower and Hobhouse Reports) and social security (Beveridge Report). Many of the commissions were concerned with the physical environment – reflecting the growing influence of the town planning lobby during the 1930s. Beveridge was given a very wide brief – all income maintenance (unemployment benefit, pensions, national assistance), welfare services and health – as was Barlow. But it is notable that no commission on the reorganization of industry or industrial relations was created.

We can sum up the growth of state intervention in the 1930s in terms of two major developments. First, an acceptance by the government of a role in regulating industrial and agricultural production, and second the beginnings of a planning movement with some recognition that the problems of society and the economy could be solved only through increased government action.

There is no doubt that these changes came about in response to the near collapse of international capitalism in the 1930s. But, crucially, recovery was seen in terms of reviving old industries (iron and steel, mining, textiles, shipbuilding) and regions which were assumed to be victims of international forces. Little thought was devoted to the restructuring of industry or to channelling investment into high-productivity, high-growth industries. Physical planning apart, the enhanced state role was perceived solely in terms of how to help declining traditional industries and, in embryo form at least, how to ameliorate the social evils of industrial decline. Within the Labour party the same issues dominated, although the Draconian solutions of government ownership and control of industry were adopted, together with state support of comprehensive welfare and health services.

Between 1936 and 1945 attitudes towards state intervention among political leaders and public alike were transformed by two events – the acceptance of Keynesian economics and the near total modification of the economy during the Second World War. The monetarist orthodoxy accepted by the National

Governments of the 1930s held that industrial development could only take place if there were general confidence in the currency, maintained by government budgets in which revenues equalled or surpassed expenditures. Keynes showed that the economy could function for long periods well below the level it might potentially attain with full use of available resources. Since one under-used resource was labour, this implied long-term unemployment for large sections of the workforce.

Governments could, however, raise the equilibrium to nearly full capacity by increasing government expenditure and therefore stimulating demand.

The war seemed to confirm the validity of this assumption. Massively increased expenditure on armaments started during the late 1930s; by June 1943 only 60,000 people were registered as unemployed. By 1945 few political leaders disputed the need for at least partial acceptance of Keynesian demand management. The war also gave planning an enormous boost, both in theory and practice. Prices, incomes, industrial relations and production were all strictly controlled by central committees. Not before or since has the British economy been so rigidly disciplined.

Being both authoritarian and comprehensive, wartime controls were always seen by civil servants and many politicians as temporary – a fact reflected by the *ad hoc* nature of the administrative reforms of the period. The old pre-war ministries remained intact, ready to resume their traditional roles once hostilities ceased. Labour politicians were much less antipathetic to controls. But as the post-war period was to confirm, even they were highly ambivalent about centralized planning of the positive variety (where the state took all important economic decisions leaving only a residual role to the market).

The Keynesian revolution and the war destroyed for ever the minimal state spending policies of the previous eras. Towards the war's end the major earlier reports plus further White Papers on employment and education laid foundations for greatly increased state spending in society and economy. This accepted, state planning through a central planning agency was rejected by the Conservatives and had won little sympathy among Labour politicians. Moreover, neither party had devoted much intellectual energy to the question of industrial reorganization and planned industrial investment. The emphasis was on *production* rather than on *productivity*; increasing total output, irrespective of how efficiently this was achieved, was the primary concern.

1945–51: Labour and the new order

The Labour government elected in 1945 passed a remarkable volume of legislation. Basic industries were nationalized, the welfare state created, regional policy strengthened dramatically and physical planning by local authorities established as mandatory. All of these policies remained until the 1980s – indeed they still constitute the core of state intervention in British society. Only recently have Conservative governments challenged the framework through privatization, the dramatic scaling down of regional policy, and the creation of 'internal markets' in education and health.

Post-war policy was dominated by a driving desire to maintain full employment. Keynesian demand management, nationalization and regional policy were either primarily or partly designed to achieve this, and in combination with a generally favourable international trading position after 1945, succeeded until 1951. Industry re-adapted to peacetime conditions quite efficiently and Britain's share of world trade actually increased during these years.

If full employment and industrial recovery were achieved quickly, little progress was made in the field of industrial organization. Various wartime reports had, in fact, pleaded for a close co-ordination of industrial location and industrial policy (Barlow) and for full blown positive economic planning (Beveridge, 1944, in his 'unofficial' report on employment). Neither were to transpire, however, in part because of opposition from established bureaucracies – and in particular the Treasury – to a new central planning agency. (There was even opposition to calling the new Ministry of Town and Country Planning just plain 'Planning' for fear it might assume a more comprehensive planning role.)

But probably more important was the absence of a coherent policy towards industrial policy within the Labour government. In the first year after the war there was much talk about the need for a national plan plus all the administrative machinery necessary to implement it, but instead the government opted to retain the wartime planning machinery. The 1947 fuel crisis came as a rude shock to the new government, bringing severe shortages of coal and other raw materials. In response, the government created a Central Economic Planning Staff (CEPS) who would implement an annual Economic Survey or short-term plan for manpower resources and economic growth.

Under the guidance of Stafford Cripps a limited and short-term form of planning actually prevailed during 1947 and 1948. Some re-assertion of direct control over labour and an effective wage freeze were part of the strategy, as was voluntary price restraint by manufacturers. From late 1948 onwards, however, enthusiasm for planning slowly declined and was effectively abandoned by the Labour government by 1950. Reasons for its demise are varied. The unions objected to wage restraint and the new austerity of 1946–8 was electorally unpopular. Perhaps more important, the administrative innovations were never more than *ad hoc* in nature. Existing departments continued much as before, the Economic Surveys were for one year only, and opposition to yet more controls and planning from within the Cabinet was mounting. Moreover, state intervention to help industrial policy was always framed in terms of centralized *planning* which, not surprisingly in the context of the wartime experience, attracted considerable opposition. More creative and less *dirigiste* means of improving economic performance were not on the agenda.

But we should be wary of underestimating the scope of Labour's efforts during these years. In social policy a comprehensive welfare system had been created providing free health care and secondary education, public housing, and a wide range of income maintenance payments for the disadvantaged. Similarly, in land use planning a comprehensive approach had been adopted –

although there was a notable failure to co-ordinate physical with economic planning. In the economic area, indeed, Labour's efforts depended more on improvisation and persuasion than on radical reforms.

> Labour leaders quite failed to see the possibilities of using the new public sector as a way of steering the whole economy in the direction they desired. They behaved as if, while carrying through their plans for nationalisation, they had no understanding of the real meaning of what they had done. Ownership changed; power did not. It had long since ceased to be true, if indeed it ever was, that the shareholders in industries like the mines and railways exercised any real power over them. (Leruez, 1975, 76)

And in economic affairs, nationalization was the only legacy left by Labour to successive governments. Keynesian demand management had already been accepted by the late 1930s, and was continued through to the late 1970s. When the Conservatives came to power in 1951, the basic relationships between government and unions and government and industry were almost unchanged from the pre-war years. The unions played no integrated role in economic or industrial policy and although big business was quite happy to accept a regulative government role – especially in foreign trade – they too were largely excluded from central economic policy-making. Administrative changes were largely confined to the creation of new bureaucracies to implement the programmes of a burgeoning welfare state. So while the public sector had expanded enormously, the basic tools available to governments to guide and control the public sector changed very little.

1951–64: the Conservatives and the state

the Conservatives fought the 1951 election on the twin themes of preservation of the welfare state and the decontrol of the economy. Decontrol meant lower income and purchase taxes (in 1951 they remained very high); an end to rationing, especially of building and other materials; abolition of the prohibitive tax (100 per cent) on land development profits; relaxation of exchange controls; and the denationalization of certain industries (notably road transport and steel). All of these were achieved by 1959, and decontrol almost certainly contributed to the growing prosperity of the 1950s.

The Conservatives also preserved the essentials of the welfare state for which there was always great public support. Some small changes were made, mainly by tinkering with some services (notably housing and charges for health services) so as to make their free availability somewhat more selective. But the changes were small.

If the Conservatives did not dismantle the welfare state or the other (by then fairly substantial) parts of the public sector, what part did they play in controlling or guiding public intervention? To answer this we have to divide the period into two parts. Until about 1960, government intervention in industry was minimal but Keynesian demand management was continued.

After 1960 Keynesian methods were combined with incomes policy and some embryonic planning devices both to control inflation and to achieve a higher rate of economic growth. The transition from the minimalist role to something approaching indicative planning, with government stipulation of general goals and priorities was inspired by an increasing disenchantment with Britain's economic performance, which was falling behind that of West Germany and France.

Using fiscal and monetary policy to stimulate or depress economic activity in the Keynesian fashion, the government soon found itself in a vicious 'stop–go' cycle. The fundamental problem was perceived as a need to defend the value of sterling by avoiding recurring balance of payments deficits (an imbalance of imports over exports which affected confidence in sterling). As the economy expanded, so imports increased, the trade deficit widened and the Bank of England was forced to buy more pounds with its foreign currency reserves to maintain exchange rates at their declared values. With reserves falling and the deficit continuing, governments felt obliged to depress economic activity by raising taxes and restricting credit in order to reduce imports and solve the balance of payment crises. But this brought a rise in unemployment and a fall in output causing governments once more to inflate the economy and thus precipitating yet another sterling crisis.

Such 'stop–go' tactics became common between 1953 and 1970. A related problem was inflation which accelerated during 'go' periods and declined during 'stop' periods. In today's terms both the inflation and unemployment rates were very low (Table 1.1) – but, crucially, were higher than those of comparable countries. Indeed, as the decade wore on the fundamental problem with the economy was increasingly defined as a failure to achieve a rate of economic growth comparable to other major industrial countries. Measured by almost any criteria – industrial investment, productivity, gross national product *per capita* – Britain was being outstripped by other countries and in particular by Germany, Italy and France.

By the late 1950s sympathy for more state intervention in industry and the economy generally was mounting within the Conservative government. Infatuated with the French experience, Selwyn Lloyd, the Chancellor of the Exchequer and Harold Macmillan, the Prime Minister, launched a limited form of indicative planning in 1961. Their main planning device was the National Economic Development Council (NEDC or Neddy) which comprised members of government, industry and the unions and whose main function would be to identify the obstacles to faster growth and then recommend ways in which these could be removed.

In its first report, Neddy estimated that an annual growth rate of 4 per cent per annum between 1961 and 1966 was possible *if* there was a change in the relationship between government and industry, *if* public expenditure could be projected ahead accurately over the five years, and *if* prices and incomes could be held down and thus balance of payments crises avoided. There is little doubt that Neddy's recommendations in this and subsequent reports were carefully worked out. However, in spite of the fact that the government accepted the 4 per cent target, few of the recommendations were implemented

Table 1.1 Unemployment and inflation, UK 1953–92

Year	Unemployment %*	Change in retail prices†
1956	1.0	2.0
1957	1.3	3.7
1958	1.9	3.0
1959	2.0	0.6
1960	1.5	1.0
1961	1.3	3.4
1962	1.8	2.6
1963	2.2	2.1
1964	1.6	3.3
1965	1.3	4.8
1966	1.4	3.9
1967	2.2	2.5
1968	2.3	4.7
1969	2.3	5.4
1970	2.5	6.4
1971	3.3	9.4
1972	4.0	7.1
1973	3.0	9.2
1974	2.9	16.1
1975	4.3	24.2
1976	5.6	16.5
1977	6.0	15.8
1978	5.9	8.2
1979	5.0	13.4
1980	6.4	15.0
1981	9.8	12.0
1982	11.3	8.6
1983	12.4	5.3
1984	11.7	4.6
1985	11.2	5.5
1986	11.2	3.9
1987	10.3	4.2
1988	8.5	5.9
1989	7.1	8.5
1990	6.9	9.8
1991	7.7	6.9
1992 (to April)	9.5	4.3

Sources: OECD, *Economic Outlook* (various years); for 1991 and 1992, *The Economist*

Notes
* Wholly unemployed, Great Britain, excluding school-leavers and adult students.
† Twelve-monthly change in weekly rates from December of previous year.

in full. Relations with industry were to be fostered via a number of Economic Development Councils or 'Little Neddies', whose job was to improve the flow of information between a range of key industries and the government. However, as with similar experiments under Cripps in 1945, these were more talking shops dominated by industry spokesmen than genuine policy instruments designed to fix targets and then set about meeting them.

Neddy also had to compete with the Treasury – a key government department antipathetic to planning and eager to defend sterling and pursue monetary orthodoxy. To be fair, the government did go so far as to reorganize the Treasury in 1962 and create a new section on the National Economy, whose job would be to liaise with Neddy. Also, for a short period between 1962 and 1964, Neddy did constitute a real rival to the Treasury and with the Chancellor (by then Reginald Maudling) on its side, led the way towards economic expansion. What Neddy and the Chancellor were unable to do was to control prices, wages and, perhaps most importantly, public expenditure. Failure with prices and incomes was understandable given the absence of a long-term legislative framework to control either (although Selwyn Lloyd had introduced a 'pay pause' during a sterling crisis in 1961). As the economy expanded so labour became scarcer and unions were better able to bargain for higher wages and to oppose more efficient, but disruptive, work practices.

Public expenditure was viewed in a way dramatically different from today. As pointed out earlier, the growth of the welfare state and nationalization had been accompanied by remarkably few administrative reforms. The system of control over expenditure in the 1950s was largely unchanged since the mid-nineteenth century. In sum it was approved annually in the budget, never surveyed systematically and never planned more than one year ahead. With the publication of the Plowden Report in 1961 (*Control of Public Expenditure*, Cmnd 1432) and Neddy's call for five-year expenditure planning, the government at last accepted the need for expenditure surveys which eventually became regular and annual in 1969 (the Public Expenditure Survey Committee or PESC). But in the early 1960s when the prevailing view was that the government could spend its way out of trouble, very few systematic controls on expenditure existed.

In sum then, the later Tory years were characterized by a new enthusiasm for economic planning, by some quite ambitious experiments in planning, but also by a failure to institute the detailed changes needed to make planning work. On the production side, targets were of the broadest macro variety, planning within specific sectors of industry being quite primitive. Incomes, prices and expenditure were at least partly beyond the government's control. Thus, as expansion set in, so inflation and trade deficits worsened yet again.

1964–70: Labour and planning

Serious overheating of the economy together with the usual sterling crisis occurred before the 1964 General Election, so on coming to power Labour inherited a difficult economic position. As a Labour government emerging from thirteen years in opposition, Harold Wilson and his Cabinet were eager to pursue reforms in social policy (mainly in housing, pensions, education and transport) all of which were expensive; to renationalize steel (also expensive) as well as to continue the Conservative policy of rapid economic growth.

Significantly, however, Labour's ideas about how to produce growth had developed very little in opposition. Their main innovation, the creation of the Department of Economic Affairs (DEA) in 1965, was inspired by a deep mistrust of the Treasury and a perception that Neddy's role was by necessity limited because it was outside the main machinery of government. Hence the DEA was a full blown government department assigned the job of long-term economic planning, the Treasury being confined to its traditional role as short-term expenditure controller. The DEA's brief was extensive: to devise a longer-term National Plan; to revitalize industry and improve efficiency (working partly through the 'little Neddies'); to work out a prices and incomes policy; and to reorganize regional policy. As it turned out this most radical administrative change lasted just four years, and as an effective policy institution the DEA was operational for less than two.

Two major reasons for its failure can be identified. First and foremost was the accelerating rate of economic crisis from 1965 to 1967. Britain's competitive position had been deteriorating for some years; balance of payments deficits were slowly increasing; and sterling was clearly over-valued, mainly because of the need to maintain the stability of the pound as an international reserve currency. Committed to economic growth and the expansion of public services, the Labour government found it impossible to reconcile its policy objectives with economic reality. In historical perspective it is clear that a bad situation was aggravated by the government's deference to the official Treasury line of giving priority to the value of sterling. So when in 1966 a serious payments crisis and a crippling seamen's strike coincided to induce investors to sell pounds, the government opted to abandon national planning and safeguard the currency by restricting credit.

Indeed, the second reason for the DEA's demise was precisely its organizational isolation from that institution, the Treasury, responsible for providing immediate advice in crisis situations.

> The structure [of the DEA] ... was such as to reinforce the Treasury's traditional weaknesses: a low concern for growth among economic priorities, a lack of knowledge of and interest in the working of industry (including the impact on industry of fiscal and monetary policies), and an overriding concern for the defence of sterling. Thus as the balance of power within Whitehall tilted away from the DEA and towards the Treasury, the ills which Labour in Opposition had diagnosed and sought to cure became embedded deeper and deeper in the structure of government. (Shanks, 1977, 34–5)

It is crucial to understand that deflation in order to defend sterling was not the only policy option open to Harold Wilson in 1966. He could have devalued and solved the immediate crisis – an option actually taken a year later in 1967. He could have cut public expenditure, but with Keynesian economics still very much alive and a host of election commitments to honour, this was never a realistic alternative. Finally, he could have frozen prices and incomes in order to cut costs, improve industry's productivity and reduce inflation. In fact prices and incomes policy was gaining in popularity as a possible solution to the country's problems. In 1965 a new independent body, the National Board for Prices and Incomes (NBPI), had been created to investigate income and prices increases and arbitrate on their fairness. But a total wage and price freeze would have been unpopular with the unions as well as with industry and was avoided – at least for the time being.

Economic planning was effectively laid to rest after 1967. The DEA together with the institutions it fostered fell into disuse. So the Industrial Reorganization Corporation, which had been set up to provide loans to industry to speed efficiency, found it could not operate in the absence of a secure and predictable economic climate. The NBPI and an incomes policy were also effectively abandoned. Instead, under the guidance of the new Chancellor, Roy Jenkins, economic policy reverted almost to a pre-Keynesian strategy – some government expenditure was cut (mainly in defence), foreign loans repaid and taxes increased. Interestingly, the Jenkins deflation was not so damaging to employment as might have been expected (Table 1.1), largely because the 1967 devaluation did produce something of an investment boom.

Labour's six years in office were characterized by continual economic crises. The reconstruction of industry and achievement of a high growth rate eluded the government. In fact, Britain's share of world trade fell from 13.9 per cent to 10.8 per cent during these years.

In spite of this, some important reforms and election pledges were carried through. Comprehensive education was launched, and public transport and physical planning reorganized. Public expenditure also increased, notably in education, health and local government. However, in comparison with the 1945–50 period, Labour had hardly been a radical reforming government. Taxation increased dramatically from 32 per cent of gross domestic product in 1964 to 43 per cent in 1970. Moreover, the government's failure to carry through a radical programme alienated many supporters within the Labour movement. By 1970 increasingly militant trades unions were demanding more fundamental reforms and were prepared to use their bargaining muscle to extract higher wages from employers.

The 1970s: plus ça change?

If the 1960s were years of periodic economic difficulties, the 1970s were years of unremitting economic crisis. For present purposes we can divide them into five quite distinct periods, each representing a sharp change in the role of the state in economy and society.

1970–2: Conservative expansionism

The first thing the new Conservative government of Edward Heath did on coming unexpectedly to office in 1970, was to dismantle the NBPI and the Industrial Reorganization Corporation, apparently disavowing both incomes policy and a strong state role in guiding industry. The government was also intent on reforming industrial relations (primarily to render the introduction of more efficient working practices easier) by imposing a more rigid framework of law on union activity. What transpired was the 1971 Industrial Relations

Act which sought to make unions accept certain legal restrictions on their activities, notably on their right to strike, and to submit themselves to a special court. From its inception this inspired the fiercest hostility from the unions.

In the absence of an incomes policy and industrial strategy, how were inflation and payments crises to be solved? Strangely, and in spite of some reforms in the control of public expenditure, *not* by reducing expenditure. Instead, a policy of economic expansion via reduced taxation and increased public spending was followed. With no controls on incomes and expenditure, inflation took off, soaring from 6.4 per cent in 1970 to 9.4 per cent in 1971 – easily the highest figure since 1950 (Table 1.1). This situation could not last long as the rapid increases were bound to undermine the balance of payments and Britain's trading position. In a famous about-turn in November 1972, Heath announced a prices and incomes freeze.

1972–4: incomes policy and confrontation

Phase I of the Heath freeze lasted until March 1973 when under Phase II all employees were to be subject to an annual increase of £1.00 per week plus 4 per cent *per annum*. The new system was to be policed by a Pay Board, and price increases were also to be carefully controlled by a newly established Price Commission. Phase II represented a highly significant break with past Conservative principles. Machinery was created to control prices and incomes for a minimum of three years implying the acceptance of a permanent incomes policy. This indicated Conservative endorsement of a highly interventionist economic policy.

Although opposed by the unions, Phase II was generally adhered to. Not so with Phase III, however, which provoked confrontation by the unions and eventually brought down the government. In fact Phase III was really quite flexible, permitting a maximum 7 per cent increase plus extra amounts for productivity payment and working 'unsocial' hours. The miners demanded more than the norm on the grounds that they were a special case. Faced with extensive picketing not only of collieries but of power stations and other energy supplies causing hardship and short term working throughout the country, with the addition of a railway strike and public disenchantment with statutory wages policy (by October 1973 only 37 per cent of the public considered stage III fair), Heath decided to call a General Election.

The government's 'u-turn' on incomes policy in 1972 was accompanied by another *volte face* on industrial policy. In spite of the liberalism and minimal state intervention which apparently prevailed in 1970, Heath very soon began to indulge in a range of policies to aid, succour and guide industrial recovery. Bankrupt companies (Rolls-Royce, Upper Clyde Shipbuilders) were bailed out, regional incentives and development grants were strengthened, a Minister for Industrial Development was attached to the new Department of Trade and Industry, and manpower retraining organized and greatly strengthened. All this did not amount to planning in the sense of economic targets being set over a fixed time period, but it did represent a new corporatism involving close liaison between government and industry.

Finally, the government was pledged after 1972 to cut public expenditure. However, by 1973 the pressures to increase expenditure (partly to compensate for the effects of incomes policy) were mounting and when they left office, the Conservatives were actually presiding over a larger public sector than in 1970 (in terms of the government share of gross national product, and number of enterprises owned by government – see Table 1.2). This is crucial because it demonstrates how much the Heath government was relying on incomes policy to harness inflation. Talk of controlling the money supply, which dominated the policy agenda in the late 1970s, was almost completely absent.

Table 1.2 Outlays of government as a percentage of GDP 1970–1990

1970	1971	1972	1973	1974	1975	1976	1977
38.8	38.1	39.3	40.4	44.8	46.4	46.0	43.5
1978	**1979**	**1980**	**1981**	**1982**	**1983**	**1984**	
43.1	42.5	44.7	47.5	46.9	46.7	47.2	
1985	**1986**	**1987**	**1988**	**1989**	**1990**		
46.1	45.1	43.0	41.1	40.9	41.4		

Source: OECD, *National accounts* (various years)

1974–5: a return to planning?

While in opposition, the left wing of the Labour party converted its disenchantment with the 1964–70 period into a set of alternative policies. Eventually published as the *Labour Programme 1973*, these called for a dominant role for the state in the British economy. Britain's industrial recovery, so the programme asserted, could be facilitated only by further nationalization, the creation of a National Enterprise Board (NEB), the introduction of planning agreements between the government and individual industries, a new deal for workers in industrial relations and the management of firms, and the protection of vulnerable industries from foreign competition.

Many of these ideas formed the basis of the 1974 Manifesto, and on coming to power the Labour government set about implementing at least some of them. The Industrial Relations Act was repealed, a National Enterprise Board whose job would be to act as a state holding company to encourage investment and improve productivity was created, and a system of planning agreements between industries and the state established. In incomes policy, a new 'Social Contract' would bind both government and unions to moderation on incomes matters. In fact, the Social Contract resulted in anything but moderation, weekly wage increases jumping from 12.2 per cent in 1973 to 29.4 per cent in 1974. Inflation too bounded ahead, reaching 16.1 per cent in 1974 and a staggering 24.2 per cent in 1975 (Table 1.1). Finally, the Conservatives' quite generous public expenditure targets for 1974 and 1975 were met in full.

1974 was a bad year for all the developed countries; the quadrupling of oil prices by the organization of oil-exporting countries (OPEC) in late 1973 had precipitated a sharp downturn in world trade and an acceleration of inflation everywhere. A good part of the 1974–5 inflation must be attributed to these international forces. But Britain suffered from additional problems peculiar only to her. British industrial competitiveness continued to decline and British unions were more successful than those in many other countries in keeping wage rates up to or beyond the rate of inflation. In fact up to the end of the 1970s, in spite of general economic difficulties, the majority of the British population enjoyed growing prosperity and a rising standard of living. From a general economic and business point of view, however, the combination of a falling national income, accelerating rates of inflation and wages, and a high level of public expenditure could not go on. Moreover, unemployment was rising fast. The assumptions of Keynesian demand management seemed no longer to apply. According to Keynesian orthodoxy, unemployment or under-capacity occurred only when prices and interest rates were low. Inflation was a product of rapid growth and labour shortages. Now, however, most countries experienced both inflation and high rates of unemployment at the same time. This fact, above all others, was responsible for the revival both of incomes policies and, crucially, of traditional monetary policies.

1975–9: monetarism and incomes policy

The Labour left's policies for radical surgery on the British economy came to very little. Surgery there was, but it was of the conservative rather than socialist variety. The first change came in July 1975 when a government now dominated by the Labour right announced a new incomes policy granting £6 a week for all workers earning up to £8,500 and nothing for those earning over this figure. This was not a statutory policy but an agreement worked out between the government and the Trades Union Congress. It was remarkably successful (strikes fell to a twenty-two-year low during the £6 a week period) and demonstrated the growing strength of the TUC. This informal agreement was renewed in July 1976 when a 5 per cent limit was agreed, and again in 1977 when a 10 per cent limit was accepted. In 1978 5 per cent was proposed but effectively rejected by the unions. Their resentment at government imposition of this 'ceiling' was shown by widespread transport and public service strikes in the 'winter of discontent' (1978–9) which almost certainly lost Labour the May 1979 election.

As important was the conversion of the government to a limited form of monetarism. During 1976 investors' selling of sterling reached panic proportions. Fixed exchange rates (the Bank of England commitment to buy sterling for fixed sums in other currencies) had been abandoned in 1971 and left free to fall – and fall the pound did, to a low of $1.57 at one point. Britain was approaching the point where the government could not meet immediate payments on outstanding debts. In exchange for massive loans from the International Monetary Fund, Denis Healy, the Chancellor, agreed to new controls on the money supply. Interest rates rose to a record 15.5 per cent and public expenditure was cut. After complex negotiations, the International Monetary Fund (IMF) and the Treasury agreed that the Public Sector Borrowing Requirement, the amount needed by the government to cover the gap between protected resources and expenditure, should be trimmed by £3 billion over two years. In fact, public spending did not fall quite as rapidly as planned (see Table 1.2) but the very idea of using public sector spending as *the* major instrument of economic policy was new (notwithstanding Roy Jenkins's more limited efforts in this direction between 1968 and 1970).

The combination of incomes policy and public expenditure cuts reduced inflation quite quickly to a low of around 8 per cent between 1978 and 1979 (Table 1.1). However, unemployment remained stubbornly high and Labour's plans both for industrial reorganization and social reform were seriously circumscribed by the spending cuts. Like its predecessor, crisis management rather than social reform became the government's overriding preoccupation.

1979–83: the new monetarism

The new Conservative government of 1979 was determined to avoid the expediency and pragmatism of the 1970–4 Heath government. With a change of personnel (the leadership plus all the key economic posts), the Conservatives were pledged to solve Britain's economic problems not by planning or incomes policies, but through rigid adherence to monetarist orthodoxy. Once given a stable operating climate (low inflation and taxes), the market would bring about recovery. Government's role in industrial revival would be minimal.

To achieve a low rate of inflation the money supply would have to be carefully controlled. So on coming to office the Conservatives attempted to cut projected public expenditure quite dramatically and raised interest rates to record levels. In order to finance lower income taxes, the indirect tax on sales (VAT or value-added tax) was also raised – a fact which partly accounted for a quickly *rising* rate of inflation during 1979–80. Unleashed from incomes policy, wage rates also increased rapidly – although little higher than the rate of inflation.

Reducing the money supply in combination with the world downturn in economic activity which occurred between 1978 and 1981 quickly lowered the level of activity in the British economy and unemployment increased from an already high 5.3 per cent in 1979 to over 11 per cent in 1982. While it would be over-simple to claim that the government's main strategy was to use unemployment to reduce wage rates and therefore inflation, there is no doubt that this was the result of government policy.

On the industrial front the NEB, while not disbanded, was quickly reduced in resources and status, and the nationalized industries were required to operate strictly according to commercial criteria. Any idea of social planning or reform involving increased expenditure was put into cold storage to await economic recovery. Unfortunately this was not even faintly visible till 1982.

As a strategy for the rapid revitalization of British industry, the new policy was hardly successful. It is important to stress, however, that at least one component (a policy of high interest rates and expenditure cuts) had been pioneered by the Labour government between 1976 and 1979. The major change was a new devotion to market principles which naturally meant rejection of a prices and incomes policy. But from 1981 this came creeping back in various forms, notably cash limits on what government departments, public authorities and nationalized industries were allowed to offer to their employees. The need for some kind of incomes policy was in line with developments under previous governments. Similarly in the field of industrial policy, even during its first year of office, the Thatcher government was prepared to continue support for lame duck industries (British Leyland, British Steel) and it actually strengthened the industrial retraining and manpower programmes inherited from Labour. This, together with increasing state payments to the unemployed, prevented the government from reducing public expenditure as a percentage of GNP (Table 1.2). The bottom of the very deep 1980–81 recession occurred in late 1981 and thereafter the economy began to show discernible signs of improvement. However, recovery was from a very low base and unemployment did not peak until 1985.

1983–7: privatization and deregulation

Until 1983 the Thatcher government favoured monetarism – a belief that control of the amount of money circulating in the economy would alone improve general economic efficiency. From 1983, however, monetary targets were rarely met and ministers became less and less dependent on the theory. They did not, however, abandon their free market philosophy. Denationalization (or privatization), reducing trade union power, and increasing economic incentives in the public sector all remained central to government policy. The British National Oil Corporation, Jaguar Cars, British Leyland, British Telecom, the Trustee Savings Bank, British Gas and British Airways, Rolls Royce and many council-owned homes were sold. In the late 1980s water companies, electricity supply and other 'natural monopolies' traditionally within the public sector were also sold off.

Major legislation in 1980, 1982 and 1984 all but transformed industrial relations law. 'Closed shops' i.e. factories where all the workforce have to join a union, had to be approved in a secret ballot by 4/5ths of the workers; secondary picketing (i.e. the picketing of firms not themselves party to an industrial dispute) was outlawed; secret ballots were introduced to approve industrial action, to elect top union officials, and to approve the collection of union political funds. These laws, together with continuing high unemployment, substantially weakened trade unions. They were further debilitated by the costly and often violent miners' strike of 1984–5, which ended with a split in the National Union of Mineworkers and an effective victory for the government.

Unemployment remained the Thatcher government's Achilles' Heel. By 1987 the number and scope of youth employment schemes, retraining programmes and other employment creation devices had increased considerably. Through all of this, however, the government never entertained the possibility of a return to an official incomes policy or to an overtly interventionist industrial policy, let alone anything that could be called economic planning. By 1985, although the world price of oil had declined, so reducing vital revenue from North Sea oil, the economy began to expand very rapidly by British standards, culminating in the frenetic 'boom' of 1987–8.

1987–93: free markets and renewed problems

In spite of its overwhelming victory in the General Election of June 1987, the third Thatcher administration was acutely aware of the political dangers from those left out of free-market prosperity, above all minority ethnic groups, inner city residents, and particularly members of these groups living in the Midlands and North. All these had suffered more than anyone else from the accumulated problems of nineteenth- and twentieth-century industrialization, and from accelerated deindustrialization in the 1980s. Intervention in these areas had traditionally involved high levels of public expenditure on housing, transport and social services, with central government relying on locally elected councils to effect its policies. The Conservatives, in line with their free-market philosophy, sought instead to remove what they saw as the dead hand of Labour-dominated local government through various measures tried out in the mid-1980s and now intensified. The centrally controlled Youth Training Scheme, channelling the energies of the young unemployed, was extended and made semi-compulsory; enterprise zones with suspension of normal planning regulations were set up under nominated boards; council house sales continued and private renting of houses was encouraged. State schools were given greater autonomy and the ability to opt entirely out of local authority control. Subsidies for public transport were effectively removed and competition encouraged. Meanwhile moral and administrative pressure was applied to those receiving unemployment benefit to take any form of work available, however low-paid and unattractive. Vigorous attempts were also initiated to break away from national pay settlements, so that firms operating in areas of high unemployment could pay less.

By such means the government hoped to render the depressed areas more attractive to private enterprise by capitalizing on their potential reserves of cheap labour. Paradoxically, however, this attempt to free the local economy involved the use of considerable coercive power by central government, particularly on local government and trade unions, the major centres of opposition to its policies (see Chapter 7). Central direction also extended to individuals, particularly the young and the unemployed. To a considerable extent, Conservative policies could be seen as changing the forms and focus of government intervention, rather than reducing the extent of intervention overall.

On a more general level, the attempt to get government out of the economy appeared by the end of the 1980s to have had real but limited success. In areas of traditional strength – finance and services centred on South-East England – free-enterprise policies had strengthened Britain's competitive position in an era of growing interdependence and internationalization of markets. They had not averted the industrial decline of the outlying areas, but no previous policies had done that either. By 1991, however, it had become clear that the recovery was temporary and linked to special conditions such as the upsurge in world trade in the mid-1980s and above all the peaking of oil revenues, which would have freed any government from the balance of payment problems which had dogged previous economic initiatives.

The stock-market 'crash' of October 1987 convinced the government that in order to avert a recession it was necessary to stimulate the economy by lowering interest rates. At the same time, the third Thatcher government was less intent on holding down public expenditure, having a surplus of revenues over expeditures and thus eliminating the annual Public Sector Borrowing Requirement (PSBR) by 1987. But the expected downturn in economic activity following the collapse of world stock prices in October 1987 never transpired. As a result, the economy became seriously overheated in 1988 culminating in an inflation rate of close to 10 per cent (Table 1.1). Remedial action in the form of punitively high interest rates followed rapidly. This in turn depressed the housing and property markets and helped precipitate another and much deeper recession.

While a number of other countries went through a similar boom/slump cycle during the late 1980s and early 1990s, in few was the initial stimulus to growth and inflation so great or the subsequent deflationary reaction so Draconian. Britain therefore experienced a longer and deeper recession than any comparable country.

1992: a return to consensus politics?

The Conservatives' surprise election victory in 1992, giving them a record fourth term, was not just a confirmation of the Thatcher policies of the 1980s. For while some of the Thatcher agenda remained – lower taxes on incomes and profits, privatization and increasing competition and self-management within the public sector – some was dropped. Perhaps most importantly, the Major governments effectively abandoned a strict adherence to orthodoxy in the national accounts. Public expenditure was allowed to rise to a point where by 1993 the Public Sector Borrowing Requirement exceeded 5 per cent of GNP. Money was, at least initially, pumped into health, education, transport and a range of other areas.

At the same time the appointment of Michael Heseltine as Secretary of Trade and Industry implied a return to a limited form of interventionism. However, there could be no return to corporatism as the abolition of the National Economic Development Council in 1992 showed. Instead, interventionist policies would be kept firmly in the hands of central government departments. By the Autumn of 1992, however, it became obvious that the Major government lacked the clarity of purpose characteristic of the Thatcher governments. In September Britain was forced out of the ERM – the system of fixed exchange rates applicable to most EC member states – which Margaret Thatcher had reluctantly joined in 1990. Major had repeatedly stressed that ERM membership was a mainstay of government policy. In October, amidst rapidly deepening economic recession, the government was further humiliated by reversing its policy on pit closures following pressure from its own backbenchers. Further evidence of indecisive leadership and policy errors were provided by the government's handling of the ratification of the Maastricht Treaty on European union and of its involvement in arms sales to Iraq.

While the Major government appeared weak and irresolute, there is no doubt that the Thatcher experience had a permanent effect on the substantial context of public policy in Britain. Large-scale re-nationalization, a return to strong trade union power and detailed intervention in industry are not proposed by any of the major political parties in Britain. Instead, the political battleground is on the extent and nature of the welfare state, levels of personal taxation and constitutional reform. The British electoral system seems likely during the 1990s to continue to deny the opposition parties an opportunity to participate in government and thus to ensure the dominance of Conservative policies in these areas.

An overview of post-war events

To provide a general background to the largely economic developments we have described, Table 1.3 gives a chronology of the main post-war developments described above, together with a brief description of international as well as of non-economic domestic events which impinged on politics. During some periods attention was deflected from economic problems to alarming foreign developments and the danger of nuclear war. In the 1950s, when the economy enjoyed a modest post-war boom and trade unions could be placated with a share of increasing profits, both the Korean War and disengagement from most remaining territories of the pre-war colonial empire preoccupied successive Conservative governments. With diminishing commitments elsewhere, entry to the European Community seemed increasingly attractive as a cure for the ills of British industry, by opening wider markets and intensifying domestic competition. After ignoring the actual formation of the Community in 1956, abortive negotiations for entry occurred in 1962 and 1968 before they succeeded under Heath in 1972 and were reluctantly endorsed by Labour in 1975 following a national referendum on the subject.

The eruption of communal strife in Northern Ireland and intensified demands for some form of autonomy in Wales and Scotland also took up considerable political energy in the 1970s. By the end of that decade, however, even these movements were being seen as tensions generated at least in part by economic malaise. As membership of the Community failed to exert any visible economic effects and governments took increasingly far-ranging action to reverse relative economic decline, they provoked more extensive reactions against their policies. Thus the moderate Labour government of Callaghan, with its muted interventionist policy, fired radical left-wing demands for control over the parliamentary leadership to ensure the enactment of social reforms and supporting measures of government economic control. Their success in getting such demands accepted in the Labour party after 1979 prompted a secession by some established leaders and MPs to form the Social Democratic Party, which in alliance with the Liberals had just over a quarter of the votes in the General Election of 1983 and over one-fifth in 1987, undermining Labour's established electoral base.

Table 1.3 Governments, policies and events, 1945–92

Labour governments 1945–51 (Attlee)

National Health Service Act 1946	German surrender 1945
National Insurance Act 1946	Japanese surrender 1945
State ownership of coal industry, gas, electricity, transport and steel	
Town and Country Planning Act 1947	Dislocation of international trade after Second World War
Full employment policy; wage and dividends freeze; control of production in many areas; rationing	Berlin crisis 1948–49 marks start of Cold War with Soviet Union and intensification of Western Alliance
Independence of India, Pakistan, Burma and Ceylon 1948	

Conservative governments 1951–9 (Churchill, Eden, Macmillan)

Deregulation of trade and financial controls	Korean War 1950–3
Limited denationalization of iron and steel industry, and road transport	World economic growth
Invasion of Suez 1956	Formation of European Community 1956

Conservative governments 1959–64 (Macmillan, Home)

Independence of most African colonies	
Wage and price freeze 1962–3	Detente with Soviet Union 1960–79
Unsuccessful application to join EC 1962	Relaxation of Cold War and arms race

---

Labour governments 1964-70 (Wilson)

Balance of payments crisis 1964–5	
National economic plan effectively abandoned 1966–7	
Increasing credit, wage and dividend restrictions 1966–9	
Devaluation of £ sterling 1966	Vietnam War 1964–73
Unsuccessful application to join EC 1968	
Plan to regulate trade union and industrial relations 1969–70 (revealed in Green Paper *In Place of Strife* 1969) – defeated by trade union and internal Labour opposition	
Intervention of British troops in Northern Ireland 1969	

Conservative government 1970–4 (Heath)

Floating exchange rate for £ sterling 1971	
Industrial Relations Act 1971 (legal regulation of trade unions)	
'U-turn' from not interfering in industry or wage negotiations to restrictions on wage and salary increases	Discovery of oil in British North Sea Rise in world oil prices 1973–4
Suspension of Northern Ireland Parliament and Direct Rule 1972	
Reorganization into larger local government units 1972–5	
Entry to EC 1973	
Easy credit and high inflation 1973–4	
Successful strikes by National Union of Mineworkers 1972 and 1974, which disrupt entire country	

Table 1.3 Continued

Labour governments 1974–9 (mostly in minority) (Wilson, Callaghan)

Major election gains by Scottish and Welsh Nationalists 1974–7	Continued rise in world oil prices
High inflation 1974 onwards	
Social Contract with trade unions, whereby limits on prices and incomes and legal concessions 1975–8	
Referendum for continuing membership of EC 1975	
Balance of payments crisis 1976	
Severe credit restrictions and increasing cuts in projected government expenditure 1976 onwards	
High and increasing unemployment 1975 onwards	
'Winter of discontent' 1979 (strikes by numerous groups of workers including transport strike)	British oil revenues from North Sea equal payments for foreign oil
Defeat of government proposals for Scottish and Welsh devolution 1979	

Conservative governments 1979– (Thatcher, Major)

Policy of restricting stock of money to bring down inflation involves further cuts in government expenditure 1979–82 and central restrictions on local government expenditure	Increasing friction between Soviet Union and West from 1979
Legal restrictions on union's rights to picket during strikes and to extend scope of stoppage	World economic depression intensifying up to 1981
Falling inflation and greatly increasing unemployment 1980–2	
Savage and extensive urban riots 1981	
Foundation of Social Democratic Party and leadership defections from Labour 1981	
Electoral alliance of Social Democrats with Liberals produces sweeping by-election and local election successes 1981–82	Falklands War 1982
Re-election of Conservatives with large majority, Alliance comes close to Labour in terms of votes but not seats, 1983	World economic recovery 1982–6
Miners' strike 1984–5 most bitter industrial dispute since war	Oil and other commodity prices fall 1986
Renewed urban riots, 1985	
Unemployment reaches 13 per cent, then begins to fall	
Renewed balance of payments problems with drop in oil revenues	Relaxation of Soviet–Western relations 1986–7, serious disarmament negotiations between the USSR and USA
'Privatization' of many nationalized industries including gas	
Single European Act projects integrated West European market mid 1990s	

Table 1.3 Continued

Re-election of Conservatives with large majority 1987, Labour fails to recover and Alliance fails to break through	Break-up of Soviet Union follows peaceful liberation of East European states
Economic boom 1987–9	Britain joins Exchange Rate Mechanism 1990
Replacement of local rates by Community Charge or poll tax provokes massive non-payment and riots	Gulf War 1991
Replacement of Mrs Thatcher as Prime Minister by John Major 1990	Maastricht Treaty on further European Union under fire following Danish referendum rejection
Conservatives returned with a majority of 21 with John Major as Prime Minister 1992	
Britain forced out of Exchange Rate Mechanism (ERM). Government policy in disarray over pit closures.	ERM comes close to collapse because of high German interest rates.

Labour support for more extensive intervention prompted Thatcherite reactions to get government out of business and industrial relations altogether. Even so, the unions felt the government was responsible for the three million unemployed and must be forced to help them through subsidies and programmes for job creation. 'Non-intervention' was almost as much a recipe for political confrontation in the industrial field as earlier governments' positive intervention had been.

The overall consequence of a declining industrial base, and uneven prosperity, was an intensification of political conflict at many levels of society. At the bottom, violent rioting in many urban centres in 1981, 1985 and 1991 warned that socially deprived groups could not be left to bear the consequences of unemployment on their own. And while the unions had been weakened by legislation and unemployment, the 1984–5 miners' strike, a bitter teachers' dispute in 1985–6, and violent picketing of News International's Wapping plant in 1986–7, showed that serious industrial problems remained even if masked and at times deflected by increased prosperity among those in work.

Since the major political developments have followed directly from government's diagnosis of the economic situation and their reactions to it, the most relevant question with which to start an overall assessment of British politics is why governments have intervened in the ways they have? What forces explain the particular forms of British government intervention in comparison with those adopted by other national governments? And why have they had such mixed success? Much of the book will be indirectly concerned with these points, and we will return to them explicitly in the last chapter.

Chapter 2
Changing networks: the bureaucratic setting for government action
Graham Wilson

Our explanation of British policy failures relates above all to the absence of adequate arrangements for co-ordinating and implementing central government policy. In this chapter and the next we will look at the processes whereby policies and decisions are made and put into effect nationally. In Chapter 7 we will look at how they get transmitted to the local level, where they begin to have an impact on the lives of ordinary people.

When we think of the British government what comes most readily to mind is the Cabinet and the ministries. These are the most obvious institutional features of government and they are very closely linked.

The Cabinet is made up of about twenty-three politicians from the majority party in Parliament, selected by the Prime Minister. All but two or three of these also act as the political head of a major ministry or department of state (the two terms mean the same thing). These include the Foreign Office, Home Office (which deals principally with police and public order) and the Treasury.

This description of British governmental decision-making highlights two aspects of the central policy process:

1. It is well organized from the point of view of having competing voices and interests heard. All the interests sponsored by government departments and the ministries themselves are able to make their points. However, there is little or no institutional machinery for getting agreement below the Cabinet level. Indeed the whole process is adversarial in nature – departments are supposed to defend their own views and to make them predominate. If two major departments backed by their ministers refuse to compromise then the matter has to go to the Cabinet. This gives the Cabinet a uniquely important co-ordinating and directing role in government and renders the question of how it operates of central relevance in any assessment of the executive. That is why we devote most of the next chapter to it.
2. It is equally obvious that civil servants are crucial. Many of the important decisions of government are actually made by them, particularly if they do not involve party politics or if both parties agree on them (measured in terms of volume, most government legislation, for example, is not contested

by the opposition). We shall examine below the extent to which ministers take political responsibility for the decisions made by 'their' civil servants. But it is clear that, whatever the constitutional doctrine, politicians only participate in, or even hear about a very small minority of the 'government's' decisions. That is why most of this chapter is devoted to the workings of the Civil Service and how individual civil servants within it relate both to ministers and to organized interest groups.

The sphere of government

The attention paid to Parliament and party politicians in the media can easily obscure the importance of these other elements in decision-making. On taking office ministers become part of a government machine which has a timetable, procedures and priorities of its own and which is staffed and run by civil servants.

British administrators have been traditionally organized into broad clerical, executive and administrative classes. Recent attempts at reform (notably the Fulton Commission in the late 1960s) tried to break down these divisions and to nurture specialist skills, such as those possessed by the statisticians, economists and scientists – each a separate career grade within the Civil Service. In spite of these attempts, British civil servants continue in the main to conceive of themselves as general administrators rather than specialists, whose job is to promote circulation between policy areas rather than dedication to a particular speciality, and to maintain broad distinctions between the hierarchy of classes. The typical higher civil servant enters directly as an administrative trainee and rises rapidly to an executive position (the principal grade) with a fairly autonomous area of operation, whether it be supervision of mortuaries in the Home Office or collation of information on southern Africa in the Foreign Office. If very successful, the principal will rise through assistant and deputy secretaryships to become permanent head of a ministry, under the title of permanent secretary.

Civil servants are grouped into administrative sections with a startling range of functions. Outside the twenty to twenty-five large ministries, most headed by Cabinet ministers, there is no agreed list. Taking departments as those agencies voted on separately in the Parliamentary Supply Estimates, there are about seventy at the present time. Table 2.1 gives a summary listing of the most important.

In his early years, a higher-level civil servant may shift between two or three departments. For most of his career, however, he will be located in one of these in spite of the 'generalist' ideology of the service.

Ministers and civil servants

In common with many nationalities, the British do not realize how odd their political institutions are. The relationship between civil servants and ministers

Table 2.1 Major departments and agencies of the central government

---

Ministry of Agriculture, Fisheries and Food
Crown Prosecution Service
HM Customs and Excise
Ministry of Defence
Department for Education
Office of Electricity Regulation (OFFER)
Department of Employment
Department of the Environment
ECGD (Export Credit Guarantee Department)
Foreign and Commonwealth Office
Office of Gas Supply (OFGAS)
Department of Health
Department of National Heritage
Home Office
Central Office of Information
Board of Inland Revenue
Law Officers' Departments
Lord Chancellor's Department
Ordnance Survey
Overseas Development Administration
Parliamentary Counsel
Paymaster General's Office
Office of Population Censuses and Surveys
HM Procurator General and Treasury Solicitor's Department
Serious Fraud Office
Department of Social Security
HMSO (Her Majesty's Stationery Office)
Central Statistical Office
Office of Telecommunications (OFTEL)
Department of Trade and Industry
Department of Transport
HM Treasury
Office of Water Services (OFWAT)

Note: in the case of Northern Ireland, the Secretary of State for Northern Ireland is responsible for law and order and for a range of services administered through the Northern Ireland Departments. Scotland enjoys wide administrative autonomy through the Scottish Office's five major departments. Wales enjoys less administrative autonomy although certain aspects of government are administered through the Welsh Office.

Source: *Britain: an Official Handbook 1992*, London, HMSO, 1992, pp. 47–51.

is no exception. Consider the experience of a newly appointed senior government minister (often called a Secretary of State). Almost without exception, the minister will have spent a significant period of time in Parliament. Most MPs develop knowledge, understanding, and (strange though it may seem to outsiders) even fondness for the folkways of the House of Commons. But new ministers will have no such knowledge of the folkways of government departments. Indeed, if our new minister's party has been in opposition for a long period, as Labour was after 1951 and after 1964, (s)he may have spent many years in Parliament without having any experience of the higher Civil Service. Except for exchanges of letters about the problems of constituents and the occasional questioning of Civil Service witnesses before Parliamentary Select Committees, contact with civil servants might have been almost nil.

After appointment, however, the new minister will begin what feels like a totally new career. Not only is the ministerial role totally different from the job of an ordinary MP, but it is spent working with a completely different set of people, civil servants, in whose selection a new minister has played no part. British ministers are dependent on career civil servants to a degree that is unusual in western democracies. Civil servants organize the minister's day as they compile the appointments diary, write letters to be signed by the minister, speeches for the minister to give, draft replies to Parliamentary questions, arrange transport and meetings, and meet their more political needs as well as implementing their decisions as the heads of department. They will even brief the minister on what is politically expedient, going so far, in the celebrated if controversial case of the Westland Affair (1986), as to leak confidential papers to the press in order to discredit their minister's Cabinet opponent. Only the most overtly partisan activities of the minister, such as giving a speech to a party conference, are outside the responsibilities of career civil servants, and even here there are well known ways of evading the ban.

All top politicians need staff support. Two features have been distinctive about the British approach. First, top politicians in Britain have had almost no control – and until recently seemed to want no control – over the selection of those on whom they are so dependent. In the United States, many of the top jobs in government departments that in Britain are filled by career civil servants go to political appointees. The President, or the President's appointee as head of the agency or department, gets to pick the people to fill the top posts. Political appointees may – and often do – have no experience of either their agency or working in Washington DC. But though the American example may seem extreme, it is not unusual in allowing politicians some degree of control over their selection of the people to play the key role in advising them. In Germany, for example, which has a strong tradition of a professional, elite bureaucracy, a change in the party in power produces a change in the top civil service. The party affiliation of top civil servants is known, and when a party loses power 'its' civil servants are placed in temporary retirement or are reassigned to jobs that are less politically sensitive. In France, where the prestige and power of the senior civil service has been legendary, there were large-scale changes at the top of the bureaucracy following the capture and the loss of the government by the Socialists.

In Britain the tradition has been that new ministers should try to work with the civil servants they inherit, with a qualified right to choose among unknown candidates for posts in their private office. Only if 'things don't work out' is a minister able to demand a change, and each minister is unlikely to be able to demand more than one change. This said, the Thatcher governments of the 1980s were unusual in favouring those civil servants most likely to advance the government's political agenda. We will develop this point later.

Second, the bureaucracy in Britain has enjoyed something much closer to a monopoly on advising the politicians in power than is the case in other countries. British political parties do little to turn their campaign policies into specific policy; little has changed since Crossman noted with dismay in 1964 that the file at Labour's headquarters on one of its longest standing commitments was almost empty. 'Think tanks' (outside centres which provide policy advice) are relatively new to Britain, and how influential they will be after the departure of Margaret Thatcher and a return to a more pragmatic style of policy-making remains to be seen. Parliamentary Select Committees struggle to make their voices heard in policy debates, and (since they lack adequate staff support) are certainly not a source, unlike US Congressional Committees, of policy innovation and ideas. In short, when British ministers need advice on how to handle the problems for which they are responsible, there is almost nowhere they can get it outside the Civil Service.

Since the 1960s, ministers have been able to appoint political advisers from outside the Civil Service, and most now do. But political advisers are relatively few in number, and their impact very limited. Indeed, one can argue that they have been 'domesticated' by the Civil Service, spending their time on tasks such as writing speeches for party rallies, which civil servants do not like to do and are supposed not to do.

The lack of background and expertise with which 'generalist' politicians enter a ministry is aggravated by the very brief length of time they usually spend there. In general, a British politician can count on being moved on to another responsibility (sometimes within the same ministry but more often outside it) every eighteen months to two years. General government 'reshuffles' (transfers of ministers between departments) take place quite regularly for various reasons – to weaken party factions opposed to the Prime Minister, to give a general impression that the government has renewed itself and is changing policies, or to get rid of incompetent ministers and promote new ones.

What can a minister do under these circumstances? In general, his or her political career depends on making a good impression in the ministry. Basically (s)he can adopt one of three roles – that of good (but essentially non-political) administrator and manager of the department; external representative of the department in the Cabinet and government; or pragmatic innovator dedicated to some basic policy change – possibly going against what the department has been doing in the past.

In the first two roles the minister can count on more unquestioning Civil Servant support than in the third. Every ministry has certain pet policies and points of view as well as certain favoured interests, which it wishes to advance. This 'departmental view' has evolved over years of internal discussion and contacts with clients and affected interests. As manager or representative, a minister can promote the departmental view in the government as a whole and perhaps get some pieces of non-controversial legislation through Parliament. This makes him/her extremely valuable to the Civil Service who after all need to have certain things done. This helps make relationships less one-sided.

However, pleasing the Civil Service in this way depends – apart from the minister's own temperament and political ambitions – on whether the department is heavily involved in government plans or not. When a highly activist government, like that of Mrs Thatcher in the 1980s, comes to power, many ministries are going to be affected. Ministers will come into a department with fairly clear ideas of what they want changed. How will civil servants respond under these circumstances?

Having a programme, even one that conflicts with the department view, is not necessarily a disadvantage for a minister. Civil Servants are socialized into responding to clear policy objectives if the minister, and government, cannot be dissuaded from them. Moreover, there are divisions of opinion among ministry civil servants themselves, so a determined minister can always find someone to do his/her bidding (often younger people who want to advance their career and are in any case inclined to criticize the established opinions of their elders). Thus, for example, the Department of Employment, traditionally the patron and friend of the trade unions in government, could be used to prepare and implement legislation designed to restrict their activities in the early 1980s. In the end this broke the department's close trade union links and changed its role to that of main provider of training schemes and re-education for the young and unemployed.

Thus, determined ministers with government backing can impose themselves on a ministry, though this does depend on their policy commitments. As the Thatcher governments were unusually committed and active in a wide variety of fields they had a proportionate effect on a wide range of ministries.

The purpose and nature of the British Civil Service

What is the character of the organization on which elected British politicians depend? Here again we find that the arrangements the British take for granted are not what might be expected. The standard definition of bureaucracy is as an organization composed of experts, organized hierarchically, acting according to clear, defined principles so that similar cases can be solved similarly.

The higher Civil Service in Britain is far removed from this ideal picture. First, as we have seen, it is composed of theoretically equal ministries in a somewhat adversarial relationship to each other. Second, far from being composed of experts, it is composed of generalists, educated in the humanities or social sciences, given little training once they have been employed, and shifted relatively frequently (about every three years) from job to job and even department to department. These characteristics also mark out the British Civil Service as quite distinct from its counterparts in other democracies. Permanent civil servants in other countries are much more likely than British civil servants to have had some education or training that is linked to their current job, although the nature of that training varies considerably.

Civil Servants in other democracies are also less likely to move between jobs and certainly between departments. The most successful civil servants in Britain can expect to change departments several times, working at some stage in a central department such as the Cabinet Office or the Treasury as well as in spending departments such as Environment, Defence or Agriculture. In contrast, a permanent civil servant in the United States would expect to pass a career within a single department or agency.

It is nevertheless a big leap to argue, as did the Fulton Committee, that British higher civil servants are 'amateurs': British civil servants feel that they are professionals in governance and administration though not experts in the substance of the policy they administer. Both civil servants and their critics would agree, however, that British civil servants do not have great *substantive* expertise.

What, then, is the Civil Service *for*? British civil servants, like the rest of the British political establishment, tend not to spend much time thinking about constitutional questions. In the aftermath of the Westland affair (an internal quarrel between two members of the government over an American as opposed to a European takeover of the last independent British helicopter firm) the hapless Secretary to the Cabinet and Head of the Home Civil Service, Sir Robert Armstrong, attempted to define the responsibilities of the Civil Service in an internal memorandum. He stated that its purpose was to assist ministers! Armstrong's formulation scarcely answered constitutional questions that had arisen during the bitterly fought quarrel over Westland. Was it, for example, the job of civil servants to assist ministers to do something that was illegal, unfair politically or contrary to the spirit of the constitution? Should a civil servant help a minister prepare a reply to a Parliamentary Question that is false in order to avoid political embarrassment? If not, how should a civil servant respond if ordered to do so by a minister?

At the routine level of ordinary administration the answer to what civil servants ought to do may be obvious. Tax collectors do their best to extract money from businesses and citizens, the Department of Social Security pays out a variety of benefits to claimants, and prison officers keep those sentenced by the courts in prison. Traditionally, the most senior civil servants have taken as little interest in such tasks as possible; the highest prestige in the civil service has gone to those who are involved predominantly in advising ministers.

But what advice can generalists who have no scientific education, little technical training and who change jobs frequently, provide? Senior civil servants have argued that the contribution they can make to policy-making, precisely because they are generalists, is to pull together the broad range of factors that should be considered in making a policy decision. These factors include normative judgments, political calculations, administrative difficulties, cost, implications for apparently unrelated but in fact affected policy areas or departments, and the reaction of interest groups with which government is in contact. The function of senior civil servants is to take the vague ideas of politicians, and, drawing on a wide variety of advice on the different issues which may be involved, turn them into policies and legislation. But before ministers commit themselves too far or publicly, senior civil servants should confront them with the likely consequences of the policies ministers think they want, so they can make informed choices. If you are about to make a decision that involves a multiplicity of considerations – economic, scientific and legal as well as political – you do not necessarily want the advice of an economist, a scientist or a lawyer; you want the advice of someone who can pull together these disparate considerations into alternatives and choices. That is a role of a generalist administrator.

Advice generally reflects the advice and opinions of the people giving it as well as the facts. Yet the British system requires that the same civil servants who have advised a minister also advise the minister's successor. Robert Armstrong earlier in his Civil Service career served as Private Secretary to both the Conservative Prime Minister, Edward Heath, and his Labour successor, Harold Wilson. Civil servants talk with pride of their success in advising a left-wing Labour minister one day and the next day, after an election, advising a right-wing Conservative. For such civil servants, the capacity to transfer loyalties so far across the political spectrum is the ultimate test of professionalism, just as it is a test of the lawyer's professionalism to be able to represent a loathsome client.

The British political system requires its civil servants not to be a-political but to be promiscuous – to sleep with whoever wins the election. The same civil servant who helped Labour nationalize the ports should help a Conservative successor denationalize them with equal enthusiasm. The civil servant who prepared a cunning answer to a Parliamentary Question for a Labour minister to use against the Conservative shadow spokesman in 1979 might well have prepared an equally cunning reply for the Conservative, now the minister, to use against the Labour former minister, now shadow spokesman, after the election.

Can civil servants really make such transitions satisfactorily? As we have seen, other democracies assume that the answer is likely to be no and allow elected politicians much greater freedom to make changes in the top bureaucracy. A number of different reasons are often given for doubting the ability of civil servants to make the required leap in loyalty from one government to the next.

The first is that civil servants are closet partisans, instinctively inimical to left-wing governments. Those who make this claim note that senior civil servants have been drawn predominantly from the ranks of Oxford and Cambridge graduates, universities that favour students from fee-paying schools in their admissions procedures.

A second argument is that civil servants are committed to existing policies and the consensus that has developed in departments about the best way to handle problems, a set of values or beliefs which we have referred to as the 'departmental view'. Civil servants, as people, cannot be expected to put full effort into reversing policies they have spent years of effort developing just before the government changed. Nor can civil servants be expected to depart easily from the departmental view of what is good policy.

A third claim is that the culture of the Civil Service encourages scepticism rather than enthusiasm, criticism of proposals rather than a determination to implement them. The Oxbridge education that shaped the style of civil servants encourages finding fault with the work of others rather than undertaking original work oneself. One of the highest attributes of the civil servant is to save a minister from undertaking a policy initiative that will produce unanticipated, adverse consequences. It is indeed a highly desirable function of a senior bureaucracy to save elected politicians from unnecessary error. However, the centrality of this task in the work of the British senior civil servants may make them overly resistant to politicians' policy proposals, more inclined to highlight difficulties with ministers' ideas than to solve the problems in implementing them.

The validity of these criticisms varies. The charge of party bias is the least plausible. There is some evidence to suggest that most senior civil servants are floating voters, supporting different parties in different elections. A series of interviews in 1989 and 1990 revealed a range of political attitudes among senior civil servants, from the left wing of the Labour party to the Thatcherite faction of the Conservative party. Most were political moderates, tempted to vote for the Liberal Democrats – should the party be credible electorally. However, all of the civil servants had a very strong professional commitment to serving duly elected governments of any party to the best of their ability; civil servants point out that it is no more difficult for them to follow this professional duty than for lawyers to represent clients whom they dislike or whose cases they disagree with. By and large, politicians who have been ministers rarely complain about the *party* bias of civil servants. Politicians with ministerial experience are dismissive of suggestions that civil servants are disloyal because they support a different party. Indeed, ministers usually do not know how their civil servants vote, and if they do know that their civil servants support an opposition party, welcome working with people with a different perspective.

Other doubts about the impartiality of civil servants are more troubling. In particular, it is hard for civil servants and ministers, let along outsiders, to be sure when legitimate and necessary criticism of policy proposals or advocacy of alternatives shades into obstructionism. Civil servants have well developed views on the policy problems for which they are responsible. Indeed, they are expected to have views, to be ready not only to criticize constructively the ideas of ministers but to produce ideas for policy initiatives for ministers who have no agendas of their own. Again, civil servants believe that their professional duty is to put aside their own values in order to serve their minister. But here it is harder for the civil servant to draw the boundary between personal views and professional responsibility. Is the vigour with which a civil servant criticizes a policy proposal a measure of a professional rigorously carrying out his duty to draw problems to the attention of the minister? Or does this shade into obstruction, raising never-ending questions and doubts about a policy to which the minister is committed?

It is in this area that politicians vary in their experience of the Civil Service. The vast majority do not think that civil servants are unduly obstructive. But those who are furthest away from the political centre on both the left and the right are the most likely to feel that civil servants are inflexible and negative. In particular, if a minister is himself out of line with general government policy, civil servants face an acute conflict of loyalty which they may resolve in various ways. On the other hand, a minister imposing policy reversals with the full support of the government seems well able to get these through, as is evident from the Thatcherites' experience of the 1980s. Because Mrs Thatcher was a radical politician, the experience of her governments in this area is particularly enlightening.

The Civil Service and Thatcherism

Mrs Thatcher entered office in 1979 profoundly suspicious of the Civil Service, believing with uncommon intensity in several of the standard criticisms that we have discussed already. Like some left-wing Labour politicians, she feared that the Civil Service was infected with centrist political attitudes and that it would work to dilute the radicalism of her policies. She thought that the Civil Service was inefficient compared with private business, a belief that is an article of faith among right-wing politicians the world over. Some of her closest friends and advisers, notably Sir John Hoskyns, saw in the Civil Service a stuffy, Establishment organization inherently unsuited to revitalizing Britain.

Relationships between the Prime Minister and the Civil Service went through several stages. Perhaps surprisingly, the importance of her policies in regard to the Civil Service increased the longer she was in office.

In the first stage, she confronted what she saw as the entrenched attitudes of the Civil Service, and tried to beat them down. These confrontations naturally occurred in areas where she had strong views that conflicted with existing policy. For example, in one celebrated incident, a civil servant from the Department of Employment who had been trying to explain the intricacies of legislating on industrial relations was reduced to asking, 'Prime Minister, do you want to know the facts?' It is thought that this exchange damaged his career permanently. Once Thatcher had consolidated her political position within the government after the 1983 General Election she placed people in charge of major departments who would destroy the prevailing 'departmental view'. Thus Lord Young, fiercely opposed to detailed government involvement in industry, was placed in charge of the interventionist Department of Trade and Industry. The strongly anti-union Norman Fowler was placed in charge of the Department of Employment, traditionally sympathetic to unions. Sir Keith Joseph and then Kenneth Baker were made Secretary of State for Education and Science precisely because their views conflicted with the department's ingrained sympathy for progressive, liberal education doctrines.

But the confrontation with the Civil Service was also more general, not limited to specific policy areas. Its overall size was reduced from around 700,000 to 560,000. The Civil Service Department, created on the recommendation of the Fulton Committee, was abolished. Thatcher thought it too easy a manager of the Civil Service. Its Permanent Secretary, Lord Bancroft, was given early retirement; his style and views were too moderate. The Thatcherite belief that civil servants were 'over privileged' because of their job security and inflation-indexed pensions resulted in a determination to resist the growing tide of union strength within the lower ranks. The Thatcher government withstood the first ever strike by civil servants. After industrial action had allegedly compromised intelligence gathering by the electronic espionage agency, the Government Communications Headquarters (GCHQ), the government banned unions from the facility. Many serving civil servants repeated in private what Lord Bancroft said in public after his enforced retirement; it was hard to maintain morale among civil servants working for a government that excoriated them.

The combination of resentment over the Thatcher government's attacks on the Civil Service and dislike of specific government policies resulted in civil servants 'leaking' documents to the media or opposition that were intended to embarrass the government. In the most famous incident a civil servant, Clive Ponting, leaked documents from the Ministry of Defence that showed that the government had given a misleading account of the circumstances leading up to the sinking of the Argentine cruiser, the *General Belgrano*, during the Falklands War. Ponting was prosecuted under the Official Secrets Act, but the jury, in a blow for liberty that recalled great acquittals of the eighteenth century, refused to convict.

In the mid-1980s confrontation gave way to attempts to recreate the Civil Service in a more Thatcherite image. The initial moves were based on personnel decisions. Here it is necessary to bear in mind that most previous governments had allowed the higher Civil Service to determine promotions with little involvement by ministers who were constitutionally empowered to make the final choice. The Thatcher government, however, decided to take a close interest in promotions at the highest levels of the Civil Service. Controversy exists about its intentions in this area. The government's opponents claim that it set out to promote civil servants who sympathized with the government politically as well as working for it professionally; the top jobs would go to people who were, in a phrase that Thatcher herself used, 'one of us'. The government's defenders argued that ministers were using their power to advance civil servants who were not so much 'one of us' in terms of their personal political values but were 'one of us' in terms of their style. Civil servants were to be favoured who were more interested in management or efficiency and who, above all, who were implementers rather than policy analysts. The style the Thatcher government favoured was one that focused on giving ministers what they said they wanted, rather than on warning ministers of difficulties and dangers.

In all events, both the admirers and critics of the government could agree that the government was changing the culture and style of the Civil Service. By 1991, there were signs that a new generation of higher civil servants was moving into and dominating top positions, a generation that stressed implementation rather than policy analysis. Typically this new generation criticized their predecessors for being 'quasi academic', people who would sit around endlessly analysing the advantages and disadvantages of a policy proposal. In contrast, the new generation gained job satisfaction from giving ministers what they said they wanted – privatization, weakening unions, or introducing the Community Charge.

Whether this 'can do' culture will survive Thatcherism and the return of politicians less certain of what they want, remains to be seen. Most politicians, after all, have a style very different from Thatcher's. Normal politicians are often short of ideas on what to do, rather than being determined to impose their policies on the country; they are less sure of the wisdom of their proposals and are more anxious to be warned about potential pitfalls. In brief, politicians want civil servants to be more actively involved in proposing and discussing policies rather than acting simply to implement them.

Structural changes

The final and most radical initiative the Thatcher government took in relation to the Civil Service was to launch the *Next Steps* initiative. Next Steps was the ultimate product of the drive for greater efficiency in the Civil Service. A first step had been to bring into government a team of business executives in an Efficiency Unit charged with identifying savings from greater efficiency. The Efficiency Unit ultimately concluded that a wholesale restructuring of government would be more appropriate than continuing to look on an *ad hoc* basis for savings. The structural change that the Efficiency Unit recommended had been foreshadowed in the Fulton Report; central government departments should be reduced in size and focus on the core needs of ministers such as developing and revising policy or preparing speeches for Parliament. The actual implementation of policy should be placed whenever possible in the hands of autonomous executive agencies that would sign a contract with the core department to provide a specified level and quality of service in return for its budget. The core department would be the customer; the agency would be analogous to an outside contractor or corporation. The Chief Executive of the agency would be responsible to the core department (ultimately the minister) for fulfilling the contract signed with it. These moves were in harmony with attempts to privatize and introduce an 'internal market' elsewhere, in local government and the National Health Service, for example.

Next Steps has an appeal that goes beyond Thatcherites and indeed beyond the Conservative party. The new agencies, able to recruit outside the Civil Service, might be able to counteract the traditional tendency in the Civil Service to neglect managerial skills. Sweden has long operated something very similar to the Next Steps system, so the system cannot be said to be inherently impractical. Senior civil servants will be able to focus more on the policy analysis and advising that traditionally has appealed to them most. Politicians, both Labour and Conservative, are attracted by the thought that they will not, as ministers, be responsible to Parliament for administrative errors committed by low ranking officials of whom they have never heard. At least since the 1970s, politicians in Britain have complained about overload and about excessive demands being placed upon them. Next Steps helps by substantially reducing the range of things for which ministers can be challenged. If MPs in the future feel that constituents have been denied pensions, benefits or licenses unfairly, they will be told to take their complaints to the relevant agency and its chief executive, not to the appropriate minister unless the treatment is a consequence of the contract with the agency the minister has approved. But herein lies the first of a number of major difficulties with Next Steps.

The accountability problem

Bureaucratic accountability in Britain has been achieved by making civil servants responsible to ministers and ministers responsible to Parliament. Everyone knows that in practice ministers do not know what social security officers in Newcastle are doing about individual cases. Following a poorly understood scandal in 1954 known as the Crichel Down affair (involving government retention of agricultural land in the West of England after it had been requisitioned during the war) a set of doctrines was enunciated by the then Home Secretary setting out a continuum of ministerial responsibility, ranging from the minister not being held accountable for some unauthorized action by an official unknown to the minister at the time, to the minister himself making the decision in question.

Ministerial responsibility varies similarly, from none to total. We now know that ministers were much more involved in the Crichel Down affair than was thought at the time, and the civil servants who shouldered most of the blame for implementing an eminently defensible policy were treated badly. Moreover, since 1954, ministers have escaped responsibility for policy failures ranging from failures of insurance companies to prison escapes in Northern Ireland for which they should have been held responsible under the Crichel Down doctrine.

However, the doctrine has provided for *some* accountability. In British government the resignations of Foreign Office ministers after the Argentine invasion of the Falklands, which they had failed to anticipate, continues to attract admiration from Americans. In contrast the US failure to anticipate or deter the Iraqi invasion of Kuwait in 1990 prompted not a single resignation. But in other countries such as the USA the bureaucracy is kept accountable by other means, such as extensive oversight by legislative committees and the judiciary. Lacking powerful Parliamentary committees and judicial review, ministers have at least to be *potentially* accountable for the actions of the bureaucracy in Britain, otherwise no one is.

It is difficult to imagine that as clear a distinction between policy and implementation can be drawn in practice as the Next Steps proposals imagine. Next Steps imagines that government policy will be embodied in the contract that departments will negotiate with their agencies. The Chief Executives of the agencies will be responsible for implementing the contract. However, policy can be defined not as the theoretical aspirations of a government department, as defined in the contract, but as the pattern of actual government action. Suppose, for example, that officials responsible for dealing with the unemployed consistently place a higher value on preventing fraud than on helping the unemployed claim all benefits to which they are entitled. The pattern of official behaviour might be regarded more plausibly as the Employment Agency's policy than a pious declaration in its contract with the

Department of Employment saying that the agency is to try to make sure that everyone receives all benefits to which they are entitled. Policy is a recurring pattern of decision-making or administration as well as major decisions made by ministers. To pretend – as does Next Steps – that governance can be divided into policy and administration is to try to make a distinction long since thoroughly discredited by political scientists. If Next Steps were not so clearly in the interests of both senior civil servants, ministers and potential ministers, more might have been made of this problem.

By the early 1990s, substantial progress had been made with the creation of Next Steps agencies. The first were set up to carry out uncontroversial tasks such as Heavy Goods Vehicle Testing and Driver Licensing. By 1991, however, Next Steps had progressed to agencies responsible for advising the unemployed and paying unemployment benefit, an area more likely to create controversy. The ultimate objective is to transfer three-quarters of civil servants into Next Steps agencies, leaving the remainder in core departments responsible for policy and parliamentary issues. Were this target to be achieved, it would be the most profound change in the Civil Service since the Northcote–Trevelyan reforms that created the modern Civil Service in the late nineteenth century.

Apart from the constitutional implications discussed above, the implications for the character of the Civil Service would be considerable. Future Civil Service careers will include a period in agency management. There the civil servant will be expected to work in an atmosphere more reminiscent of industry than of Whitehall; it was claimed at least that chief executives would be recruited from industry and finance as well as from the Civil Service and by 1992 several such appointments had been made. Apart from any immediate consequences, Next Steps agencies are intended to promote the 'can do' implementer style that was developing in the 1980s.

Change and continuity

The higher Civil Service undoubtedly changed under Thatcher; if Next Steps is implemented fully, her promotion of managerialism among administrators will be institutionalized. But the policy adviser role of civil servants in regard to ministers has also proved enduring. Even after the radical Thatcher governments, ministers remain extraordinarily dependent by international standards on permanent civil servants. While this situation endures, one may query how much has changed fundamentally in British government.

Ministers, departments and interest groups

The second network that ministers enter into after they leave behind the world of Westminster for the world of Whitehall – one in which civil servants are continuously involved – is the one linking government and interest groups.

It is likely that MPs will have had some experience of interest groups before becoming ministers. Most of the well-run interest groups maintain contacts with MPs – not so much in order to influence specific policy decisions as part of their general attempts to influence the climate of opinion among the political elite. Briefings, lunch invitations and appearances before Parliamentary Select Committees are commonly used by interest groups with the requisite resources. Some interest groups do focus on Parliament more seriously. Mass membership 'cause' groups, particularly in areas such as abortion policy, Sunday observance and campaigns against blood sports (all issues on which MPs have a 'free' vote, i.e. are not told how to vote by their party's whips) make Parliament a central target in their strategy.

The most effective interest groups, however, make government departments, not Parliament, their major target. This is particularly true of 'producer' groups representing economic interests (farmers, employers, trade associations and specific industries such as chemicals). The director of a trade association representing a specific industry, or the directors-general of organizations representing broad sectors of the economy, such as the Confederation of British Industry (CBI) or National Farmers' Union (NFU) spend far more time and effort on relations with the government departments of most importance to them than they do on talking to mere MPs.

The reasons for the interest groups' focus on departments rather than Parliament are obvious. Parliament generally ratifies what ministers have decided; it is therefore vital to influence what ministers are thinking before they announce what they will present to Parliament. Moreover, many detailed issues in the interpretation of laws or policies by government departments will be of little interest to Parliament but may be of considerable importance to the interest groups affected. It may seem less obvious why government departments spend so much time talking to interest groups. A variety of explanations have been offered. These include cultural, practical and institutional elements.

Political scientists have long stressed the importance attached to interest groups in British political culture. There is a strong belief that interests affected by a policy should have the opportunity to comment on it before it is developed fully. The consent of affected interests is likely to reduce the controversy that attends the introduction of a new policy. It is therefore in the interests of ministers and departments to comply with the norm of consulting 'the relevant interests'.

The practical reason why departments consult interest groups is that this can save departments a great deal of trouble. Consultations can reveal that a proposal is likely to run into practical problems that the department has not foreseen; the timing of payments of an agricultural subsidy may come too late to influence the decisions of farmers about what to produce the next year, a tax might be extraordinarily difficult or complex to collect, and a proposed environmental regulation might increase production costs massively for an industry already in financial difficulty. The department concerned needs to learn all this before it is too late and an ineffective policy has been put in place. Even political feedback has a practical value. Ministers need to know if interest groups will greet a policy change with praise, indifference, criticism or outrage; ministers might go ahead with a policy whatever the response, but they want to be forewarned.

The institutional reason why departments co-operate with interest groups is that British central government has a sharply limited capacity of its own. Although the Civil Service includes a large number of technical specialists such as economists, accountants, scientists and statisticians, it does not have enough, and perhaps could not conceivably ever have all the experts it would need, on all the technical issues that it handles. Indeed, the generalist administrator tradition of the Civil Service has made it particularly dependent on interest group advice; the French Civil Service, composed of graduates of the Grands Écoles, including Ponts et Chausées, may have a much better idea of where to place new roads than the British generalist administrator, who is therefore more likely to look for advice to interest groups with the relevant expertise.

Even where complicated or technical considerations are not involved, a government department may feel that it has little chance of success without the co-operation of interest groups. In the 1960s and 1970s, British governments tried to impose restrictions on the rate of increase of prices and incomes; the policies stood no chance of success without co-operation from unions and employers, for otherwise the administrative burden would be too great. British regulation of health and safety at work, and of environmental and consumer protection, has depended heavily on the co-operation of the interest being regulated, for without this co-operation government would not have nearly enough inspectors to impose compliance on industry. The institutional limits of British government have compelled co-operation with affected interests.

How close have British departments been to such groups, and how effectively have these been organized?

British interests have succeeded quite well by international standards in creating 'peak associations' representing broad sectors of society that are well staffed, are generally respected by government organizations, and have close, effective relationships with major government departments. The National Farmers' Union and the Confederation of British Industry compare favourably with foreign equivalents in terms of the quality of their work and the degree to which they have established close relations with government departments. The Trade Union Congress (TUC) has done almost as well, though it is noticeably under-funded compared with the CBI.

This is not to say that relations with all governments are equally warm. At times groups such as the CBI and TUC have been so closely consulted on major economic and social policies that commentators have expressed fears that Britain was becoming a corporatist or neocorporatist country – one in which major policy decisions are made after what approximate to negotiations with groups accepted by the government as the sole authoritative voices of the sectors of society they claimed to represent. The 1970s were perhaps the high-water mark of neocorporatism in Britain. In more recent years, as we shall see, the situation has been very different.

Beneath or within the peak associations, however, producer groups in Britain take on a more complicated character. There is immense variation in unity, expertise and effectiveness. It is certainly the case that peak associations in Britain such as the CBI or TUC have little or no control over their members. The CBI cannot command individual corporations or trade associations representing specific industries to comply with its policies. The TUC has little control over individual unions, which in turn often struggle to control the local shop stewards within the union. Although government departments found contacts with groups such as the CBI, the NFU or the TUC valuable, relationships with other groups such as the trade associations of individual industries were frustrating, because they lacked the staff, skills and expertise to make discussions worthwhile. Moreover, the limited integration of trade associations into the CBI or of unions into the TUC reduced considerably the value of bargaining between government and peak associations. Promises of co-operation or help from the TUC or CBI could be made worthless by the refusal of member firms, unions or trade associations to accept the deal.

The British producer or economic interest group system is therefore uneven. It contains organizations such as the NFU that are well run and well staffed. It also contains under-funded trade associations or unions that are struggling to survive and have little to give the Civil Service.

Though they are less celebrated in British political culture than in American, interest groups mobilizing ordinary citizens outside their economic interests have increasingly flourished in the post-war period. The Royal Society for the Protection of Birds (RSPB) has more members than any political party in Britain. The Royal National Lifeboat Institution (RNLI), supported entirely by voluntary contributions, provides the primary surface sea rescue service, a function that in the United States is provided by the Coast Guard, a government agency. Consumer organizations, environmental protection organizations ranging in radicalism from the National Trust and the Council for the Preservation of Rural England to Greenpeace and organizations promoting causes as varied as opposing British possession of nuclear weapons (CND) to keeping shops closed on Sundays, all flourish.

Interest groups and policy-making

How do these varied interest groups try to influence policy? On the one hand there is the 'insider' strategy of cultivating close relations with government departments. Groups pursuing this strategy avoid confrontational tactics and rhetoric; they value confidential and regular discussions with ministers and top civil servants so much that they avoid tactics that might disrupt the relationship such as leaking controversial ideas or material to the media, even when there might be a short-term advantage in doing so. The insider group aims to change policy by argument and negotiation in private before ministers are committed to a particular policy. The outsider group such as CND is much more in the public eye as it attempts to change policy by changing the climate of opinion rather than working discreetly behind the scenes.

Some groups shift uneasily from one category to another. It was the proud boast of one former General Secretary of the TUC that he had led the unions out of Trafalgar Square (traditional rallying ground for demonstrations) and into Whitehall, i.e. the government offices. Yet within a few years of this comment, unions were once again rallying in Trafalgar Square as their relationship with government became more confrontational.

There is great variety too in government behaviour towards interest groups. British governments ask a series of questions about interest groups in deciding whether or not to accord them insider status. First, is the interest group capable of providing government with a needed service or information? The CBI provides surveys of industrial activity useful in economic forecasting, the Royal Society for the Prevention of Cruelty to Animals (RSPCA) and the National Society for the Prevention of Cruelty to Children (NSPCC) operate inspectorates that, did they not exist, the government would have to provide. Consequently, they are accorded insider status.

Second, does the group pursue 'reasonable' goals, i.e. are its policies sufficiently close to government policy that it is worth bargaining with them? Radical penal reform groups are not given insider status; the moderate Howard League for Penal Reform is. Third, how badly does the government need the co-operation of the group? A government trying to restrain the growth of wages during a period of full employment may feel that it is worth a high price to secure the co-operation of the TUC. A government that allows higher unemployment to control wage increases as the Thatcher government did, will not value the co-operation of the TUC as highly because it will not need an incomes policy.

British governments enjoy a tremendous advantage in relations with insider groups. There is a continuum between true insider status and outsider status rather than a clear division. Groups can be given more or less insider status according to their current status with the government without any overt, let alone legal, change occurring. Thus an insider group that displeases government might find itself moved towards outsider status almost without realizing what is happening. Instead of frank discussions in confidence with the minister and senior civil servants about policy options, the government may allow the group to present its case to a senior civil servant who will offer tea, listen politely and promise to report to the minister. The opportunity to influence the government's thinking will have been minimal, even though consultation has formally occurred.

The impact of Thatcherism on relations with interest groups

We saw earlier how the eleven and a half years of government under Margaret Thatcher affected the relationship between politicians and the permanent bureaucracy. Was there a similar effect on the relationship between government and interest groups?

The Thatcher administration had a clear strategy of governance. The state would become strong by shrinking its activities. The humiliations endured by British governments in the 1960s and 1970s at the hands of trade unions and other interest groups, resulted from governments trying to do things that they were inherently incapable of doing well, such as controlling wage increases in hundreds of industries and thousand of companies. If government attempted to control inflation by relying on monetary and fiscal policies, even if those policies resulted in high unemployment, there would be no need to try to operate an incomes policy. If there were no incomes policy, the government would not need the co-operation of unions.

Indeed, the Thatcher government was antagonistic to economic interest groups of all kinds, even those that might have seemed to be its natural friends. The CBI, for example, was viewed with intense suspicion by Thatcher; proper business executives should have been out competing in the market place, not sitting in committees with senior civil servants. Relations were not improved when, during the deep recession of the early 1980s, the Director General of the CBI promised a 'bare-knuckle fight' with government unless it reversed policies that he believed were damaging manufacturing industry. The Department of Trade and Industry under the leadership of one of Thatcher's closest protégés, Lord Young, produced a White Paper that claimed that Britain's comparatively poor economic performance was due to an excess of corporatism, a rather astonishing conclusion in view of the economic success of countries that are much more corporatist than Britain (such as Sweden, Austria and Germany). The spirit of the Thatcher government was not to work in partnership with groups, however, but to redeem the nation by imposing solutions on them. Even business needed to be reformed by government, not placated by bargaining with it.

Not surprisingly, the government moved to weaken the interest groups and the interest group system it disliked. The National Economic Development Council (NEDC), which brought together government and major economic interest groups, was downgraded in importance. Meetings between the TUC and ministers became rare. The supremacy of the CBI was threatened by the government promoting the Institute of Directors as a rival to it. The Department of Trade and Industry was reorganized with the explicit goal of reducing the closeness of the links between trade associations and units within the department. Civil servants were encouraged to talk directly to companies and not to use trade associations or the CBI as intermediaries.

In consequence, large numbers of companies opened offices in London to represent their political interests, and there was a boom in 'contract lobbying', the hiring of professional lobbyists by interests, usually companies, to handle a particular political problem. The world of business lobbying began to look more like its counterpart in Washington than British practices in the recent past. The NFU found that it could often receive a more sympathetic hearing from other Ministers of Agriculture in the European Community as a whole than from its former friends in the Ministry of Agriculture, Fisheries and Food (MAFF).

Again, we should ask how enduring the changes made by Thatcher are likely to be.

We noted before that the fall of Thatcher in 1990 brought to an end an unusual period in British politics, one in which an ideological government acted with a high degree of certainty in the correctness of its policies. The Thatcher government was thus much less likely than its predecessors or successors to value advice from either the Civil Service or the bureaucracy. We might anticipate, therefore, that its termination would restore some of the importance of both the senior bureaucracy and interest groups. However, just as the Civil Service will never be exactly the same after Thatcher, so the system of interest representation will not simply revert to its previous practices. The unions will almost certainly not return to their previous strength; the CBI may forge new links with government departments, but a revival of the corporatist experiences of the 1960s is unlikely.

Putting it all together

We have shown that central decision-making in Britain brings together elected politicians, career civil servants and interest group representatives – who may themselves be a very mixed bag of people. The relative importance of the various actors changes according to circumstances. Civil servants are always present, but in certain cases they are more autonomous than in others. The nature of the issue helps determine the way it is handled. Changes in local taxation from a property basis (the rates, weighing more on the better-off) to the Poll Tax (a flat-rate Community Charge on everyone regardless of income) involved politicians very heavily. Safety and health at work are handled predominantly by the interests concerned.

Second, governments may be more or less ideological. The Conservative governments of the 1980s were unusually so, although the subsequent Major government has proved to be more pragmatic in style. But as governments spend longer in office they tend to run out of ideas and may be grateful to civil servants who have their own agenda of problems to be tidied up. This may be more the norm in the mid- and late 1990s.

Third, as we have seen, the importance attached to negotiations with interest groups varies from government to government.

The traditional interpretation of British politics has emphasized the centralization and cohesion of the system. The Cabinet, elected on a party programme, supported by a disciplined majority in the House of Commons, aided by a highly competent, obedient Civil Service, is capable of making far more coherent policy than emerges from the coalition governments of Continental Europe or the American division of powers between legislative, executive and judicial branches.

The traditional stress on the coherence of central decision-making in British government needs to be modified for a number of reasons. First, political: British political parties, and so Cabinets, are coalitions of people of clearly differing views. Differences between 'wets' and 'dries' in the Thatcher government had their counterpart in divisions between left and right in the Labour governments of the 1960s and 1970s: such differences can be profound. Second, in attempting to win votes within occupational groups and regions, British governments have been prepared to make promises that are not always in line with party ideology or the rest of its programme. Promises as diverse as devolution for Scotland and Wales, continuing tax relief on mortgages, a bridge across the Humber, and subsidies for farmers and Austin Rover, have all been made by governments of different parties anxious to win the support of some supposedly strategic block of votes. British governments play the vote-catching game as well as most.

Another factor disrupting the supposed unity of British government, as we have stressed in this chapter, are divisions within the administrative sector itself. Departments differ in their attitudes and concerns. The Ministry of Agriculture is much more supportive of farm subsidies, as is the Ministry of Defence of military spending, than is the Treasury. As a major part of the job of ministers is to represent the interests and attitudes of their departments, such differences create conflicts not only between civil servants but also between their ministers in the Cabinet. It is interesting to note that these centrifugal tendencies of government have created major problems in controlling expenditure. Numerous experimental techniques such as the Public Expenditure Survey and Programme Analysis and Review have broken down – in large part because of the determination of each minister to fight for his department's programmes. Indeed, any minister who gallantly offered to cut his department's budget in order to help the government reach its general objectives would be seen by Cabinet colleagues as showing such weakness or quixotic behaviour as to lose political strength permanently.

The administrative style of British government has always been to entrust the implementation of most policies to other people – local notables serving as Justices of the Peace until the late nineteenth century, local authorities, and, in some policy areas, interest groups. Such devolution limits the degree of control that central government enjoys. It was traditionally said that a French Minister of Education could tell you at any hour of the day what every child in France was studying; Conservative governments were never able completely to break local control of education in Britain even though they wanted to do so. Administrative devolution saves central government the expense and difficulty of running schools directly; it also limits the degree to which the Secretary of State for Education can make real decisions about what happens in schools. The 'internal market' in education will decrease this power even further.

The coherence of central decision-making in Britain has also been limited by the weakness of 'umbrella' interest groups speaking for broad social groups, particularly unions and employers. As we noted, the CBI and TUC have very little control over their members: British governments thus deal with interest groups which have not themselves achieved the same degree of unity as interest groups in, say, Austria or Sweden. In consequence, they have to broker more conflicts than their counterparts in countries with more centralized interest group systems. At times central decision-makers are themselves disorientated by contending and conflicting claims from groups.

Central decision-making in Britain still offers the opportunity for politicians who know what they want and how to achieve it. The Thatcher and Major governments show that elections can indeed make a major difference in British politics. Yet behind the apparent simplicity lies the complexity of interactions between different spheres – political, administrative, and interest – groups.

Within each sphere there is also less unity than might be expected. British government is formally and constitutionally highly unified. In reality it is substantially fragmented.

Chapter 3

Cabinet co-ordination or prime ministerial dominance? A conflict of three principles of Cabinet government
Anthony King

Our previous discussion has uncovered a number of contradictions at the heart of British government. It is highly centralized but at the same time remarkably fragmented. On the one hand, the state is unitary, Parliament is sovereign, and the executive (in the form of the Prime Minister, the Cabinet and the great Whitehall departments) is dominant. But, on the other hand, the departments themselves are often in conflict, there are no mechanisms for 'concertation' among different economic and social sectors, and in recent years there have often been profound disagreements among Britain's political parties, not just about the details of policy but about what the broad outlines of the country's economy and society should be.

Some of the difficulties this poses for coherent and consistent policy-making have been explored in the previous chapter. In particular we have commented on the absence of effective co-ordinating arrangements or institutions below the level of the Cabinet itself. Given the Cabinet's unique importance in the executive and the link it provides, through the majority party, between government and Parliament, we devote this chapter to an analysis of its current modes of operation.

We should not however expect that the Cabinet can wholly escape the contradictions and conflicts that abound at other levels of government, for they are to be found in Downing Street and Whitehall as much as in the rest of the political system. They find expression in a conflict of three principles.

The principle of collegiality

When the Founding Fathers wrote the American constitution in the summer of 1787, they decided that the United States should have a unified executive. They thought that only if all executive power were vested in a single individual, the President, could the new country's government have the necessary capacity for decision and action. In doing so, the Founding Fathers were modelling their new system on what they were used to. Executive power in most of the British North American colonies had been vested in a single individual, the colonial governor, who was solely responsible for the colony's affairs, even though he usually had associated with him some kind of council of advisers or informal cabinet.

The system in Britain, however, was evolving in the opposite direction. The monarchy in eighteenth-century Britain was fast relinquishing its monopoly of executive power. But it was relinquished not to one man, but rather to that group of men who could, collectively, command the confidence of a majority in the House of Commons. A group of men was necessary because only a group comprising a dozen or so could win and maintain the support of enough of the numerous factions into which the eighteenth-century House of Commons was divided. A hydra-headed executive was needed in order to mirror an even more hydra-headed assembly. All governments were, of necessity, coalition governments, in fact, if not in name. Frequently these governmental coalitions fell apart under the pressure of personality conflicts, policy differences and changes in the balance of interests and opinion in the House of Commons itself. The best hope of any government having the will to remain in power was for its individual members to submerge their differences, at least in public, and to present a united front to Parliament. In the famous words attributed to Lord Melbourne, an early nineteenth-century Prime Minister, 'It doesn't much matter what we say, so long as we all say the same thing.'

Thus, out of political necessity, was born the 'principle of collegiality', one of the principles that informs British constitutional practice to this day. The principle had, and has, three linked components. The first was that the 'best', the most authoritative, decisions in British government must be collective decisions – decisions of the whole Cabinet, not just of one member of it or of any group of members. The second was that, if the best decisions were to be collective decisions, then the collective's members had the right to be consulted about the most important of them and to participate in the taking of them. The third was that, collective decisions having been taken, all the members of the Cabinet and the government had the duty to defend them publicly. Political strength lies in unity. The best way of achieving unity, and of increasing the chances that it could be publicly maintained, was collective deliberation. British government was not to be a one-man band; it was to be like an orchestra.

This collegial mode of operation, the product of eighteenth- and nineteenth-century political circumstances, is still the dominant norm in the British constitution today. The Prime Minister still has few decisions that (s)he can take alone. The best decisions are still Cabinet decisions; indeed a decision that does not have the Cabinet's sanction behind it is, in a strict sense, not a decision of the government at all.

Moreover, institutions have grown up to reinforce the Cabinet's collegiality and special constitutional status. The country's principal civil servant is the Cabinet Secretary. The government's principal co-ordinating mechanism is the Cabinet Office (not the Prime Minister's office). The most authoritative record of the government's decisions is the Cabinet Minutes. Not all government business, even in the upper echelons of Downing Street and Whitehall, is Cabinet business, of course. For reasons of convenience, speed, secrecy and political expediency, much high-level business is transacted by small groups of ministers (some formally constituted as Cabinet committees, some not); by groups of civil servants and ministers meeting together; and by means of ministerial correspondence. But the principal focus of governmental decision-making is still, in the 1990s as it was in the 1790s, the Cabinet.

The principle of collegiality also finds expression in the language of Downing Street and Whitehall. Members of a collegial body are, in a literal sense, 'colleagues', and that is the word that British Cabinet ministers use in referring to one another. The use of the word 'colleagues' implies that Cabinet ministers are associated together in a common political enterprise. It also implies a degree of equality: colleagues are people who work together; they are not people who work for one another. Ministers correspondingly refer to the Cabinet and to the government as a whole as 'we'. The doctrine that imposes a vow of silence on dissenting Cabinet minsters (unless they care to resign) is the doctrine of '*collective* ministerial responsibility'.

The principle of collegiality is thus formally dominant in the British system. It is enshrined in institutions and in language. It is spelled out (although the specific term is seldom used) in a hundred textbooks. It does not, however, go unchallenged. Two other principles of British government compete with it, and the competition between them can be cut-throat. One of the two competing principles is the 'principle of departmental autonomy'.

The principle of departmental autonomy

We have already gone into this in some detail in Chapter 2. Most of the time British government departments do not have much to do with one another. Why should they? The Home Office imprisons prisoners. The Department of Transport builds roads. The Department of Social Security pays pensions. The Department of Health runs the National Health Service. The Ministry of Agriculture subsidizes farmers. And so on. Most departments' business requires little contact with other departments. Reference is often made to 'the Whitehall machine'. In fact, for most purposes there is no one great Whitehall machine: there are dozens of little (and some not so little) Whitehall machines.

This separation of government departments is reinforced in a number of ways. One already described is the structure of the British Civil Service. Although most policy-making civil servants are initially recruited into the Civil Service at large rather than into a single department, they are then assigned to one department and, after some initial transfers, spend all or most of their subsequent careers in that department. Permanent secretaries are among the very few who are shifted sideways. The result is that the great majority of civil servants imbibe the ethos of their department, are socialized into its norms and come to accept its institutional goals as their goals. Their view is thus seldom government-wide and their relations with civil servants in other departments are apt to be antagonistic and adversarial rather than co-operative. They brief their ministers to 'go into battle' on behalf of their department and against rival departments.

Relations between government departments are often antagonistic and adversarial because, on the occasions when different Whitehall departments do come into contact, they are likely to do so because they disagree or because they are laying claim to the same quantum of scarce resources. The annual public expenditure round, to take the extreme case, pits every spending department against every other spending department and every spending department against the Treasury. The question that each department normally asks in its dealings with other departments is not 'What would be best for the government?' or 'What would be best for the country?' but 'What would be best for the department?' This is not as selfish as it sounds: 'best for the department' usually means best in terms of some departmental conception of the public good (like spending more money on the National Health Service). All the same, this approach means that inter-departmental relations are usually competitive relations.

Not only do government departments compete; their political heads do too. Ministers may call each other 'colleagues' and may genuinely feel themselves to be; but they are also, almost invariably, rivals. They are rivals for funds, rivals for places in the parliamentary timetable, rivals for a share of the political limelight, rivals for the favour of the Prime Minister, rivals for the plaudits of the House of Commons, rivals not least for promotion in the ministerial hierarchy. This competitiveness among ministers – 'there is little friendship at the top' – compounds and is compounded by the competitiveness among departments. Ministers become their department's champions in the inter-departmental wars. They win their battle honours – in their own eyes, in their civil servants' eyes, in their colleagues' eyes – by fighting vigorously on their department's behalf and, more important, by winning. It is small consolation for a defeated minister – whom everyone in Whitehall will know has been defeated – to be able to say that perhaps, after all, his defeat was in the government's or the public's interest.

One consequence of the principle of departmental autonomy is that in Whitehall, as in most other human institutions, 'where you stand depends on where you sit'. Ministers see the world from their department's point of view. They stand where the department stands (or where they want it to stand). Not surprisingly, when, as frequently happens in Britain, a minister is transferred from one department to another, he almost invariably ceases to be his old department's champion and becomes his new one's. As Chief Secretary to the Treasury, John Major was passionately opposed to increased public spending and was responsible for freezing child benefit. Once he became Prime Minister, he could see the advantages of higher public spending, including on child benefit.

We have explored the consequences of departmental autonomy for general decision-making processes in British government, but it also has subtle effects on the operation of the Cabinet and Cabinet committees. Under the principle of collegiality, those who serve on bodies like the Cabinet should have as their principal concern the interests, especially the political interests, of the collective as a whole. They should attend Cabinet and Cabinet committee meetings, and conduct all their Cabinet-related affairs, as *members* of the

Cabinet, not as Cabinet (i.e. departmental) *ministers*. They should be above the inter-departmental battle, concerned solely to advance the government's interests and those of the political party that sustains the government in office. Under the principle of collegiality, the Cabinet collectively should function, in effect, as a kind of 'council of elders', not merely shrewd and wise, but also, and above all, detached. The Cabinet should be a genuine council of state (or at least a governmental council or party council).

The principle of departmental autonomy, however, exerts a powerful contrary pull on ministers. Under the principle of departmental autonomy, their duty – and also their role, since that is what others expect of them – is not to rise above the battle but to take an active part in it. Viewed from a distance, the Cabinet may seem like the board of directors of a small private company, its various members anxious to work together to advance the company's interests. Viewed from closer up, the Cabinet often appears more like a meeting of the United Nations Security Council, with the representative of each member state concerned to protect and promote the interests of that state. For 'Secretary of State for Transport', read 'Ambassador from the Department of Transport'. Under the principle of departmental autonomy, the Cabinet minister who fights and loses on behalf of his 'country' has lost; but at least he has fought. The Cabinet minister who actually volunteers to sacrifice his departmental interests in the interests of the collective is thought to be behaving oddly. He has 'let down the side', 'broken the rules'.

The contradiction between these two principles – those of collegiality and departmental autonomy – inevitably poses problems for individual ministers. What role should they play? When should they play it? How hard should they play it? It also poses problems for the collective institutions within which ministers operate, notably the Cabinet. The outcomes that best serve the interests of individual ministers and their departments may not be the outcomes that best serve the interests of the collective body as a whole. An outcome that the Cabinet can live with internally, for example, may not be an outcome that the government or the governing party can live with electorally. Hard bargaining does not always make for good policy, whatever one's definition of 'good'.

Because a system of pure inter-ministerial and inter-departmental competition would produce unsatisfactory results, there has grown up in the British system (and in most others) an alternative set of political roles that is less department-centred. If departmental ministers are 'players', the occupants of this alternative set of roles are 'referees'. They are referees in the sense that they are in a position to referee political and policy fights among individual ministers and groups of ministers; but they are also referees in a more extended sense. They are in a position to bring, and are likely to see it as part of their job to bring, the interests of the collective as a whole to bear on inter-ministerial and inter-departmental disputes. Their role is to be more detached and more disinterested than most departmental ministers are capable of being. Their role is also, amid the governmental fray, to try not to lose sight of 'the big picture': the governing party's electoral interests, the national interest, Britain's interests in the European Community or whatever. Those playing referee roles, more than other ministers, are the bearers of the principle of collegiality.

All ministers are likely to be referees on occasion. Almost all ministers are genuinely concerned about the collective and will step from time to time out of their purely departmental role. On occasion one or more departmental ministers will have no personal or departmental stake in what is currently at issue and may well opt to function as referees on an *ad hoc* basis. But in practice most referee roles are more institutionalized. In the modern British system, the Leader of the House of Commons, with wide-ranging responsibilities for the government's legislative programme and without any department of his own, is likely to be a referee. So are the Chancellor of the Duchy of Lancaster and the Lord Privy Seal, also ministers who usually have no department of their own. If he has time, the Foreign Secretary may function as a referee on domestic matters. In the Labour governments of the 1970s, Edward Short, Harold Lever and Shirley Williams sometimes took on this role. In the Thatcher governments of the 1980s, William Whitelaw frequently did so.

But of course the principal referee in every government – the referee of referees – is the Prime Minister. The third of our three principles is the 'principle of prime ministerial authority'. This principle may on occasion reinforce the principle of collegiality, but at the same time it can be its most powerful competitor. This principle has been the greatest single source of change at the centre of British government in recent years.

The principle of prime ministerial authority

To understand the place of the Prime Minister in the British system, it is useful to begin by imagining someone called 'the Prime Minister' with none of the real Prime Minister's more formidable powers. Suppose that this notional Prime Minister could not hire, fire and reshuffle ministers. Suppose that (s)he could not create and destroy government departments. Suppose that (s)he was not the head of the Civil Service and the security services. Suppose, in other words, that (s)he was merely the chair of the Cabinet, possibly elected by its members. (After all, if there were no Prime Minister, the members of the Cabinet would probably want *someone* to act as chair and there is a good chance that they would want that someone to act as chair for a period of time. They would not want to have to elect somebody new every week or month.)

Such a scenario is improbable; but it points to the fact that even such a powerless Prime Minister might still have an important role to play, especially if the individual in question was a senior politician and was taken seriously by those around him. The role (s)he would be asked to play would probably be the one just referred to: the role of referee. After all, even in the absence of a proper Prime Minister, the members of the Cabinet would in all likelihood still want someone, not merely to take the chair at their formal meetings but to referee fights among them and to have a continuing concern for the group's collective interests. The Prime Minister, in other words, is not to be seen solely (or even mainly) as someone imposed on the Cabinet from outside. If the referee roles the Prime Minister plays did not exist, they would have to be invented. Small groups *need* leadership – or, if not leadership, then refereeship, with a leading individual responsible for keeping order and concerned for the group's common interests. Groups that do not produce leaders and referees, in however informal a way, seldom persist for long.

In the real world of British government, the Prime Minister's referee roles are an important source of his authority. (S)he is not merely a source of 'power'; (s)he is also a source of 'order'. Colleagues look to the PM to settle their disputes and disagreements. They expect the PM to do what they customarily find it difficult to do for themselves: namely, to focus on, and constantly to bear in mind, the 'big picture'. More than any other minister, the Prime Minister sits astride a flow of business – of meetings, papers and telephone calls – that encompasses the full range of the government's activities. More than other ministers, (s)he is therefore in a position to see the connection among aspects of the government's work that are widely dispersed and may not seem to be related. (S)he also has a powerful incentive to keep the big picture in focus, being the member of the government who, more than any other, is blamed when things go wrong. In short, the Prime Minister is uniquely well placed to be not merely *a* bearer but *the* principal bearer in the government of the principle of collegiality.

So far, so good. The Prime Minister as referee emerges as a neutral, detached, disinterested person, concerned only for the common weal. And (s)he may often be all these things. Cabinet ministers frequently pay tribute to their Prime Minister's 'kindness', 'consideration' and 'wisdom' in playing their referee roles. The head of government is seen by colleagues, more often than might be supposed, as a considerate parent or kindly uncle.

But of course, in the real world, there is more to it than that. The Prime Minister is not merely a referee; (s)he is also a player, in two distinct senses. In the first place (s)he often has views, possibly strongly held views. (S)he does not merely want to referee arguments: (s)he wants to win them. In the second place, the real Prime Minister is not in fact the mere chair hypothesized a moment ago. On the contrary, history and custom have contrived to endow the office with formidable executive powers.

One of these powers is peculiarly important. It is the power not merely to appoint but also to promote, to demote, to move sideways and ultimately to dismiss every other individual member of the Cabinet and the government. It is the power, in other words, to make or break men's and women's political careers; and it is especially formidable in the 1990s, when most politicians are career politicians, people whose political careers matter to them a great deal, sometimes more than anything else. The Prime Minister alone possesses what almost all the other politicians around him desperately want: ministerial jobs. And this possession is his or her power. 'I have had people in here weeping and even fainting,' Ramsay MacDonald said in the 1920s. Someone who can make members of Parliament weep and even faint is someone to be reckoned with.

And here we come to the greatest contradiction of all at the top of the

British system: the contradiction between the principle of collegiality and the principle of prime ministerial authority. On the one hand, the Cabinet is a collective body, a collegial executive; all its members, including the Prime Minister, are 'colleagues'. But, on the other hand, one minister, the Prime Minister, has far greater power over his ministers than they have over him – and, to the extent that he has such power and authority, British government at the top ceases to be a collegial government and becomes, if not a single-person government, then at least a single-person-dominated government. A collective executive argues for a high level of equality among its members; but the relations among the members of Britain's collective executive are anything but equal. They are those of superordination and subordination, at least so far as the Prime Minister is concerned. The Prime Minister is not a 'colleague'; (s)he is the boss. It is as though the chairman of the board of a public company had the right to sack all of his fellow directors or the head of a trade union had the right to dismiss his entire executive committee.

Prime ministerial authority has, of course, many other buttresses: the prestige that attaches to the office, the Prime Minister's control over senior civil service appointments, control over the organization of central government, control over the conduct of Cabinet and sub-Cabinet meetings, and the authority that flows naturally from the fact that, as the Cabinet's most visible member, (s)he is likely to be held to account by the press and the public for everything that goes wrong. But the buttress (s)he can least easily do without is undoubtedly his control over ministerial posts. That, more than anything else, is what sets the Prime Minister apart.

A conflict of principles

The three principles we have been outlining – those of collegiality, departmental autonomy and prime ministerial authority – are clearly in competition with one another, potentially at least. Collegiality is likely to compete with departmental autonomy. Collegiality is also likely to compete with prime ministerial authority. Prime ministerial authority in turn is likely to compete with departmental autonomy, as the demands of the Prime Minster's job impinge on those of departmental ministers'.

How do these actual and potential tensions work out in practice? What balances (or indeed imbalances) are struck? The answers go to the heart of many of the long-standing debates about 'prime ministerial government'.

One way of resolving the tensions among the three principles is for the Prime Minister to become wholly dominant, at the expense of the principles of collegiality and departmental autonomy. So powerful, however, are the latter two principles that periods of total prime ministerial dominance in the twentieth century have been quite rare. They have existed all the same. One was during the premiership of David Lloyd George in the latter half of the First World War. Another was during Winston Churchill's premiership through most of the Second World War. The most recent was during most of Margaret Thatcher's premiership between 1979 and 1990.

A pattern of prime ministerial dominance seems to assert itself under one or other of two sets of circumstances. One occurs only when the country as a whole, or at least the government as a whole, confronts a grave emergency. If everyone in the government is agreed that there is such an emergency, and if they are all further agreed on the broad steps that need to be taken to deal with it, then ministers may tacitly agree that they will, in effect, hand over their policy-making powers to the Prime Minister for the duration. In other words, they agree to suspend (in practice) the principle of collegiality and also (in so far as it is possible to suspend it) the principle of departmental autonomy. Individual ministers become for the time being the Prime Minister's agents rather than his colleagues. He is the leader; they are, and for the time being acknowledge that they are, his subordinates. Such a picture simplifies, but does not greatly distort, the system of government that operated during most of Lloyd George's and Churchill's wartime premierships. The ability to adapt in this way is a testimonial to the flexibility of Cabinet government and to its ability to adapt to changing circumstances.

A pattern of prime ministerial dominance may also assert itself when (1) the Prime Minister has goals that he or she wants to achieve, which are separate from the goals of other members of the government; (2) he or she is absolutely determined to pursue those goals; (3) he or she is prepared to use every power available, including the power to hire, fire and relocate, to get his or her way; (4) he or she does not care a fig for the principle of collegiality; (5) those members of the Cabinet who do not share the Prime Minister's goals are too weak and/or divided and/or demoralized to assert their rights as Cabinet 'colleagues'. Such a combination of circumstances is rare in British politics. But it defines quite precisely the character of most phases of the remarkable eleven-year premiership of Margaret Thatcher in the 1980s, which we shall examine more closely below.

Another way of resolving the tensions among the three principles is for the Prime Minister to be active and assertive, and even in some ways 'dominant', but for him to be at the same time highly collegial in his mode of operations. A Prime Minister may have strong views of his own, and he may be confident in his expression of them; but he may at the same time believe, or calculate, that the best way of achieving his ends – and also of keeping his government together and himself in power – is by working with his Cabinet colleagues rather than against them or around them. In their different ways, Harold Macmillan, Harold Wilson (at least during his first few years), Edward Heath and James Callaghan were all strong Prime Minsters, with a great deal of personal authority, who nevertheless took the principle of collegiality seriously.

They did so for different reasons. Macmillan genuinely believed in the principle (and, in addition, he had seen Sir Anthony Eden come a cropper partly as a result of violating it). Wilson and Callaghan were conscious of deep divisions within their Cabinets, and also within the Labour party, and probably chose collegiality as the best available means of holding their administrations together. (A Thatcher-like approach on their part and their governments might well simply have fallen apart.) By contrast, Heath could easily afford to be collegial: his administration was one of the most united of modern times and suffered no ministerial resignations despite its policy failures and its innumerable U-turns (and also despite the presence in it of Margaret Thatcher, who, whatever her subsequent protestations, sat uncomplaining throughout).

One reason for drawing attention to the Prime Minister who is at once strong and active but also highly collegial is because there is a tendency on the part of some writers to suggest that strong Prime Ministers are also Prime Ministers who invariably ignore their Cabinet colleagues or ride roughshod over them. This is not so. A few do; Mrs Thatcher often did. But the majority of strong Prime Ministers appear to be quite ready to play by the rules of the Cabinet game. It is the game they know. It does not prevent them, if they play it well, from achieving their purposes.

Not all Prime Ministers choose, however, to be activists. Some either do not want to, or see no need to, assert themselves unduly *vis-à-vis* their ministerial colleagues (whom they genuinely regard as colleagues). In the Labour government of 1945–51 Clement Attlee was perfectly capable of asserting his authority and from time to time did so, sometimes with devastating effects; but for the most part he was content to be the relatively passive chairman of a Cabinet that contained a large number of able ministers, that was reasonably united and that, until its last year or two, had an unusually strong sense of direction. Churchill in his post-war phase was also relatively passive. Like Attlee, he had as senior ministers a number of men of stature whom he trusted; and, in addition, towards the end of his last administration he was often ill. Sir Alec Douglas-Home was almost entirely passive, and Harold Wilson lapsed into passivity in his second term. Under passive Prime Ministers, the principle of collegiality comes into its own and the principle of prime ministerial authority falls largely into abeyance. Attlee enjoyed the job, but the peacetime Churchill, Douglas-Home and Wilson between 1974 and 1976 all showed signs of finding it irksome, even boring. Wilson eventually quit.

The danger for governments with passive or recessive prime ministers is, of course, that the principle of departmental autonomy, always present, may assert itself at the expense not just of the principle of prime ministerial authority but also of the collegiality principle. Governments of this kind are liable to become deeply divided, given the ever-present conflicts between departments and disagreements among ministers; and, if a Prime Minister is so passive (or ill) that he cannot or will not play even his minimal role as a referee, he is liable to find that his administration drifts into disorder. The Wilson government 1974–6 was a disorderly, departments-centred, ministers-centred affair. So was the Callaghan government in its last months, as Callaghan, after a strong start, grew tired and disillusioned.

From Thatcher to Major

British government at the top is to be understood in terms of the tensions among our three principles. The principles of collegiality and departmental autonomy are almost always in competition with one another. The principles of collegiality and prime ministerial authority often are. How have these principles played themselves out in recent years?

Under Margaret Thatcher, as we have seen, the principle of prime ministerial authority was in the ascendent, if not in all phases of her premiership then in most of them. Thatcher knew what she wanted. She was determined to get it. She used the powers of her office to the fullest extent in order to get her way. In particular, she was ruthless in dismissing or demoting ministers who either disagreed with her or did not display sufficient zeal in pursuing the objectives closest to her heart. By November 1990 the tally of dismissed Cabinet ministers was a long one: Norman St John-Stevas, Sir Ian Gilmour, Mark Carlisle, Lord Soames, Lord Young, Francis Pym, David Howell, Patrick Jenkin, Peter Rees, John Biffen, John Moore, Paul Channon.

The principle of departmental autonomy occasionally asserted itself; for example, prior to the Madrid European summit in 1989 the Chancellor of the Exchequer, Nigel Lawson, and the Foreign Secretary, Sir Geoffrey Howe, by threatening to resign, forced Thatcher to concede the principle that Britain would ultimately join the European Exchange Rate Mechanism. But assertions of departmental autonomy were fairly rare; and the principle of collegiality fell largely into disuse. The forms of collegiality continued to be observed, of course (the Cabinet continued to meet on Thursday mornings during parliamentary sessions); but 'Cabinet government' as a genuinely collaborative enterprise had become largely an empty shell.

It is impossible to be sure, but Thatcher's contempt for the principle of collegiality seems to have played some part in her downfall in 1990. It appears to have done so in two ways. In the first place, one of the political advantages of the collegiality principle is that, if ministers are able to speak freely and to fight their corners vigorously, they can, individually and collectively, act as a kind of early warning system for the Prime Minister, alerting him or her to the probable adverse consequences of, and the political dangers in, lines of policy the Prime Minister and government are considering pursuing. By 1990 Mrs Thatcher's personal early warning system was seriously defective. She herself had largely destroyed it. The introduction of the ill-fated Poll Tax was only the most notorious example of a number of policies that had not been adequately 'pre-tested' with ministers and other senior Conservative politicians.

In the second place, Thatcher's contempt for the collegiality principle almost certainly irritated (at the very least) a considerable number of her ministerial 'colleagues'. They were proud people. They were conscious of their ministerial prerogatives. They did not greatly enjoy the public and semi-public dressings-down to which they were sometimes subjected. Michael Heseltine, Secretary of State for Defence, resigned in January 1986. Nigel Lawson, Chancellor of the Exchequer, more dangerously, resigned in October 1989. Sir Geoffrey Howe, Foreign Secretary, more dangerously still, resigned in November 1990. At the end, only five members of Thatcher's Cabinet believed that she should continue in office and that she could win the second ballot in the Conservative leadership contest that followed Howe's resignation. Most of the rest told her that, in their judgment, she could not win; and it seems probable that, in at least some cases, their judgment was influenced by the fact that they did not desperately want her to win. She had been a dominant figure for a long time. Some people like being dominated. Some do not.

When John Major became Prime Minister it was as though he had read textbooks on British constitutional theory, had observed very closely the circumstances of Margaret Thatcher's downfall, and had come to the conclusion that he was going to do things differently – very differently. He knew that Thatcher's political early warning system had collapsed. He knew that many Cabinet colleagues had resented her style of leadership (he may secretly have resented it himself). He was determined to reunite both the government and the Conservative party, and he knew that one of the best means of accomplishing these linked objectives would be to be as collegial as Margaret Thatcher had been uncollegial. He, unlike her, would listen. He, unlike her, would consult. He, unlike her, would take his fellow Cabinet members seriously and would respect their right to represent the interests of their departments and to take an independent view.

The result was the re-enthronement, under Major, of the principle of collegiality. The Thatcherite experience with prime ministerial dominance, like many other aspects of Thatcherism, proved transitory. The government's decision in early 1991 to replace the Poll Tax with a Council Tax was a genuinely collective effort, and before the Maastricht European summit in December 1991 Major took care to see every member of the Cabinet in order to gauge how far each was prepared to go in the direction of European political and economic union. In the months immediately prior to the 1992 General Election, the formal weekly meeting of the Cabinet was frequently followed by an informal meeting at which members of the Cabinet, meeting as party politicians and in the absence of civil servants, were invited to discuss the details of election strategy.

None of this is to say that John Major is a weak or passive Prime Minister. To be sure, he has Cabinet colleagues like Michael Heseltine and Douglas Hurd who are politically more powerful *vis-à-vis* him than, latterly, any of Thatcher's Cabinet colleagues were *vis-à-vis* her; and, as a new and relatively inexperienced Prime Minister, he has been forced to tread somewhat warily. But, that said, Major has clearly been determined from the beginning to be an active Prime Minister – one who, so to speak, 'reaches out' for collegiality rather than having it thrust upon him. In the case of the Poll Tax, he was determined that, even though it had been the 'flagship' of the Thatcher administration, it had to be abolished – and be seen to be abolished. He appointed Michael Heseltine Environment Secretary towards that end, and through several months of Cabinet discussions and negotiations in early 1991 he worked, patiently but single-mindedly, towards the goal of a replacement tax that would minimize the electoral damage the Poll Tax had inflicted on the Tory party and at the same time have a reasonable chance of being accepted, at least in the long run, by the opposition. The full Cabinet and all the relevant ministers were involved in all the discussions. The process was collegial in the fullest sense. But the Prime Minister dominated it. His style was akin to that of James Callaghan during the 1976 IMF crisis. Both men knew what they wanted, and one of the things they wanted was to carry a united party and government with them. Both were successful.

John Major's collegiality undoubtedly owes much to his instincts and temperament, but it also represents a conscious rejection of Margaret Thatcher's authoritarian style – on his own part and on the part of her erstwhile colleagues. Indeed, in a paradoxical way, Margaret Thatcher may, in spite of herself, have strengthened the principle of collegiality and given it a new status and legitimacy. Thatcher largely rejected the principle, in practice if not in theory. Her rejection was viewed with dismay, not merely by many Conservative politicians but also, from a somewhat greater distance, by most Labour and Liberal Democrat politicians. They saw her extreme assertion of the principle of prime ministerial authority. They did not like what they saw. And they made a mental note that no Prime Minister in their political lifetime was going to be allowed to get away with anything like what she had got away with. Such a blatant assertion of prime ministerial power was not to be allowed to happen again. As we have noted in other contexts, the most enduring legacy of Thatcherism may be the reaction against it.

For all these reasons, the principle of collegiality is alive and well and living in Downing Street. Margaret Thatcher did not remake the prime ministerial office in her own image. On the contrary, by the manner in which she comported herself in office she did much, however paradoxically, to ensure that collegiality as an operating principle at the top of British government would live on from the eighteenth century into the twenty-first.

Renewed fragmentation

What consequences do these developments have for the problems of central co-ordination and policy cohesiveness that we have noted as being central to British policy-making processes? Does the current reassertion of collegiality imply greater fragmentation at these levels or less?

The answer is that it depends on how far the government can maintain its unity and programme in the face of pressures from departmental autonomy and personal and other rivalries among Cabinet ministers. Collegiality is likely to be reinforced by them: but policy agreements obtained on a fully collegial basis will not be less binding than those imposed by prime ministerial power. However, they will almost certainly be more considered.

Perhaps the major problem for Cabinet co-ordination of policy-making lies less in how decisions are taken in Cabinet, however, than in how decisions are monitored and implemented within the government machine. Most policy is made either within departments or through a labyrinthine structure of committees, many of which involve only civil servants, or non-Cabinet ministers. Many may nevertheless have implications for general policies the government wishes to pursue. The sheer task of keeping track of them involves more resources than the Cabinet as an entity, or the Cabinet Office, have.

Prime Ministerial dominance under Mrs Thatcher included her acting as a one-woman enforcer of the policies she was interested in. She would frequently talk to and contact junior ministers and others, in the administration or outside it, to get advice, information and opinions. She would also draw on right-wing policy centres for alternative views.

Her interventions were largely personal, however, and not supported by any institutional base. Indeed, in pursuit of governmental economies (and perhaps distrustful of their advice) she abolished both the Civil Service Department and the Central Policy Review Staff, which might have provided Prime Minister and Cabinet with additional resources for enforcing their collective policies. Without this the Cabinet, like its individual members, becomes heavily dependent on department civil servants both for information and implementation. While adversarial relationships between departments and ministers may enable the Cabinet to hear opposing points of view and decide between them, they do not expose the Cabinet to a continuing stream of information from its own agents: and they leave it dependent for the implementation of its decisions on departments which in some cases have bitterly opposed them.

Chapter 4
The place of Parliament
Melvyn Read

British governments are formed by the party which wins most seats in the House of Commons. Usually, but not invariably, this is the party which also controls the majority of seats. The growth of third parties (Liberal Democrats, Welsh and Scottish Nationalists, Ulster Unionists and Social Democrats) means that a 'hung' parliament, where no clear Conservative or Labour majority exists, is always a possibility. The more usual situation is that of the 1980s and early 1990s, however, where Conservative governments with majorities respectively of 44, 144, 100 and 21 dominated the proceedings.

Clearly these different situations have different consequences for relations between government and Parliament, and relations within Parliament itself, which we shall explore below. Besides supporting governments, however, and providing their members (all members of a government have to be MPs or Peers) Parliament has the equally important role – at least in constitutional theory – of scrutiny, discussion and, if necessary, criticism of executive actions. It is this aspect we shall concentrate on in this chapter. There are grounds for believing that the obsessive secrecy of British governments and their desire to manipulate information to their own advantage undermine Parliament's role as a forum for informed criticism and constructive debate. Together with the majority party's (i.e. the government's) control over procedures and legislation, they may deprive ordinary MPs of any real political influence at all. In order to investigate these points we have to look at the structure of Parliament and the nature of its business, before examining the pressures for reform which may come to the fore in the 1990s.

The structure of Parliament

The Lords

Although we generally equate 'Parliament' with the elected House of Commons, it also comprises the nominated and hereditary House of Lords. Britain is the only country in the world to contain such a chamber within a democratically elected Parliament. Its inappropriateness in this context has been clear since 1911, when the Parliament Act (restricting its previous power of veto to one of delay over legislation) promised fundamental reform later. At the end of the century it still exists, with the same delaying powers.

Yet the pressure of legislation does render necessary a 'revising' chamber to consider Bills more carefully than the House of Commons (which under 'guideline' procedures often passes legislation without properly debating it). It must also be said that although the Lords is dominated by hereditary peers, most of its more active members are those nominated by the government to a 'life peerage'. In addition, an active role is played on certain issues by judges and bishops who have attained their position by merit. While hereditary peers still attend (some of course being distinguished in their own right) they do not dominate discussion although they may crucially influence voting – usually in favour of a Conservative government.

The House, being composed of generally elderly and privileged people, does incline towards the Conservatives and it grew increasingly out of sympathy with the minority and small majority Labour governments of the 1970s, obstructing much of their legislation. (Its delaying powers give it an effective veto if a government is approaching the end of its term or fears defeat from a reintroduction of the Bill in the House of Commons to override the Lords.)

However it must be said that the House also fell out of sympathy with the Thatcherite policies of the 1980s, particularly as they involved a torrent of badly conceived and drafted Bills which markedly increased its pressure of work. On technical Bills in which members took a personal interest the government suffered notable defeats which they could not reverse in the Commons: the Wildlife and Countryside Bill (1981); the Sunday Trading Bill (1986); and on provisions to allow the Secretary of State for Education to intervene on certain university teaching decisions.

Despite these and other notable stands against the current of New Right reforms, the Lords' major influence is through persuasion and correction of details rather than direct defiance of the government. It is still worthwhile to get the support of its members because of their personal influence and weight, and the publicity this attracts for views promulgated in the House. In the last analysis, however, the role of the Lords is peripheral, and it is in the House of Commons that governments are formed and major debates take place.

The Commons

The mechanics of legislation

The House of Commons meets for about 200–250 days of the year, on a reasonably continuous basis from late October to July or August. General debates, questions to and statements from ministers, and certain stages of legislation are debated in full meetings of the House from mid-afternoon to around midnight. Much work is done in specialized committees which meet both in the mornings and later, in tandem with meetings of the whole House.

Such committees are of two general kinds. Standing committees consider the technical details of legislation. Each government Bill put before Parliament receives a formal first reading and then a second reading on its general principles. This involves the whole House of Commons. By definition since a government normally has majority support in the Commons, government Bills are almost always approved. After the second reading the Bill goes to a standing committee for a clause-by-clause review of its details. Occasionally the whole House of Commons may constitute itself as a committee for this purpose. Generally, however, standing committees consist of 40–90 members. A few of these are specialized (for example, the Scottish and Welsh Standing Committees, to which Scottish and Welsh legislation is referred) and have a relatively permanent membership. Generally, however, the question of which standing committee a Bill goes to is arbitrary, and membership shifts. Each is selected to reflect the balance of parties in the House of Commons so that a government party normally has a majority. After the technical parts are approved the Bill goes back to the full House of Commons for its report stage and subsequently its third reading. All Bills pass through the Commons. Bills can be introduced first in the Lords but this is not usual. If the Lords amend the Bill, then it returns to the Commons which considers those amendments but can override them.

Private Members' Bills introduced by MPs without government backing, and Private Bills sponsored by an outside body (normally some local government) also go through these general stages. Without government support, however, it is unlikely that they will survive all these stages to become law.

Since the government in office so strongly dominates legislative proceedings, the process of passing legislation does not provide much of an opportunity to affect executive action. By and large, legislative bills pass as originally drafted by the government. The considerable amount of time given to legislation might indeed be regarded as a device whereby the two major parties' leadership keep their restive followers occupied and concentrated on the main party battle.

The major instrument through which the legislature independently scrutinizes the executive is the other main type of committee, the select committees. These are bodies whose membership is selected to serve for a Parliamentary session. They are often chaired by an opposition MP, and are expected to produce non-partisan reports on detailed aspects of government administration. They may concentrate on the financial side (as with the Public Accounts Committee) or on a particular region (Scottish or Welsh Affairs). The committees examine documents and witnesses and issue reports on aspects of policy, which can attract widespread newspaper and television comment.

The role of committees in scrutinizing administration is supplemented by the time allotted to questions which individual MPs can put to ministers, including the Prime Minister. Ministers are bound to reply, although their answers may be evasive. Verbal questions put in the House are supplemented by written questions and answers which are reported in *Hansard* (the transcript of parliamentary proceedings published each week). On certain days back-bench MPs can also raise questions for a short adjournment debate at the end of the day's proceedings.

The opposition parties also debate broad aspects of government policy on the supply days allotted to them on the parliamentary timetable. These are used to criticize selected aspects of government policy, and to promote the opposition party's alternative policy, although at a very broad level. Given the secretiveness of both government and Civil Service and the influence of party rivalries, it is difficult for set debates to be really informed.

Government and Parliament

The presence of both the actual government and of the alternative government (the official opposition) in the House of Commons has both advantages and disadvantages. It means that the chief policy-makers directly face elected representatives for most of the year, which makes for close and intimate communication. On the other hand, it means that proceedings are dominated by ritual quarrels between government and opposition which makes it difficult for the House of Commons to organize itself as a distinct entity, or to express an independent point of view.

All one hundred or so ministers in a British government have to be Members of Parliament or peers. In practice a large majority are MPs. The government continues so long as it is supported by a majority of MPs, normally all members of the majority party. Indeed party cohesion is central to the functioning of parliamentary democracy as it exists at the present time in Britain. It is secured by various devices, such as the existence of a special office and officials (Whips) to maintain agreement and discipline, weekly party meetings to discuss policy and distribution of party and government patronage. We consider these along with evidence of some weakening on cohesion below. Of course the emergence of some 40–50 MPs belonging to minority parties with whom it is sometimes necessary for governments to deal in a close parliamentary situation may also contribute marginally to undermining the major party leadership's dominance of proceedings. The basic reality, however, is tight control by the majority party leadership.

Party unity in the Commons

Party unity and the need to keep 'their' government in office implies that even if a minority of government supporters disagree with the majority in their party, they will still normally vote with them against the other party or parties. The presence of most ministers in the Commons means that out of the 350-odd members in a majority party, a proportion approaching a third actually form the government. The presence of so many ministers actually in the House of Commons clearly encourages party unity. Conversely, of course, it acts against the House developing views independent of the government in office. Although the leaders of the other party (recognized as the official opposition) are much more in the position of ordinary MPs, their constant desire to criticize their rivals along party lines with a view to winning the next election also inhibits the House from developing a 'Commons' view of most matters.

Within the government there is a hierarchy of ministers, from parliamentary private secretaries who act as factotums for the more important ministers, through ministers of state who are normally second in command in a large department, and non-Cabinet ministers heading their own departments, to Cabinet ministers who normally take responsibility for running important departments or ministries and also participate in discussions of overall government policy.

Whatever their status or role in the government, all its members are, as we have seen, formally bound by the doctrine of collective ministerial responsibility, even if the practices have been changing to some extent over time.

Internal party disputes, with occasional spectacular exceptions, are generally fought out in Cabinet committees and spill over into the press, rather than provoking debates in Parliament. The last thing major parties want is to have internal clashes aired in general debate. Collective responsibility and party cohesion still operate to maintain the semblance, at least, of the united effective government so important to the British political tradition; and in doing so reduce the accountability of British government to Parliament.

Parliamentary scrutiny of government

Parliamentary scrutiny of government actions, in the sense of critically reviewing what ministers and civil servants do or intend to do, is important for two reasons. First the wider discussion, sometimes by experts, may improve the quality of the policies being pursued. And second, Parliament is, in constitutional theory, the main national institution representing the views of the population and (potentially at least) able to express them more freely than press and television, not being constrained by censorship and libel laws. In other words, the government is *accountable* to the people through Parliament.

The leader of the party with the largest number of elected members in the House of Commons is assumed to have had his or her policies approved and therefore has a 'mandate' to carry them through in government. However, many problems unforeseen at the time of the election campaign emerge in the three to five years separating most elections. Many of these relate to what is an on-going tension between the electoral mandate and continuing parliamentary scrutiny.

Electoral mandate versus continuing scrutiny

We should start by noting two major obstacles to informed debate on policy alternatives. The first is the way in which parliamentary processes and procedures are designed to facilitate the Conservative and Labour battle. The domination of business first by the government, and second by the official leadership of the next largest party, constitutes perhaps the major obstacle to independent collective initiatives by the House of Commons as such.

This institutional monopoly is buttressed both by constitutional doctrine and the entrenched attitudes of many MPs. They consider that the government's ultimate responsibility to serve popular interests is guaranteed by exposure to a general election at the end of its term. In the interim, decision-making will only be disrupted by undue parliamentary interference. The task of the parties in Parliament is, therefore, to support their government, or, if out of office, to keep up morale by attacking the office-holders. As Parliament is simply an arena for partisan encounters it can have no collective and independent role *vis-à-vis* the government.

This belief is in turn linked to a broader, traditional emphasis, also embedded in constitutional theory, that government knows best what to do in the public interest, and should be left (at least between elections) to get on with it unhindered. This colours opinion on a wide range of practical questions besides the nature of parliamentary debate. It covers government secrecy (desirable, because it prevents too much outside intrusion into government business); reform of the relationship between party votes and seats in the House of Commons (undesirable, because the present system, though grossly unfair to third parties, generally allows one major party to take clear responsibility for forming government) and accountability of the leadership to members inside parties (undesirable because it renders leaders, who may become ministers, less able to act decisively on their own initiative).

Support of strong, unfettered government thus tells against effective day-to-day scrutiny in Parliament. The justification is that 'the public interest' (a term often used to justify government action) can only be served this way. Governments must not be put under pressure to meet immediate demands, for to do so might result in an inability to plan for the future. In turn the opposition should set out an alternative government programme for the next election, supported by its MPs: nobody in the major parties should engage in independent action outside the party line.

These views are very characteristic of Thatcherite thinking in the 1980s. Conservative back-bench opposition to government measures was regarded as disloyal. There is no evidence, however, that current Labour leadership thinking is more relaxed.

The case for MPs adopting a more independent and critical attitude to what government is doing, is that most of what is done during its tenure is only tenuously related to the broad lines of policy presented at the election. Implementation of these demands requires many intermediate decisions, as we have seen, some of which may be debatable. Moreover, much of the business of government is unrelated to electorally endorsed party policies and carried on by un-elected civil servants. Wider and more informed discussion might in any case help improve them, rather than hampering the business of government. The growing belief that this is the case has spurred MPs to develop procedures for discovering and then discussing the justification, and likely outcomes, of government policy.

The obstacles to establishing even the simple facts about what the government is doing can hardly be exaggerated, given the administrative secrecy already discussed. The selective management of information by government is best illustrated in the parliamentary context by the 'lobby system' of specialist journalists attached to Parliament. (Incidentally it is significant that British political reporters, almost without exception, are concentrated within Parliament rather than in the executive offices, where they have of course no official place assigned to them. This means that news about government comes second-hand rather than directly from within the system itself.)

The parliamentary lobby itself is a name given to specially privileged parliamentary correspondents of the main newspapers and television and radio channels who spend most of their time in the 'lobbies' of Parliament. They are given confidential information and have ready access to ministers (rarely to civil servants). It is understood that in return they will reveal only what they are expressly authorized to publish, and use the rest solely as background material in preparing their reports. Failure to observe the understanding leads to exclusion from their privileges. A further consequence is that the information which gets published is that divulged at the initiative of the government and therefore consists of what it wants to reveal rather than what it wants to keep hidden. Two developments have undermined this way of managing news. One is the increasing practice of ministers and administrators briefing selected journalists, usually in order to have the story published as part of an attempt to resist or push policy proposals within the administration. This is an especially common tactic when resisting budget cuts, even on the part of such figures as the Joint Chiefs of Staff, the supreme military commanders. The briefing shades into the 'leak' of unauthorized news in the case of nominally subordinate administrators opposed to policies backed by their superiors.

Briefings still represent selective management of information in someone's own interest. The other process undermining the lobby system is the development of a more independent stance on the part of political journalists and their increasing practice of so-called 'investigative journalism' where stories are pursued at the initiative of the newspapers or television companies and followed through without buying information for silence. In line with this trend, journalists and newspapers have also been prepared to risk prosecution under the Official Secrets Act, the D notices circulated by governments to editors to prevent discussion of topics relating to national security, or the severe British libel laws, while refusing to reveal the sources of their information. The editors of some newspapers have recently withdrawn from the lobby and now explicitly quote their official sources.

In spite of these breaches, however, the ethos of the lobby system still predominates in British government. Information is for insiders rather than outsiders and government (or at least its constituent ministers and administrators) determines who shall be insiders. As peers and MPs depend heavily on published material for their own information, to supplement erratic personal contacts and the selective confidences of party leaders, government management of news deprives them of a major source of information just as much as it does the general public.

Live radio or television coverage of parliamentary proceedings has not changed this situation, as what is broadcast tends to be set debates which are covered by the quality newspapers anyway. Only if Parliament itself develops procedures for uncovering and evaluating important information will broadcasts be more illuminating.

This accepted, the set-piece exchanges typical of debates of the weekly Prime Minister's Question Time do perform a democratic function. They oblige Prime Ministers and ministers to state their positions clearly and to make some defence of them. In so doing they have to be convincing to their own supporters and to put up a good fight against opposition attacks and taunts.

For most of the time these exchanges are simply theatre. On some occasions, however, such as the attack by Geoffrey Howe on Margaret Thatcher following his resignation as Foreign Secretary, they can contribute to major political changes.

Scrutiny through select committees

One way to make information more widely available is to utilize parliamentary privileges to force investigation of important policy areas and publish the findings, in a way in which press and television themselves are not able to do. Attempts to do this in the last twenty years have concentrated on extending the remit, and strengthening the organization, of an old parliamentary institution – the select committees. As mentioned earlier, these are bodies with a relatively permanent all-party membership often chaired by an opposition MP and traditionally non-partisan, which are designed to investigate detailed policy areas and to produce agreed reports. In these, if anywhere, a parliamentary view can be expressed, and technical detail accumulated.

At the beginning of the 1990s there were 14 select committees covering a particular department of government. These included Agriculture; Defence; Education, Science and Art; Employment; Energy; Environment; Foreign Affairs; Home Affairs; Social Services; Trade and Industry; Transport; Treasury and Cabinet Services and the Scottish and the Welsh Office. Other Committees included: Broadcasting; European Legislation; Administration; Privileges; Procedures; Public Accounts; and Statutory Instruments. Despite this impressive list their role is limited. Committees derive their power from the House of Commons. Governments try to ensure that select committee membership reflects the political balance of power. Indeed, as happened with Scottish Affairs in 1987, where this cannot be ensured the committee is not formed.

However, government can be held accountable to some extent because it must be seen to be at least attempting to co-operate with the select committees. By refusing to allow civil servants to appear before a committee, it may appear to be attempting a cover-up. Furthermore, committees are not only endowed with general powers to choose their area of inquiry but they also have the right to summon persons and papers to appear before them and to answer all questions which the committee sees fit to put. In addition, witnesses cannot constitutionally excuse themselves on grounds that this may subject themselves to civil (legal) actions.

This is the theory but the practice can be quite different. When seeking to elicit information from Ian and Kevin Maxwell (suspected of massive embezzlement of pension funds to prop up their own business) the Social Security Committee divided across party lines on how hard to push. At least one Labour member was worried that it would strengthen the hand of Conservatives who want more general restrictions on the right to silence. However, precedents had already been set by at least two Conservative government ministers – Lord Young over the privatization of Rover and Sir Leon Brittan over the sale of Westland Helicopters, who successfully refused to answer select committee questions.

It also became clear that the ability of committees to elicit information from civil servants was limited following the Armstrong memorandum, which was adopted by the Head of the Civil Service, Sir Robin Butler. When Sir Robin appeared before the Treasury and Civil Service Committee in 1988 he explained that the duty of the civil servant to his minister was similar to that owed by military personnel to their commanding officer. Thus civil servants could only respond to committees (or indeed appear before them) if this had been approved by the minister.

Despite such well publicized confrontations, much of the work of investigating select committees is necessary but dull. Many MPs suspect them of being no more than a 'gravy train' for a few individuals favoured by parties and Whips. Only certain MPs are regarded as suitable for particular committees. The Foreign Affairs Committee appointees come from back benchers who can be trusted not to leak information to the media and to endorse current defence policy. It is argued that this method of selection ensures that important committees enjoy a strong sense of cohesion. In contrast, less favoured committees – for example, Environment, Education and Social Services – are perceived as less cohesive. They have fewer secrets, commitment is less robust and there is a higher turnover of members.

The methods of selection of committee members are nicely illustrated by membership of the Defence Select Committee. Prior to 1987, this committee enjoyed a close relationship with the Ministry of Defence. The three Labour MPs were considered 'sound'. The appointment of a left-winger opposed to the British nuclear deterrent would have jeopardized that relationship. Following the 1987 election, the Labour party increased its overall number of MPs in the House of Commons, compared to 1983, which gave it an additional place on committees, with a corresponding loss by the Conservatives. The threat to the Defence Committee came when the Labour Whip removed Dr John Gilbert (Labour MP for Dudley, East) following his criticism of the party's stand on unilateralism. The two other Labour members threatened to resign if he was replaced by a unilateralist.

This is not the only problem which has occurred following elections. Critics of current select committee procedures point to the length of time necessary to reconstitute select committees for the new parliamentary term. Following the 1983 General Election, it took nearly six months to set up the various committees, owing to party objections. First, the Labour leadership refused to nominate members until after the shadow Cabinet (i.e. the parliamentary leadership in opposition) was elected. Second, the minority parties claimed to be under-represented. Third, a problem arose with the 13-person Scottish Affairs Committee. Because of the limited number of Scottish Conservative MPs there were too few to allow the government to form a majority.

In part these manoeuvres themselves reflect party jostling for position in Parliament. From the government party's point of view, if committees are not quickly put in place they relieve departments from immediate scrutiny. Increased representation of the opposition would also cause closer scrutiny and opportunities to embarrass government. Third, if the government majority on a committee is only one, the willingness of many back benchers to criticize government means that a favourable majority might not always be certain.

Party interference with other aspects of committees is also extensive. We have seen that, in some cases, 'sound' members only are regarded as suitable. Further evidence suggests that party Whips influence the choice of chairpersons. Following the 1987 General Election, the Whips connived to nominate Audrey Wise (Labour MP for Preston), who had been re-elected to Parliament after eight years' absence, as chairperson of the Social Services Committee. Similarly, Tory whips tried to have Sir Anthony Grant, a former minister, installed as chairman of Trade and Industry to replace Kenneth Warren who had supervised critical reports in the previous Parliament. In both cases they failed, but it has been suggested that there is a general practice of offering former ministers such positions in order to 'keep them sweet'.

Party influences naturally also make themselves felt in internal divisions on the committees. For example, the Foreign Affairs Committee divided on party lines in a report on the sinking of the Argentine cruiser *General Belgrano* in the Falklands War, with the loss of over 700 lives. This was attacked on the grounds that the sinking was unnecessary. In the committee seven Conservatives argued there had been no cover up while four Labour members believed there was evidence of ministerial deception of Parliament. (This was the Committee to whose Conservative chairman Clive Ponting leaked papers showing that the government was lying, only to be reported back by him to the Ministry of Defence!)

In similar cases the Home Affairs Committee divided on party lines in a report on the police Special Branch; and the Employment Committee on whether or not British Coal should reinstate miners sacked during the 1984–5 strike, with one Conservative MP siding with Labour on this issue.

The major parties thus use committees to carry on their controversies just as they use Parliament, which threatens their ability to express an independent view.

Nevertheless, the committees do provide an opportunity for back benchers to participate, even in a limited way, in government. Inexperienced newcomers have an ideal opening to learn about government and, perhaps, to start making a name. Those who might be considered to be 'has-beens' or 'never-will-bes' are able to participate actively and are more likely to take independent positions (this applies also to members of third parties). And all back benchers have the potential of putting forward the views of particular interests. Thus committees offer a forum for various interests whose views might otherwise be excluded from Parliament.

One controversial factor associated with the working of Select Committees has been the prevalence of leaks (the passing on of confidential information, usually to the newspapers for publication). This has taken place both from government and Civil Service to Select Committees and from these to press or television. Typical examples are the *The Times*'s reports in 1990 (on the basis of internal discussion in the Social Service Committee) on errors in government statistics which affected social security payments and the *Independent*'s reports from the Home Affairs Committee on the weaknesses of the Crown Prosecution Service.

Of course, given the use of secrecy by government and Civil Service to stifle independent discussion of their action, the occurrence of such leaks from Select Committees might not be regarded as a bad thing. It counteracts selective official leaks to justify government policy, which reached their apex in the later Thatcher years. Nevertheless, leaks can undermine mutual confidence between members of the committees and so undermine their effectiveness. It may be that reforms of the Official Secrets Act will ease this problem by vastly extending the amount of information publicly available.

Probably the major problem of Select Committees, however – as with Parliament itself and the Cabinet – is the lack of any real administrative or research support. Operating with the minimal assistance of a Clerk of Parliament and a couple of secretaries, possibly with a seconded part-time researcher, they rely heavily on published reports and the evidence which witnesses are willing to provide (and as we have seen, witnesses cannot in practice be effectively compelled to reveal information).

This makes the Select Committees, like the government itself, heavily dependent on what civil servants are willing to provide or reveal. As they will not wish to embarrass either their department or their minister, it is clear that this is going to be limited. Without independent resources of their own, Select Committees are bound to be severely restricted in what they do.

As their activities cut across the major parties' partisan battles in the House of Commons, and have the potential for unexpectedly undermining one side or the other's positions, the Conservative and Labour leaderships will want to keep the committees weak and dependent. This is particularly true when they have a weak parliamentary position and are straining every nerve either to keep themselves in or get the other side out.

Summing up, it is clear that the committees have provided an independent standpoint within Parliament and adopted a reasonably critical approach to government within Parliament. They have also provided useful information which would otherwise not be available. Over the two sessions of 1987–9, for example, the Social Services Committee published a detailed report about resourcing the National Health Service while the Energy Committee criticized the proposals to privatize electricity. In the meantime, the Defence Committee pursued mismanagement in defence procurement, while the Transport Committee uncovered the complex and hidden world surrounding the computer reservation system for airlines.

These cases from recent sessions make it clear, however, that the committees, like the House of Lords, are only operating at the margins of power. Without more resources and powers, the parliamentary scrutiny of executive action will remain ineffective and largely ignored by the very people who are supposed to respond to it.

Party cohesion

Much of the preceding discussion has emphasized the key role of party cohesion and loyalty, both in maintaining the authority of the government and its mirror image, the relative impotence of Parliament. Party loyalty or discipline raises two crucial and related questions. What mechanisms are available to enforce loyalty? and under what circumstances can loyalty break down? Both issues are related closely to problems of democratic theory. Tight party discipline is, many argue, the prerequisite for strong and effective executive action. As a result, the electorate can make a rational choice on the record of an incumbent government at the general election.

Members often break with party discipline, however, in order to vote with their conscience or to reflect the interests and preferences of their constituencies. As we will see, this tension between electoral mandate and individual members' duty to conscience and constituency has increased over recent years.

Enforcing cohesion

Parties act to enforce internal cohesion through a variety of strategies and mechanisms. Within the majority party the party leader is also Prime Minister and can therefore appoint MPs to government office as a reward for loyalty (and oust them for disloyalty). (S)he can also award honours and make other appointments. So, to a lesser extent, can the leader of the opposition. The Prime Minister has the power to dissolve Parliament and call a general election through a formal request to the Queen. The uncertainty of the result prevents this threat being made very often but it can promote cohesion on a particular issue. Edward Heath, Conservative Prime Minister from 1970 to 1974 – who was widely unpopular among back benchers for his technocratic approach, lack of personal warmth, and failure to distribute honours more widely – still secured a majority of 309 to 301 on the second reading of his much opposed Bill to join the European Community (February 1972) by making the issue a vote of confidence, and thus indicating his willingness to hold an election if defeated. Similarly, Mrs Thatcher's uncompromising attachment to her measures usually brought Conservative rebels into line.

Supporting the leadership in its efforts for unity are the party officials known as Whips, selected from MPs not in the government (or alternative government, in the case of the opposition party). The picturesque name comes from the analogy with the whipper-in of foxhounds, hardly a flattering analogy for back-bench MPs! One of the Whips' powers is withdrawal of the whip from a dissident, with resulting loss of access to parliamentary order papers and back-bench party committees. The ultimate sanction is expulsion from the parliamentary party, with an almost inevitable loss of party endorsement at the next election and near-certain electoral defeat. On the side of positive inducements, while the Whips do not control access to office they do in effect allocate members to standing committees on government Bills, recommend members for standing committees on Private Members' Bills, and choose members for parliamentary and party delegations abroad. Once again, such incentives can be used to improve the atmosphere on the back benches and thus encourage cohesion. Probably the Whips' most important function, however, is to act as a source of information for the selection of junior ministers. Prime Ministers rely on them for appointments to these vital junior posts which are the stepping stones to more senior positions. Margaret Thatcher's failure to select ideologically 'sound' Whips contributed to the emergence by 1990 of a Cabinet which was out of tune with many of her own policy positions.

'Ideology' (adherence to a particular doctrine or a programme) is often associated exclusively with the Labour party. In considering the Conservative party, the shared social and educational background of Conservative members is more usually given as the reason for unity. In fact this explanation is really ideological as it implies that this common background leads to a shared set of political values, which then predisposes most members to support the front-bench position. Not just support of party views but also dislike for those of the other side may play a powerful part. Although there may be ideological splits, particularly in the Labour party, it can be argued that parties remain cohesive because no matter how much they dislike the other wing of their own party, they dislike the opposition more. This is an explanation often given of the reluctance of the left wing to split away from Labour, and is frequently linked to the argument that the British electoral system would prevent a party formed from the left of the Labour party having any access to power. This argument is reinforced by the failure of the right-wing Social Democrats who split from Labour in 1981–2 to form an effective independent party.

Factionalism has been more evident in the past among the Labour party than among the Conservatives – one reason possibly why the Conservatives have not experienced a secession similar to Labour's. There is, however, at least one area in which Labour is noticeably more cohesive that the Conservatives. On major unwhipped issues (i.e. those where party leaderships do not take an official stand) such as abortion, capital punishment, divorce and homosexuality, there is still a very strong relationship between party and vote. Labour MPs tend to support the extension of abortion and divorce, and freedom for homosexuals, and to oppose the death penalty. Conservative MPs tend to take the opposite line. Labour is almost totally united on its point of view (with the exception of abortion on some occasions), but the Conservative party is split, with roughly one-third agreeing with Labour and two-thirds opposing. This indicates that there are some shared values among Labour MPs which aid rather than hinder cohesion.

A last element of ideology which has united members inside both major parties is belief in the necessity and desirability of strong, effective government. The general prevalence of this view has already been noted but it is particularly influential among Conservatives, because they see themselves as the 'natural party of government'. This implies that a Conservative government has a particular claim on the party in performing the task incumbent on it: to govern.

Dissent within parliamentary parties

Governments cannot rely for ever on unquestioning support if things go too badly wrong. The British belief in strong government relies on it being successful, at least in the long run, and the lacklustre economic record of the last twenty years has undermined this belief.

Along with a decline of deference towards government has come a decay of the other force making for party cohesion: for example, constituency parties will be less inclined to blame rebels when they themselves feel critical of the leadership. And if his own leaders are not achieving what an MP wants, the prospect of voting to weaken the government and allowing another party to gain power is less alarming than it used to be.

The secession of the Social Democrats was the culmination of increasing factional tensions among Labour MPs in the 1970s. This extended even to the traditional consensual and hierarchic Conservatives, though internal tensions there did not show themselves in quite so dramatic a form. Conservative factionalism is obviously on the increase, however. Under the aloof prime ministership of Edward Heath (1970–4) an identifiable body of Conservative MPs emerged with a hard line on monetary policy and social issues. When they took over the leadership with the victory and premiership of Mrs Thatcher, semi-public dissent from the prevailing monetarist orthodoxy became common, and increased in extent after 1980.

Under Heath there were 69 divisions in which more than 10 MPs dissented during the period 1970–4. At the same time there were more persistent dissenters, with 41 MPs (12 per cent) casting 6 or more dissenting votes and 17 MPs dissenting on 20 or more occasions. In fact one Conservative MP (perhaps not surprisingly it was Enoch Powell) dissented 115 times (for a discussion see Norton 1980).

Dissent has always been more widespread in the Labour party, but it became almost epidemic in the 1974–9 Parliament. No less than 45 per cent of all whipped divisions in the 1978–9 session saw some Labour MPs voting against the government (whipped divisions being those where the leadership requires MPs to vote in a certain way). What is more, only 62 Labour MPs (19 per cent of the total) cast no dissenting votes, while 40 cast more than 50, and 9 more than 100 dissenting votes.

All this continued when Margaret Thatcher was elected Prime Minister in 1979. Although dissent was not as widespread as under Edward Heath, it was still common and on occasions spectacular. Under the first Thatcher government at least one MP dissented on 10 per cent of the votes and there were 16 occasions on which more than 10 Conservative MPs defied the whip. On these 16 votes in fact a total of 393 dissenting votes were cast. The two most spectacular concerned the immigration rules. On the two occasions when there was a division, more than 50 back-bench MPs took a less liberal line that the Conservative front bench. When the Conservatives were re-elected in 1983 dissent still persisted. There were rebellions in 1984 on the Trade Union Bill (40 dissenters) and the Local Government Bill (19 dissenters) and in 1985 on the Water Fluoridation Bill (48 rebels). In all these cases, however, the large government majority carried the day. They were not so fortunate in 1985 when there was a major rebellion over the siting of the third London airport, or more spectacularly in 1986 when the Shops Bill failed to obtain a second reading.

So many Conservatives objected to the inspector's report on the siting of the third London airport that the government Whips, certain that they were going to be defeated on an adjournment vote (a vote to end discussion on the topic) instructed Conservative MPs not to vote. In the end 70 back-bench Conservatives defied these instructions and voted with the opposition against the inspector's report which the government, of course, supported. The government's biggest débâcle was on the 1986 Shops Bill, where they were committed to extending hours for Sunday trading. 'Liberalization' was opposed by a strong, if unusual alliance, between the churches, the trade unions, the National Chamber of Trade and the Co-operative Society. Many Conservative back benchers believed that the Bill would 'change the nature of Sundays' and many more were under considerable pressure in their constituencies. In the end no fewer than 72 Conservative MPs dissented and the government lost a bill which had been a significant element in the Queen's Speech.

Following the Conservative's election victory in 1992 which resulted in a reduced majority of twenty-one, Tory back-bench rebels forced major changes in government policy on pit closures and the management of the Maastricht Treaty legislation in the House.

There can be no doubt, therefore, that dissent within both major parliamentary parties has shown a major increase up to and beyond the secession of the Social Democrats in 1981–2 and that the 1970s were the crucial turning point in the process (which still continues). Can any reasons for dissent be identified beyond pervasive economic problems?

A plausible explanation is found in the changing nature of MPs and the critical attitude of younger entrants towards the government. From around 1967 on, younger MPs demonstrated stronger feelings of dissatisfaction about both their own role and the domination of the executive. In all 35 Labour back-bench rebellions – both in the full House of Commons and in standing committee – which defeated the government over the three sessions from 1974–6, the background and date of entry of MPs into Parliament were related to rebellion. Newer middle-class MPs, less imbued with traditional notions of party solidarity and discipline, were more likely to dissent and subsequently influenced many older members. New MPs, on both the Labour and Conservative sides, are more interested in their local position and hence see their role less as a parliamentary party voting machine and more as a representative of local party and constituency interests.

As we have noted, this change of mood is related to the conspicuous failure of governments to solve the economic and other problems of the last decades. It is difficult to believe in the infallibility of government when governments constantly prove fallible. While dissent has also had an ideological base in the internal disputes within parties, these themselves rest on opposing prescriptions for solving national problems. As the problems pile up internal disputes between adherents of a controlled or mixed economy, of social concern versus economic freedom, of European Community versus national sovereignty, become increasingly widespread and bitter. The outcome is an increasingly critical attitude to the government of the day.

While dissent has not been confined to minor issues, governments can still expect to win the vast majority of votes if they have a clear majority, and can still rely on back-bench support on votes of confidence. But MPs are no longer lobby fodder. Dissent, moreover, is a politicizing experience; once MPs rebel they are more likely to do so again and their example will encourage others. In reaction, ideological opponents then assert a similar right to dissent over questions on which they feel strongly. This means that governments with small majorities will have to consult their back-benchers or be more prepared to accept defeat on a variety of votes. While dissent has most dramatically manifested itself in the Labour party, it is not confined to it. All this will make the future role of party leaders and Whips more difficult than in the past, even discounting the possibility of minority or coalition governments under a three-party system. John Major was quick to learn this lesson. Unlike Margaret Thatcher, he played very careful attention to the Whips' Office both after his selection as Prime Minister and after his election victory in 1992. Even so with a majority of just 21, he soon became aware of the need to accommodate Tory rebels.

The House of Commons in the 1990s

There is, therefore, no likelihood that dissent and cross-party alliances will abate. As MPs express their own views rather than those of their party's leaders, this reinforces their own propensity to take a more critical and independent stance, and encourages others to do so. Second, governments have increasingly come to accept dissent. At one time a defeat on the floor – certainly a defeat on a major Bill – would have been a resigning matter. Now a government is unlikely to resign except on an issue of confidence, and it will choose such issues carefully. For MPs this must in many cases legitimate dissent.

All this will produce more defeats for the government on the floor of the

House and even more in standing committees, particularly with a small majority. Experience with the minority Labour governments of the mid-1970s indicates, however, that the government will still win most votes. It is significant that the Thatcher administrations of the 1980s, so active in trying to centralize power inside the government and to dominate the localities, obviously felt quite comfortable with their position in Parliament and even extended the role of the Select Committees. This is an eloquent testimony to the almost absolute dominance of party in the House of Commons, despite marginally greater internal dissent and opportunities for cross party scrutiny.

Despite continuing pressures for a relaxation of the hold of the two main parties in the House of Commons and on individual MPs, it is unlikely that this can be broken without major constitutional change – above all, a change in the electoral system in the direction of reflecting popular votes in the share of seats. Any move in this direction would increase the probabilities of coalition and minority governments emerging, instead of the one-party majority governments which have dominated the post-war period. These would constitute such a radical break with the past, however – as well as permanently shifting the balance of political power from Conservatives and Labour to Liberals – that it is likely to be resisted to the last ditch by the two major parties, and by the Conservatives in particular. In the end, effective parliamentary scrutiny of the executive depends on other far-reaching changes which would radically transform the whole British political system, rather than just Parliament alone. For that reason, we are unlikely to see it come in the 1990s, any more than in the previous post-war decades.

Chapter 5
Parties and electors
Ivor Crewe

Our discussion of Parliament decisively demonstrates that British government is party government. It is formed by the largest party elected to the House of Commons, directed by a Cabinet drawn from its leading members, and headed by the person whom the party – not the people – has elected as its leader. The government's legislative programme furthers party goals and is passed by a Parliament that votes on party lines and was elected by voters casting a verdict on the national parties. Without party backing, politicians and political ideas do not get far. What applies to Westminster applies with almost equal force to town and county hall. The British political system, nationally and locally, is dominated by party.

The role of parties

Democratic parties are associations of like-minded people who by means of popular election compete for state power to further their common goals. Parties serve the dual functions of government and representation. As instruments of government they form the executive that seeks to steer the state, they recruit and groom politicians, they implement policies and they mobilize popular support. As instruments of representation they promote the interests and values of sections of the electorate, translate their demands into state policies and give them a sense of place within the wider society. Most important of all, they represent the government or the opposition, the 'ins' or the 'outs', thereby rendering the government of the day ultimately accountable to the electorate. Parties offer the public a scapegoat for government failure (or, more rarely, a totem of government success) enabling it to 'throw the rascals out' or 'keep the winning team'. As instruments of government and representation the major parties therefore perform a third function: political integration. To win elections parties must attract support from many different groups in the electorate. By aggregating their separate interests, parties identify and create consensus across large segments of the population. They must also respond to people's expectations or persuade people to modify them, thus limiting the ever-present gap in a democracy between what people expect of a government and what it can provide. Horizontally, parties act as a bridge across groups; vertically, as a ladder between citizen and state.

The parties: what they stand for

The media frequently depict the parties as disciplined armies moving in perfect order on the political battleground. Reality could hardly be more different. As with all voluntary organizations, people join with dissimilar objectives and protest or quit if these are not met. Parties have an inner life, marked by ideological divisions, personal rivalries, and tensions between the leadership and the rank and file. All parties are uneasy coalitions.

The modern Conservative party was formed by a gradual merger from the 1870s to the 1920s between Tories, representing the interests of the state (the 'Crown') and land, and the Whigs, representing the interests of industrial capital. The core values for Tories were social order and national unity, and the protection of the institutions that sustained it: the central state (Crown, Parliament and Civil Service), the armed forces, the judiciary and the Church of England. The core values for Whigs were economic growth and the free market, the core institutions were property, the limited liability company and the law, encapsulated by the City of London.

The faint cleavage lines of the modern party still reflect the old Whig–Tory distinction but have been overlaid by more recent divisions within each camp (see Figure 5.1). Tories believe in a strong state to secure social order but differ over its role: authoritarians see the state as an instrument of law and

	Traditional Toryism	Tory paternalism
Strong		
Role of state in relation to the economy	Disraeli J. Chamberlin (1900+)	Macmillan Heseltine (Major?)
	Thatcherism	Traditional Whiggism/ Liberal Conservatism
Weak	Powell Thatcher	Heath (1970-2) Lawson (Major?)
	Strong	**Weak**
	Role of state in relation to society	

Figure 5.1 Historic ideological cleavages in the Conservative party

order through the police, the courts, the schools ('discipline') and religion ('morality'); paternalists see the state as an instrument of economic amelioration through protection of home industry and welfare. In the wake of the Depression, wartime economic planning and Labour's 1945 victory, there emerged an influential group of progressive Tories, the One Nation group, who regarded the state as a regulator of the country's economy rather than its morals or culture. The Whig tendency eventually bifurcated in the 1970s in reaction against the collectivist economic and social policies of successive post-war governments. It agreed on the need to restore market forces in the economy but divided on whether an authoritarian state was needed to deal with the consequent social dislocation of strikes, riots and crime. Mrs Thatcher welded together the economic liberals and social authoritarians and under her patronage they held sway for most of the 1980s. John Major's position is more ambiguous in relation to the economy but he is clearly more permissive in regard to society.

These fault lines in the Conservative formation tend to produce minor tremors rather than major upheavals. They reveal themselves most clearly when national traditions conflict with the demands of a modern economy on such issues as Sunday trading, the protection of the countryside against commercial development, the sale of major British companies to foreign buyers or the merging of regiments to save on defence spending. They partly account for the deepest division of all, over Britain's relations with the European Community. Traditional Tories, who regard European institutions as a threat to the autonomy of the British state, are pitted against traditional Whigs, who regard economic integration into the European Community as essential for economic growth. It would be wholly misleading, however, to depict the Conservative party as neatly divided into warring factions. Dividing the party into 'right' and 'left' or 'dry' and 'wet' grossly over-simplifies. Ideological differences are complex and indistinct, matters of style as much as substance, and expressed in code. Most Conservative MPs cannot be slotted into any of the categories in Figure 5.1: they join private dining clubs rather than political blocs. They suspect doctrine, put their faith in 'men not measures' and give first priority to the electoral success and unity of the party. Ideologies are for legitimating the government's record, not determining its future programme. Despite her convictions, they voted for Mrs Thatcher in preference to Edward Heath as leader in 1975 because he lost elections; and despite her convictions they stayed loyal to Mrs Thatcher for the next fifteen years because she won elections.

The Labour party was formed in 1900 by trade unions, socialist societies and the radical Independent Labour Party, for the purpose of electing working-class men to represent working-class interests in Parliament. It has always been an alliance of organized labour and 'socialists', although the former has come to embrace white-collar and professional workers and 'socialism' encompasses many beliefs.

The core value that unites all strands of the Labour party is equality. The party stands for the elimination of poverty, a steady improvement in ordinary people's living standards, the narrowing of income and wealth differentials, equality of opportunity, and the abolition of social and legal distinctions based formally or informally on social status. In recent years it has paid growing attention to racial and sexual equality, alongside class equality. Its international outlook also originates in egalitarian values: traditionally it has supported trans-national organizations, collective as opposed to national defence, anti-colonial movements and the elimination of Third World poverty.

The main divisions within the Labour movement reflect its origins as a coalition of trade unionists and socialists. The former stand for 'labourism'. They regard the party as the political means for promoting the interests of a class within a system whose principles, including capitalism, they accept. Its job is to improve inch by inch the circumstances of working people through the welfare state and public services, paid for by progressive taxation and economic growth. For socialists, by contrast, the party's principles are defined by ideology not interests. Its purpose is not simply to represent part of existing society but to transform it.

This basic division between gradualists and radicals, pragmatists and theorists, goes particularly deep in two areas: the economy and defence. Socialists have traditionally wanted a state-directed economy insulated from international forces ('socialism in one country') in the form of centralized economic planning, nationalized industries, administered prices, physical controls and protective tariffs. Labourists give first priority to economic growth and accept free market forces, a large private sector and indirect steering of the macro-economy towards that end. In the 1950s this division was crystallized by the bitter dispute occasioned by Hugh Gaitskell's attempt, as leader, to eliminate from the constitution 'Clause 4', which formally committed the party to wholesale nationalization. In the early 1980s a similar conflict arose over the 'Alternative Economic Strategy' advocated by the resurgent left.

The Labour party's periodic splits over defence and foreign policy are produced by two separate but related divisions between 'pacifists' and 'realists', and between 'neutralists' and 'Atlanticists'. For the pacifists peace is the prerequisite of defence and is best secured by unilateral disarmament which would signal Britain's peaceful intentions towards other nations and serve as a model for them to follow. For the realists defence is the prerequisite of peace and is best secured by weapons and forces sufficient to deter potential aggressors. The two sides differed over appeasement and rearmament in the 1930s and, more bitterly, over unilateral nuclear disarmament in the 1950s and 1980s. Neutralists opposed Britain's involvement in the Cold War, both out of sympathy for the 'socialist' Soviet Union and antipathy to American capitalist imperialism. Atlanticists admired the social egalitarianism and democratic culture of the Americans, and saw the 'special relationship' with the United States as the most practical form of collective security. The two sides divided over Britain's membership of NATO in the late 1940s, German rearmament in the early 1950s, the Labour government's support for American involvement in Vietnam in the 1960s, and American military bases in Britain in the 1980s.

Internal conflicts last longer and bite deeper in the Labour party than the

Conservative party. This is partly because opposing sides on economic and defence policies overlap rather than cross-cut, producing an identifiable left and right (while still leaving many MPs and activists in between), and partly because conflict is conducted more openly. But the bitterness of the party's feuds arises from a third division, that between the parliamentary leadership and the rank and file members. Labour governments, wrestling with global forces and powers beyond their control, have generally fallen short of their aims and principles, and the disappointed rank and file have responded with accusations of 'betrayal'. Thus after the defeat of a Labour government the party has lurched to the left (e.g. 1931–5, 1952–5, 1970–4 and 1979–83) but it has returned to more pragmatic positions after long spells in opposition have left it hungry for office (1963–4, 1988–92). A classic case is the Labour party's 1989 Policy Review, produced after three successive election defeats, which advocates a highly pragmatic programme.

The Liberal Democratic party was formed by the fusion of a breakaway wing of the Labour party (the Social Democrats, who left the party in 1981) and the Liberals, an old party which had been gradually squeezed out of power by Labour and Conservative competition in the inter-war period. Dissatisfaction with the other two parties led to the Alliance of Social Democrats and Liberals receiving from a fifth to a quarter of the national vote in the 1980s. The two parties merged in 1988, and the Liberal element predominated in the combined party.

The Liberal party's preoccupation with individual freedom led it after the war to oppose censorship and support the liberalization of abortion, while advocating welfare legislation on the ground that it enlarges freedom of action for the masses. The Liberals have always been firm on regional devolution, on extending ownership of industry to the workforce, with workers having control with management, and, most important of all, have always supported the full integration of Britain into the European Community.

The parties: whom they represent

Speaking in Parliament shortly after the 1918 election the then Prime Minister, Lloyd George, said he felt he had the Trades Union Congress in front of him and the Association of Chambers of Commerce at his back. Parties represent segments of society not only by promoting their interests but as ladders of mobility for particular groups into positions of influence.

As Table 5.1 shows, the Conservative and Labour parties are wholly unrepresentative socially of the public in general and their voters in particular. The MPs of both parties are largely middle-class, preponderantly university-educated, overwhelmingly male, and almost universally white. In social, if not political, terms Conservative and Labour MPs have more in common with each other than with the party members who selected them or the voters who elected them.

Table 5.1 Social composition of MPs, members and voters of the Conservative and Labour parties, 1987

	Conservative party			Labour party		
	MPs %	Members %	Voters %	MPs %	Members %	Voters %
Social class						
Salariat	90	46	31	66	56	14
Intermediate	9	41	39	15	18	23
Working class	1	12	31	19	26	63
Education						
Independent schools	68	n.a.	9	14	n.a.	3
Further education	82	14	13	79	32	10
University	70	n.a.	11	56	n.a.	6
Oxbridge	44	n.a.	n.a.	15	n.a.	n.a.
Women	5	58	52	9	41	52
Ethnic minorities	0	n.a.	2	2	n.a.	9

Sources: Butler and Kavanagh (1988), p. 202, 204; Rose and McAllister (1990), p. 56

The social distance between the two parliamentary parties has gradually narrowed since Lloyd George made his comment, mainly because the parliamentary Labour party has ceased to be working-class: the proportion of manual workers on the Labour benches has steadily fallen from 72 per cent between the wars, to 36 per cent in the 1950s, to 29 per cent in 1987. Over the same period the proportion of graduates has risen from 17 per cent between the wars to 40 per cent in the 1950s and 56 per cent in 1987. In 1987 twice as many Labour MPs were teachers as miners. The Conservative party has also lost some of its patrician element, although only very gradually. In the 1950s 75 per cent went to public schools and 22 per cent to Eton alone; in 1987 the figures were 68 per cent and 11 per cent.

Thus the two parliamentary parties do not so much comprise two social classes, as two strata within the middle classes. Most Labour MPs come from the less privileged and moneyed middle classes: compared with their Conservative counterparts they are more likely to be first rather than second generation middle-class, educated at state rather than private schools, at polytechnics rather than universities, 'red brick' rather than Oxbridge, and to have worked in the public sector and the new professions rather than the private sector and the traditional professions. At a lower level the Labour party is more middle-class than the Conservatives: a development of the past two decades is the steady replacement of working-class members by the public sector, university-educated, salariat.

In two important respects the social composition of the House of Commons has failed to reflect important social changes in the country outside. First, the number of women MPs remains tiny. Despite the growth of the women's movement, the rising number of women graduates and career women and Mrs Thatcher as a role model, the number of women MPs fluctuated between

17 and 29, under 5 per cent of the Commons, throughout the period 1945 to 1983. In 1987 the number jumped to 38 (6 per cent) and in 1992 had risen again to 60 (9 per cent) –the largest number in the history of Parliament but, at 9 per cent, still a very small proportion. Second, the ethnic minorities are under-represented in Parliament. Proportional representation would result in 26 Afro-Caribbean and Asian MPs; but there were none until 1987 when four black MPs, all Labour, were elected. In 1992 the number increased to six – five Labour and one Conservative. The reasons behind the under-representation of women and the ethnic minorities are complex. Prejudice on the part of selection committees (sometimes rationalized as a response to the alleged prejudice of voters) is one factor; financial, occupational and psychological constraints on putting themselves forward for selection as candidates is another. Probably the most important factor is mundanely institutional: only about 60 safe seats become vacant at each election so the composition of Parliament is bound to lag behind social change.

The parties: how they are organized

The party ladder contains four main rungs. At the top is the party leadership, a group of no more than twenty to thirty parliamentarians occupying or hoping to occupy a senior government position as a Cabinet minister. Their primary interest is in their party winning the next election. A little further down is the parliamentary party of elected MPs and active peers in the House of Lords, from whom the party leadership is drawn. They too place enormous importance on electoral success, but their priorities are subtly different from those of the leadership. Most MPs represent safe seats and have more to fear from de-selection by their local parties or from an unfavourable re-drawing of their constituency boundaries than from an adverse national swing against their party. Much further down the ladder is the party in the country: the unpaid officers and active members of local parties, many of them elected councillors on the local authority. For most activists the reward is not career advancement but the furtherance of the party's broad goals, on which they tend to take a more principled stand than the party's leaders and MPs. On the bottom rung is the party in the electorate – stalwart supporters who, while not formally members, can be relied upon to vote for the party in elections and to accept the party line on most political issues.

Superficially, British parties are organized in much the same way. A branch of the party exists in each parliamentary constituency and, where support is strong enough, in each local ward making up the constituency. Its main function is to contest elections – to raise campaign funds, engage in electioneering and, most important of all, select the candidate who in the 500-plus safe seats will become the MP. Political education and policy debates are intermittent and secondary: in most local parties political agreement is taken for granted and politics is not discussed much. The local parties send delegates to the national party's annual conference whose formal role is to discuss party policy but whose real purpose nowadays is to display the party, in particular its leadership, to best effect on television. The conference elects a national executive which oversees the day-to-day running of the national party. Policy is formulated by specialist groups recruited from the party headquarters, MPs, sympathetic research institutes, and the leadership's personal contacts. The leader of the parliamentary party is the effective party leader in the sense of being the party's spokesperson, its chief campaigner at elections and the prime minister if the party wins. The Conservative leader is elected by MPs only, the Labour leader by Labour MPs and the annual conference (on behalf of the wider Labour movement), the Liberal Democrat leader by the party members.

Despite these superficial similarities, the Conservative and Labour parties differ significantly in their constitutions and ethos. The contrasts owe something to the two parties' very different historical origins. The Conservative party began in the nineteenth century as a parliamentary faction which gradually built up a party in the country. The Labour movement existed outside parliament before it put up parliamentary candidates of its own. The Conservative party has a unitary and hierarchical structure and a deferential culture; the Labour party a federal and democratic structure and a dissenting culture.

The first structural difference to note is that the Conservatives are a party of individual members whereas Labour is a party of 'affiliated organizations' as well as of individual members. These organizations – overwhelmingly trade unions – are entrenched in the party's decision-making bodies and they exercise a vote at the annual conference and in local parties roughly proportionate to their membership (strictly speaking, to the number of Labour-dues paying members they claim to have when they contribute to Labour party funds). In the 1980s affiliated trade unions accounted for 89 per cent of the vote at the annual conference and the five largest unions commanded a majority (55 per cent of the vote) between them. Because of the way the vote is exercised the leaderships of the big unions wield enormous power in the Labour party. The vote is cast as a 'block' and not in proportion to the division of opinion among union members; indeed union leaders generally do not know what their members' views are. Moreover, the trade union vote dominates the election of 18 of the 28 places on the national executive. There are plans to reduce the influence of unions in the party, which have already been implemented for the selection of parliamentary candidates, but even after these reforms trade union leaders will continue to wield considerable and largely unaccountable power in the Labour party.

A more important constitutional difference between the parties is the much greater power given to the Conservative leader. In the Conservative party, the shadow Cabinet, the party chairman and vice-chairmen, the Chief Whip and deputy Whips are all in the leader's gift. In the Labour party the shadow Cabinet and Chief Whip are elected by Labour MPs and on becoming Prime Minister a Labour leader must include the sixteen-member shadow Cabinet in his full Cabinet (although he determines their ministerial responsibilities). The general secretary of the Labour party (the closest counterpart to the Conservative chairman) is appointed by the national executive while the treasurer is elected by the annual conference. The Conservative leader's policy-making powers are equally extensive. He is solely responsible for the party's election manifesto (the party programme circulated during each election campaign) and can incorporate or veto specific proposals without consulting the rest of the party, as Mrs Thatcher's 1983 manifesto commitment to abolish the Greater London Council testifies. The Labour manifesto is drafted by a joint sub-committee of the NEC and the shadow Cabinet (themselves elected bodies) and must incorporate any policy passed by a two-thirds majority of the annual conference.

A second, related, difference lies in the formal powers accorded to the party in the country. The annual Labour conference is the electoral college for the party leader and deputy leader (with trade unions allocated 40 per cent of the vote and the constituency parties and parliamentary Labour party 30 per cent each). It is also the sovereign policy-making body with the right to determine party policy and incorporate provisions in the manifesto. The annual Conservative con- ferences have no such rights. They can pass policy motions or resolutions critical of the leadership (though they rarely do) but these have no constitutional power. Labour conferences decide; Conservative conferences confer.

A parallel difference exists at the constituency party level. Local Labour parties can instruct their delegates to the annual conference on how to vote in elections for the national executive or the leadership and increasingly do so on the basis of ballots of local individual members. They not only choose the local parliamentary candidate but, if their constituency has a Labour MP, require the MP to submit to a formal process of re-selection before each election. Conservative associations do not mandate those attending the conference and Conservative MPs are automatically re-selected unless their relationship with the local party has badly deteriorated.

These constitutional differences are reinforced by quite distinct party cultures. Conservatives value party unity and loyalty above all else, including ideology. Conservative conferences are rallies rather than debates. Most resolutions from the constituencies are paeans of praise for the party leadership or, if critical, expressed in muted and deferential terms. The Labour party takes ideological principles ('socialism') more seriously and most activists accord them priority over party unity, loyalty to the leadership or even electoral success. For most Conservative activists, conservatism is an instrument for winning elections; for most Labour activists elections are an instrument for implementing socialism.

Thirty years ago, Robert McKenzie argued that the Labour party was much less democratic and the Conservatives somewhat less oligarchic than their respective constitutions suggested; in reality the distribution of power was similar in both. The late 1980s seem to confirm this scepticism. The ousting of Mrs. Thatcher in November 1990 was a graphic reminder that the Conservative leader, however extensive her powers, depended on the continuing confidence of her MPs, and that the Conservative party constitution gives MPs ample opportunity to withdraw that support. Until 1965 Conservative leaders were not elected if the Conservatives were in office; they 'emerged' after secret consultations between the Chief Whip and senior figures in the party. After the controversial emergence of Lord Home as leader in 1963, the system was changed to one of election by Conservative MPs, with two amendments in 1974 that proved fatal for Mrs Thatcher. The first allowed a leadership contest to take place annually and at the beginning of each new Parliament so long as the challenger could secure a nominator and seconder; the second stipulated that to be elected in the first round the candidate with most votes had to secure a majority of at least 15 per cent of all Conservative MPs, irrespective of the number who voted. In November 1990 Mrs Thatcher won most votes in the first round but fell two short of a 15 per cent majority and thus came under pressure to go.

Ironically, the 1981 'democratization' of the election of the Labour leader has almost certainly made it more difficult for a challenger to succeed. Selection by an electoral college requires three months' notice, the convening of a special conference, and a campaign by the challenger not only among MPs but among trade unions and local parties. Moreover, Neil Kinnock's leadership between 1983 and 1992 demonstrated how powerful a determined leader can be. Under his predecessor, Michael Foot, the fundamentalist left was in the ascendant, internal conflict was rife and the party was unelectable. In the space of six years, Kinnock and his personal allies expelled the Militant faction, marginalized the socialist left, jettisoned the party's long-standing (but unpopular) policies of nationalization, trade union legal immunities, withdrawal from Europe and nuclear unilateralism, and reunited the party behind a pragmatic, mild, social-democratic programme. The other constitutional reform of the early 1980s, mandatory reselection, has not led to its intended democratic consequences either. Very few Labour MPs have been deselected, and an increasing number of constituency parties in Labour-held seats have reselected their MP from a shortlist of one.

However, to dismiss the Labour party's democratic reforms as inconsequential would be premature. Kinnock could not have transformed the Labour party without the support of sympathetic trade union leaders who, desperate to see the return of a Labour government, turned a blind eye to the autocratic practices of Kinnock's personal office and used their block-votes to ensure a pliable national executive and an acquiescent annual conference. But such support would not long survive a period of Labour government that presided over a recession or inflation and without it the Labour leader, and individual Labour MPs, would be threatened by an alliance of left-wing activists and dissatisfied trade unions exploiting the democratic reforms.

The rules of party competition

The rules of party competition – the 'electoral system' – are not neutral technicalities. They systematically help some parties and hinder others. By far the most significant are the counting rules for determining how votes are translated into seats. Unlike the rest of Europe, Britain uses the single-member simple-plurality (SMSP) system, misleadingly known as 'first past the post' (because the post is not fixed!). The country is divided into parliamentary constituencies (651 of them in 1992) of about 60,000 electors each; voters place a cross against their single most preferred candidate; and the candidate with the most votes (the 'plurality') is declared the winner, irrespective of whether that plurality constitutes a majority, (i.e. at least 50 per cent) of all the votes cast.

The origins of SMSP elections lie in the eighteenth century before the establishment of the universal franchise, organized mass parties and a national economy. They were appropriate for the pre-democratic and pre-industrial era when the function of Parliament was to vote monies to the Crown in return for local privileges and patronage, and local coteries of landowners and merchants elected one or two of their own to protect and enhance their wealth. Because parliamentary government in Britain has been uninterrupted by war or revolution, the SMSP system has been adapted rather than abolished. Britain's modern party system has been shaped by pre-modern electoral arrangements.

SMSP is a system of territorial rather than popular representation. It was not designed to ensure that the national vote for each party was proportionately translated into parliamentary seats, and it radically fails to do so. What determines the number of seats a party wins is the distribution of its popular vote, not its overall level. The system rewards parties whose vote is concentrated locally and penalizes parties whose support is evenly spread.

The disproportionate relationship between votes and seats in British general elections is shown in Table 5.2. Some post-war elections have thrown up bizarre anomalies, including the 'wrong' winner and 'undue' rewards. In 1951 the Conservatives won fewer votes than Labour but more seats, and therefore formed the government; in February 1974 Labour got its revenge by the same means. In 1983 the Conservatives' share of the popular vote fell by 1.5 percentage points but they gained an additional 58 seats and saw their parliamentary majority triple from 43 to 144. The Liberal–SDP Alliance vote rose by 11.6 points (compared with the Liberals at the previous election) but their reward was a niggardly 12 gains. Altogether they won a mere 23 seats with 25.4 per cent of the vote. Labour, with 27.6 per cent of the vote, won 209 seats.

Table 5.2 reveals three consistent and crucial biases in the relationship between seats and votes in British elections. The first is a plurality bias: SMSP always over-rewards the single most popular party at any election, converting a plurality of the popular vote into a majority of the parliamentary seats. In October 1974, for example, Labour won only 39.2 per cent of the popular vote but 50.2 per cent of the seats (319 out of 635). In 1983 the Conservatives won 42.4 per cent of the vote but 61.1 per cent of the seats (397 out of 650). Since 1945 no single party has ever won a majority of the vote but, excepting the single case of February 1974, one party has always obtained a majority of the seats.

The second bias, the multiplier bias, is related. SMSP converts small net shifts of the popular vote into a much larger turnover of seats. In a system of perfectly proportional representation each 1 per cent swing in the vote (a 1 per cent drop for one party and a 1 per cent rise for the other) would result in 6 or 7 seats changing hands (i.e., 1 per cent of a Parliament of 650 seats). In Britain during the 1980s and 1990s, each 1 per cent swing under SMSP

Table 5.2 Share of the vote and share of the seats under Britain's electoral system, 1945–92

	Excess of % share of seats over % share of vote for:[1]				
	Cons.	**Lab.**	**Lib.[2]**	**Other parties**	**Mean difference**
General election					
1945	−6.8	+13.4	−7.1	+0.5	7.0
1950	+4.3	+4.3	−7.7	−0.8	4.3
1951	+3.4	−1.6	−1.6	−0.1	1.7
1955	+5.1	−2.4	−1.7	−0.9	2.5
1959	+8.5	−2.8	−4.9	−0.7	4.2
1964	+4.9	+6.2	−9.8	−1.3	5.6
1966	−1.7	+9.8	−6.6	−1.4	4.9
1970	+6.0	+2.6	−6.5	−2.1	4.3
Mean 1945–70	+3.0	+3.7	−5.7	−0.8	
Feb 1974	+8.9	+10.2	−17.1	−2.3	9.6
Oct 1974	+7.8	+11.0	−16.3	−2.6	9.4
1979	+9.5	+5.5	−12.1	−2.9	7.5
1983	+18.7	+4.6	−21.9	−1.4	11.7
1987	+15.5	+4.4	−19.1	−0.9	10.0
1992	+9.7	+7.4	−14.8	−2.4	8.6
Mean 1974–92	+11.7	+7.2	−16.9	−2.1	

Notes
1 i.e., the differences between the share of the parliamentary seats and the share of the
  UK vote obtained by each party.
2 Lib/SDP Alliance in 1983 and 1987.

resulted in 9 or 10 seats changing hands because of the concentration of seats with small majorities. SMSP is more sensitive than the proportional representation system to small movements in the popular vote although, as we shall see later, not as sensitive as it once was.

The third bias is well known but less well understood. It is often described, falsely, as a bias against small parties, third parties or centre parties. SMSP penalizes parties whose vote is both relatively small and evenly spread. But it does not necessarily discriminate against small parties with local concentrations of support. For example, in 1992 a system of proportional representation would have allocated three seats to Plaid Cymru, the Welsh nationalists, and four seats to the moderate Catholic party, the SDLP: in fact they each returned four MPs. Plaid's support comes mainly from Welsh-speakers, who are concentrated in north-western Wales, and the SDLP's comes from Catholic areas. Nor does SMSP discriminate against all parties with an even spread of support; on the contrary, once such a party rises above the 37–38 per cent level, it is disproportionately rewarded. But that is a very steep popularity threshold and national parties with a minority but still substantial following such as the Liberals (and, in the 1980s, the SDP) and the Greens are punished. Thus in 1983 and again in 1987 the Liberal–SDP Alliance won about a quarter of the vote but only 3 per cent of the seats; and in the 1989 Euro-elections the Greens won 15 per cent of the vote, outmatching any of their sister parties elsewhere in Europe, but unlike them they failed to win a single seat. This under-representation is a double penalty: because the centre parties cannot convert votes into seats, they find it difficult to convert support into votes. Substantial numbers of sympathizers reluctantly vote for a major party for fear of 'wasting their vote'.

In recent years the SMSP system has attracted growing controversy in political circles, although less among ordinary voters. For reasons of party interest it is fiercely criticized by all the minor parties and stoutly defended by the Conservative and Labour parties. As an instrument of representation SMSP is undeniably unfair but as a means of forming governments it can be defended. It usually manufactures a single-party majority government and thus government which is powerful, durable and accountable. It excludes or marginalizes small, extremist parties of the racist right and revolutionary left which in a multi-party coalition government might enjoy a leverage out of all proportion to their popular support. Its moderately strong gearing ensures that genuine changes of popular sentiment produce clear changes in the direction of government, as in 1945, 1964 and 1979. None the less, criticisms of SMSP have gathered pace in recent years, especially in the Labour party after their defeat of 1992, and there is a serious possibility of its being replaced by some system of proportional representation by the end of the decade.

Other electoral arrangements

The counting rules are overwhelmingly the most important rules of party competition. But other electoral arrangements count too. A case in point are constituency boundaries. The procedures for drawing them are designed to be impartial. Responsibility is vested in independent, quasi-judicial Boundary Commissions and gerrymandering – party-inspired artificial boundaries – is therefore unknown. But the statutory guidelines by which the Commissions operate benefit the Labour party, in two ways. First, Scotland and Wales are deliberately allocated proportionately more seats than England. On a strict population basis Scotland is entitled to 59 and Wales to 32; in fact they are allocated 72 and 38 respectively. Given its dominance in both countries, Labour gains: in 1992 it 'won' 13 of the 19 bonus seats. Second, the boundaries lag behind population changes by anything from five to twenty years. The Boundary Commissioners are encouraged to give priority to 'natural community boundaries' over equality of size (within reason); required to re-draw the boundaries only every fifteen years; allowed to allocate seats to counties on the basis of out-of-date census figures and precluded from incorporating future population projections into their decisions. As a result constituencies vary massively in size, ranging in 1991 from the Isle of Wight (101,784 electors) to the Western Isles (23,073) – a mere quarter the size. Since these disparities arise mainly from population drift from the Labour fastnesses of the inner city and industrial North to the Conservative heartlands of the suburban and small-town South, it is Labour that benefits. In 1992 the average size of a Labour seat was 61,672 electors, the average size of a Conservative seat 70,882 electors, the equivalent of the Conservatives forfeiting twenty-one seats to Labour.

Other electoral arrangements give the Conservatives a potential advantage. In Britain, unlike much of the European Continent, parties receive no state funds and must therefore rely on membership subscriptions, private gifts and, in the main, on institutional donations. The Conservatives rely for about 70 per cent of their income on business donations which, in the case of public companies, must be notified in the accounts but do not need to be approved in advance by shareholders. The Labour party relies even more heavily on trade union donations, although since the 1985 Trade Union Act these are subject to much stricter regulation than party contributions from business. Trade unions are obliged to ballot their members every ten years on whether to establish a political fund and individual members are allowed to contract out of contributing to it.

The Conservative party's individual and institutional backers are richer than Labour's and it therefore spends more money on elections. Both major parties are in turn much wealthier than the Liberals or the now defunct SDP, which have had no institutional funders to speak of and rely almost wholly on small subscriptions. The ratio of central party election spending between the Conservatives, Labour and the Liberal/SDP Alliance was 12:7:6 in 1983 and 12:6:3 in 1987. However, the Conservatives derive little or no advantage from spending more, because of legal controls on many aspects of campaign expenditure. In the constituencies it is restricted to about £6,000 (depending on the size of the constituency). Nor are parties allowed to buy political commercials on radio or television. Instead the broadcasting authorities offer the main parties time and facilities for election broadcasts, an indirect public subsidy which neutralizes the impact of the unequal resources commanded by the parties. Most of the Conservatives' financial advantage is devoted to newspaper and poster advertising and the hiring of expensive advertising agencies. Surveys consistently show that such spending has a negligible impact on the vote.

The permanent pro-Conservative bias of the press is a more serious advantage which we shall go into in the next chapter. Throughout the post-war period a majority of newspapers have supported the Conservative party and after the death of the pro-Liberal *News Chronicle* in 1960 and pro-Labour *Daily Herald* in 1964 the Conservative bias became overwhelming. By the 1980s three-quarters of all newspapers sold supported the Conservatives and the majority of working-class readers read a Conservative paper. Moreover, as television has emerged as the dominant medium of political communication the tabloids have countered its bland impartiality with a more strident partisanship of their own. Recent estimates suggest that press bias is worth a swing of about 1 per cent to the Conservatives at each election, a not insignificant advantage when cumulated over the long-term. Press impact would be stronger but for the fact that voters' partisanship determines what they read rather than vice versa. In the majority of cases newspapers reinforce their readers' existing partisanship rather than convert them from other parties: for example, the *Sun* and the *Star* persuaded their relatively non-political readers to return to the Conservative fold in the run-up to the 1983 and 1987 elections (Miller *et al.*, 1990) and appear to have contributed to the last-minute swing to the Conservatives in 1992.

Other electoral arrangements might be thought to advantage whichever party is in office rather than the Conservative or Labour party *per se*. For example, television is required to be non-partisan and during election campaigns gives the two main parties (and in 1987 all three) exactly equal coverage. But between elections, including the crucial run-up to the campaign, news values result in television giving the government and Prime Minister far more exposure than the opposition parties and their leaders. This is a double-edged weapon for the government, however: government failures capture as many headlines as government successes.

Another potential advantage to the governing party is the Prime Minister's right to choose the election date, which enables it to go to the country whenever opinion polls and economic indicators suggest the time is ripe. None the less, the fact that the government has lost 6 of the 14 elections since the war suggests that the practical advantage to the party in office is slim. A government's control over bad news from the economy, the City, trade unions or abroad is limited; and Prime Ministers can misread public opinion as Wilson did in 1970 and Heath did in February 1974. It may seem anomalous to give reigning champions the starter's gun but as often as not they shoot themselves in the foot.

The electoral strength of the parties: a return to two-party politics?

A defining feature of a party system is the electoral strength of the main parties. Table 5.3 sets out their electoral support at each election since 1945 and suggests that the post-war years can be divided into a period of two-party dominance from 1945 to 1970 and a period of partisan dealignment from 1970 to the present. The 1992 election suggests that Britain might be returning to something like the former era of two-party dominance.

From 1945 to 1970 the Conservative and Labour parties commanded the overwhelming allegiance of the British electorate. They took 98 per cent of the parliamentary seats, usually over 90 per cent of the total vote, and the first two places in the vast majority of individual constituencies. Strictly speaking, it was not a pure two-party system, because the Liberals, and in Wales and Scotland the Nationalists, contested some seats and very occasionally returned an MP, especially at mid-term by-elections. But in practical terms it was a two-party system, because elections effectively guaranteed that one or other would govern on their own without help or hindrance from a minor party. Indeed, the Liberals and other minor parties were not national parties with activists throughout the country and the organization and resources to fight every seat. What Britain had was not only a two-party system but two-party politics.

The period after 1970 was marked by a steady erosion of that two-party

Table 5.3 Electoral support for the Conservative and Labour parties, 1945–92

Date of general election	Share of *vote* obtained by:				Share of *electorate* obtained by:			
	Cons.	Lab.	Cons. + Lab.	Other parties (no. of MPs)	Cons.	Lab.	Cons. + Lab.	Other parties
	%	%	%	%	%	%	%	%
1945	39.8	47.9	87.6	12.4 (30)	30.2	36.4	66.6	9.2
1950	43.5	46.1	89.6	10.4 (12)	36.5	38.7	75.2	8.7
1951	48.0	48.8	96.8	3.2 (9)	39.6	40.3	80.0	2.6
1955	49.7	46.4	96.1	3.9 (8)	38.2	35.6	73.8	3.0
1959	49.3	43.9	93.2	6.8 (7)	38.8	34.5	73.3	5.4
1964	43.4	44.1	87.5	12.5 (9)	33.5	34.0	67.5	9.6
1966	41.9	48.1	90.0	10.0 (13)	31.8	36.5	68.2	7.6
1970	46.4	43.1	89.5	10.5 (12)	33.4	31.4	64.4	7.6
Feb. 1974	37.8	37.1	74.9	25.1 (37)	29.5	29.0	58.5	20.3
Oct. 1974	35.8	39.2	75.1	24.9 (39)	26.1	28.5	54.7	18.1
1979	43.9	37.0	80.9	19.1 (27)	33.3	28.1	61.4	14.6
1983	42.4	27.6	70.0	30.0 (44)	30.8	20.1	50.9	21.8
1987	42.2	30.8	73.0	27.0 (45)	31.8	23.2	55.0	20.3
1992	41.9	34.2	76.1	23.9 (44)	32.5	26.5	59.0	21.0

dominance. Three features stand out. Firstly, the two major parties steadily loosened, without relinquishing, their grip over the electorate. Both major parties lost support. Their combined share of the vote fell from 90 per cent in 1970 to 73 per cent in 1987 and their combined share of the total electorate – the more telling statistic – fell from 66 per cent to 55 per cent. In three of the last four elections little more than half the electorate have turned out to vote Conservative or Labour.

Secondly, Labour's electoral decline in the period of partisan dealignment was steeper than that of the Conservatives. From 1970 to 1987 its vote fell by over a quarter (down 12 per cent), the Conservative party's by under a tenth (down 4 per cent). Moreover, the Conservative vote displays no clear long-term trend. Since 1979 it has recovered to well above its 1974 nadir and returned, if not to its 1950s peaks, at least to its 1964–70 level. Labour's vote, by contrast, has been in almost continuous decline since the war. Its share of the electorate fell at each successive election between 1950 and 1983, apart from a small blip in 1966. In 1987 and 1992 it recovered, but only slightly, and to nowhere near its pre-1983 levels.

Thirdly, since 1970 support for the minor parties has clearly, if erratically, grown. In 1983 the Liberal–SDP Alliance took 26 per cent of the vote and 23 seats – the centre's best performance since the 1920s – and in 1987 23 per cent of the vote and 22 seats. In 1992 the Liberal Democrats won almost as many seats (20) but on a smaller vote (18 per cent). In by-elections and local elections tho.centre vote has been higher. Britain appeared to be moving towards something like a three-party system in England and a four-party system in Wales and Scotland.

Again, the term 'three-party system' is not perfectly accurate. With barely more than twenty seats the prospects of the Liberal–SDP Alliance forming a government were clearly slim and certainly not equal to that of the two big parties. Yet it was a force to be reckoned with. It contested every seat (as, indeed, the Nationalists did in Wales and Scotland) and it had a much stronger, more professional, national organization than the old Liberal party did. It replaced Labour as the main if often distant challenger in the majority of Conservative seats. Britain may not have had a fully fledged three-party system; but it undoubtedly had three-party politics. The slippage of the Liberal vote to 18 per cent in 1992, together with the continuing weakness of Nationalists of all persuasions, indicates that the party system may be changing yet again.

Party identification

Long though it lasted, Labour's electoral decline might have arisen from a succession of essentially short-term problems rather than a diminution of long-term allegiance. However, the trend in underlying party loyalties (see Table 5.4) suggests that the reservoir of Labour loyalty in the electorate gradually dried up after 1964 (when it was first measured). Conservative party loyalties, by contrast, have stayed remarkably level, whatever the party's fortunes at the polls, remaining within a narrow 35 to 40 per cent band throughout the period. As a result Labour has relinquished its head start in the electorate's loyalties: in 1964 there were 3 per cent more Labour identifiers than Conservatives; by 1987 there were 7 per cent fewer.

Table 5.4 The incidence and strength of party identification, 1964–87

	1964	1966	1970	Feb./ Oct. 1974*	1979	1983	1987
	%	%	%	%	%	%	%
% with a party identification	93	91	92	90	87	86	86
% identifying with Con.	39	36	40	35	38	36	37
% identifying with Lab.	42	45	43	40	36	31	30
% of all electors who are:							
'very strong' identifiers	45	44	43	28	22	22	20
'fairly strong' identifiers	37	38	38	45	46	40	41
'not very strong' identifiers	11	10	12	17	19	24	25
without any identification	7	9	8	10	13	14	14

* combined

Source: Heath *et al.* (1991), pp. 12–13.

Two other features in the party identification trends stand out. Firstly, identification with the minor parties – mainly the Liberals and, in the 1980s the SDP – rose much more slowly than their votes, because a substantial proportion of centre-party support in the 1980s was a protest or tactical vote by people who remained Conservative or Labour at heart. The fragility of the centre vote was illustrated by its rapid collapse after the divorce of the Liberals and SDP in 1988.

Secondly, British voters have become less partisan, rather in the way they have become less religious. Overwhelming numbers continue to volunteer a party affiliation, but agnosticism is on the increase. In 1964 only a fifth of the electorate regarded themselves as anything other than Conservative or Labour; by 1987 fully one-third had psychologically opted out of the two-party system. In particular, the strength as well as incidence of party allegiance has diminished. In the 1960s nearly half the electorate were self-declared 'very strong' identifiers; by the mid-1980s the proportion had fallen to a fifth, while the number of 'not very strong' identifiers had more than doubled. This increasing detachment from parties is reflected in the steady decline in membership of all political parties despite the growth in leisure time and real incomes in British society. Between the early 1950s and 1990 Conservative party membership has fallen from about 2.8 million to about 720,000 and Labour party membership from about 1.0 million to about 275,000. Party loyalists are getting scarcer, unreliable fainthearts more common.

These trends should not be overdramatized. Long-term allegiance to the Conservative and Labour parties remains the dominant fact about the British electorate, the psychological anchor of a stable, slow-moving party system. But the anchor is drifting: as electors' attachments to the major parties, especially Labour, have weakened, the short-term influences of the campaign have strengthened and the vote has become more volatile.

Electoral volatility

A feature of the two-party system in the 1950s and 1960s was the rock-like stability of support for the two parties. From 1950 to 1970 both the Conservative and Labour vote fell within a narrow six-point band of 43 to 49 per cent and the average two-party swing was under 3 per cent. Between elections, the picture was equally serene in opinion polls and at by-elections where there was none of the media razzamatazz that there is now.

In the 1974–92 period there was more turbulence. The opinion polls fluctuated much more wildly; there were more by-election upsets; more voters made up their minds at only the last moment; and swings at general elections became stronger. It was a period of electoral volatility.

The reasons were not difficult to fathom. As partisan and class ardour cooled, considerations other than habitual party and class loyalties began to influence the voting decisions of more and more voters: short-term factors specific to the campaign such as the issues of the day, or the leaders' personalities, or the outgoing government's economic record took on more significance. More voters treated elections as an occasion for personal choice, not class or parental loyalty. Television had an impact, too: by bringing national politics into everybody's home it made day-to-day politics more salient and had a direct influence that often outweighed that of the family, neighbourhood and workplace.

Britain's return to a form of two-party system has not been accompanied by a return to electoral stability. As Table 5.5 shows, the average fall in support for the government at by-elections since 1987 is similar to that for previous Conservative governments since 1970 and higher than that for the Conservative governments of the 1950s. Recent opinion polls have shown a similar turbulence. Fluctuations of Conservative and Labour support in the monthly polls since 1987 are similar in range to those for previous Parliaments since 1970 and are considerably greater than for the 1945–70 period. A spectacular instance of such volatility occurred in November 1990, the month Mrs Thatcher resigned, when a Labour lead of 16 per cent in the polls turned into a Conservative lead of 12 per cent in the course of three weeks: such is the power of television in an age of declining party loyalties. So far, at least, the electorate has not reverted to a new settled pattern of party support.

Table 5.5 Indicators of volatility, 1945–92

Parliament	National swing (%)[a]	Mean fall in support for government in by-elections (%)	Mean annual range in monthly opinion polls (%)[b]
1945–50	+2.9	4.5	n.a.
1951–5	+2.1	1.9	8.5
1955–9	+1.2	8.8	13.6
1959–64	−2.9	13.5	11.0
1966–70	+4.7	16.8	18.9
1970–Feb. 74	−1.3[c]	13.1	15.3
Oct. 1974–9	+5.2	9.5	25.7
1979–83	+3.9	11.4	26.8
1983–7	−1.7	13.9	21.5
1987–92	−2.1	11.2	23.3

Notes:
a The national swing shown relates to the relevant pair of consecutive elections and refers to Great Britain. The 'Butler' swing is adopted, i.e. the average of the change in the Conservative percentage of the vote and the change in the Labour percentage of the vote. A '+' sign denotes a swing to the Conservatives; a '−' sign a swing to Labour.
b Range is measured by the difference between the highest and the lowest support of the Conservatives in any one month *plus* the difference between the highest and lowest support for Labour in any one month.
c In one sense this is a misleading figure because there was a substantial fall in the vote shares obtained by both the Conservative *and* Labour parties.
n.a. = information not available.

The social basis of the vote

Long-term partisanship is rooted in the enduring features of voters' everyday lives: their class or ethnicity, their community and their fundamental values.

Trends in partisanship reflect changes in these underlying structural foundations. It is important, however, to distinguish firmly between structural change, such as a shift in the size of the social classes, and behavioural change, such as a shift in the voting patterns within classes.

A fierce academic controversy rages over whether or not the class basis of partisanship has diminished (Denver and Hands, 1992). Anthony Heath and his colleagues argue that the long-term pattern in class voting is one of 'trendless fluctuation', not inexorable decline. Much of the debate turns on definitions, measurement and statistical inference. By conventional measures of class voting, such as the proportion of all voters voting along class lines (i.e., non-manual workers for the Conservatives plus manual workers for Labour) class voting has undoubtedly subsided (see Table 5.6). In the 1945–70 period, about two-thirds of all voters voted for their class party. After 1970 the link slowly and fitfully weakened and since 1983 the proportion has been under half (47 per cent); the majority voted for either the 'class enemy' or for one of the non-class parties like the Alliance or the Nationalists. This trend should not be exaggerated, however: class remains the single most important social factor underlying the vote.

Class dealignment in Britain is graphically illustrated by comparing the pattern of class voting in 1987 with that in 1959, when Macmillan beat Gaitskell. They were uncannily similar elections: in both cases the Conservatives won with a majority of a hundred; in both cases it was Labour that fought the slicker, more professional campaign, but to no avail because in each case the Conservatives benefited from presiding over a period of prosperity at home and peace abroad. They were both 'you've never had it so good' elections.

Yet the class basis of the Conservative and Labour vote at the two elections was very different. Among non-manual workers the Conservative lead over Labour narrowed from 46 to 29 per cent whereas among manual workers the Labour lead over the Conservatives fell from 27 to 10 per cent. The Conservative vote fell from 67 to 51 per cent among non-manual workers but increased from 30 to 35 per cent among manual workers. And, more dramatically, the Labour vote stayed the same among non-manual workers but slumped from 57 to 45 per cent among manual workers. In other words between 1959 and 1987 both social classes shifted away from their 'own' class party.

Changes in the social composition of both classes are the main explanation. The growth of the public service professions – civil servants, local officials, Health Service managers, social workers, teachers, planners – has eroded middle class solidarity with the Conservative party. Many in this new middle-class have risen from a working-class Labour background by means of higher education, which tends to promote liberal rather than conservative values. Their jobs promote the ethic of public service and professional standards above wealth-creation and authority. In the 1980s they came to regard the Thatcher governments as hostile to the public sector and its values and many joined white-collar trade unions. Social and demographic changes within the working class have worked in the opposite direction. The rapid spread of

Table 5.6 Class and vote, 1945–92

Election	Cons.	Lab.	Lib./SDP and other	Total	Non-manual Cons. + manual Labour voters as a % of all voters
1945–70 (average)					
Non-manual classes	66	24	9	99	63
Manual classes	30	62	8	100	
1959					
Non-manual classes	67	21	12	100	61
Manual classes	30	57	13	100	
Feb. + Oct. 1974					
Non-manual classes	52	24	24	100	55
Manual classes	24	57	20	100	
1979					
Non-manual classes	60	23	17	100	55
Manual classes	35	50	15	100	
1983					
Non-manual classes	55	17	28	100	47
Manual classes	35	42	22	99	
1987					
Non-manual classes	55	19	26	100	48
Manual classes	35	41	24	100	
1992					
Non-manual classes	50	25	25	100	48
Manual classes	34	46	20	100	

Note: Figures do not always add up to 100 because of rounding.
Sources: 1945–87: Heath *et al.* (1985), p. 30; 1992: Harris/ITN exit poll.

home-ownership, the migration from North to South and from inner city to suburb, and the expansion of non-union private-sector employment have undermined working-class loyalty to the Labour party. Unionized council tenants in the North remain solidly Labour; but they are increasingly outnumbered by the 'new working class' of non-union home-owners in the South who, in the 1980s and 1990s, voted Conservative.

This decline in class voting has not necessarily altered the long-term Conservative–Labour division of the vote: both parties have lost support in their own classes. Structural changes in the size of the social classes is a different matter. The embourgeoisement of British society has undoubtedly tilted the balance of partisanship in the Conservatives' favour. Almost all the predominantly Conservative groups in the British electorate have expanded; almost all the predominantly Labour groups have contracted. Between 1964 and 1987 the working class – defined as manual workers excluding the self-employed, supervisors and technicians – declined from 50 to 36 per cent of all voters and contraction has continued since then. Over the same period the professional and managerial salariat grew from 19 to 29 per cent. There are parallel trends in housing: between 1951 and 1990 home-ownership more than doubled, from 31 to 66 per cent of the electorate and, through the sale of council houses under the Thatcher governments, the majority of working-class voters (56 per cent) owned their own homes by 1987. The trend in trade union membership is different. It gradually grew between 1951 (45 per cent of the workforce) and 1979 (51 per cent) but since then has fallen below the 1951 level, to 38 per cent, as a result of the decline in manufacturing industry. The changing size of these class, housing and trade union groups reduced the Labour vote by about 6 per cent and increased the Conservative vote by about 4 per cent between 1964 and 1987, independently of any voting shifts within these groups. However, other social changes such as the steep decline in church attendance, has hurt the Conservatives, so the overall advantage to the Conservatives from changes in social structure is somewhat less.

New social factors

Class has diminished, without disappearing, as a basis for party choice. Have any new social divisions emerged in its place? Economic self-interest, community pressures and party policies have combined to make housing – in particular the division between owner-occupiers and council tenants – a better predictor than occupational class. But housing is closely correlated with class and some of its impact disappears once class is taken into account. Following the West Indian and Asian immigration of the 1950s and 1960s, another new factor is race: the ethnic minorities vote along ethnic rather than class lines. In 1987 the overwhelming majority of Afro-Caribbeans (86 per cent) and Asians (67 per cent) voted Labour compared with well below half their white neighbours. But under 4 per cent of the electorate is black, so the impact of race is confined to a few areas. The slow spread of higher education has created a new but still weak value cleavage within the middle classes: broadly speaking, materialist, nationalist and authoritarian non-graduates who vote Conservative versus libertarian, internationalist and anti-commercial graduates, who voted for the centre parties or Labour (Heath et al., 1991). The most powerful political division apart from class (partly, however, because it reinforces it) is territorial: the North and South-West of England, Scotland and Wales give disproportionate support to Labour, Liberals and Nationalists. In the case of Scotland and Wales this leads to a minimal return of Conservatives thus reinforcing demands for autonomy and devolution of powers from Westminster.

These new divisions, however, have cut across and weakened class voting, but not replaced it. By 1987 four out of five voters belonged to 'mixed-class' categories – working-class home-owners, or middle-class trade unionists, or the white-collar wives of blue-collar husbands. For such voters their group identity, including class, is ambivalent and thus their group interests unclear. As a result, the electoral impact of the social structure taken as a whole has steadily declined. There has been a general social dealignment as well as a specific class dealignment.

The ideological basis of partisanship

Partisanship is rooted in what people believe as well as what they do. It is sustained if a party's basic positions match those of its supporters; strained if they do not. Underlying beliefs have a structural impact if their distribution within the electorate changes; a behavioural impact if their influence on the vote strengthens or weakens.

Simplifying drastically, the political beliefs of British voters can be described in terms of two dimensions: collectivist-individualist and liberal-authoritarian. The first refers to the relative roles of the state and the market in matters of production and distribution. Nationalization *vs.* privatization, economic planning *vs.* the free market, universal *vs.* selective welfare, progressive *vs.* flat-rate taxation are among the perennial issues that fall along this dimension. The second dimension is less clear-cut, but broadly refers to issues of citizenship concerning the rights of the state versus the individual, minorities and foreign states. Issues of crime and punishment, censorship, racial and sexual equality, immigration, nuclear defence and war loosely cluster along this dimension. In popular discourse, both dimensions are conflated into a single 'Left–Right' spectrum, but this confuses more than clarifies because a very substantial minority of voters are on the 'left' of one dimension but on the 'right' of the other.

Figure 5.2 maps the location of the three parties and their supporting voters on the two-dimensional ideological map. Three features stand out. First, the middle classes are more ideologically polarized than the working class,

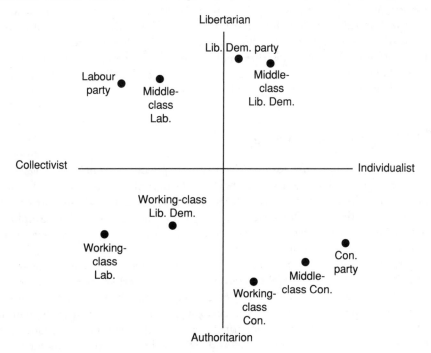

Figure 5.2 The ideological map of the British electorate

especially along the liberal-authoritarian dimension. Second, the party system corresponds to the political divisions within the middle classes, not the whole electorate. All three parties are ideologically closer to their middle-class supporters than to their working-class supporters. This may well be the result of the overwhelmingly middle-class composition of the parties at both parliamentary and activist levels. Third, this ideological gap between parties and their working-class supporters poses a particular problem for the Labour party because the working class provide it with the great majority of its votes while the middle classes provide it with the great majority of its activists. Class differences on policy are particularly wide among Labour voters, most notably on immigration, nuclear disarmament, capital punishment and the rights of women, blacks and gays. This periodically presents the Labour leadership with electoral dilemmas.

It is difficult to judge how much the ideological map has changed in recent years: reliable measures of long-term trends in voters' beliefs do not exist. The scraps of available evidence offer a mixed verdict. Between 1964 and 1979, a period of mainly Labour governments, the electorate appears to have moved to the right. Support for Labour's collectivist trinity of nationalization, trade union power and an expanding welfare state fell dramatically (if unsteadily). A major rift between the Labour party and its working-class supporters opened up on economic issues alongside citizenship issues. But since 1979, during an uninterrupted period of Conservative government, ideological undercurrents in the electorate flowed back to the left. The electorate became less Thatcherite, not more, especially on issues of social expenditure and welfare provision, but also on job creation, trade union legitimacy and a range of 'civil liberties' issues such as abortion, the death penalty, racial equality and women's rights. Moreover, the Labour party's abandonment of its old positions since 1987 has closed the policy gap with its supporters. In the 1990s it is unlikely to be said, as it was in the 1960s and 1970s, that the Labour party won votes despite its policies.

Britain's changing electoral geography

Partisanship is not only fostered by the jobs people do and the things they believe; it is also based on where they live. Geographical factors have become increasingly important since the 1970s (Johnston *et al.*, 1988). Once again, we need to distinguish between the structural impact of a geographical redistribution of the electorate and the behavioural impact of a change in the importance of geographical factors.

The steady post-war population movements have of course changed the constituency map. In the short term, as we saw earlier, the Labour party benefits because it normally represents depopulating areas and thus under-sized constituencies while the Conservatives normally represent expanding areas and thus over-sized constituencies. In the medium term, however, migration should have no structural effects because the boundaries of constituencies are adjusted to population changes. Thus between 1955 and

1992 the number of seats in the South grew from 334 to 351; the number in the North of England declined from 177 to 173. Glasgow, Birmingham, Liverpool and Manchester together were represented by 46 MPs in 1955 but by only 30 in 1992.

These long-term structural changes would be immaterial if the way people voted was unaffected by where they lived. In the 1950s and 1960s constituency and region made an apparently negligible difference once their socio-economic composition was taken into account. Wales was more Labour than the South-East but because it was more working-class, not because it was Wales. Behind this assumption was the remarkably uniform swing across all constituencies: election results appeared to be the product of strictly national forces. (Swing is one party's gain plus the other party's loss divided by two.)

In fact a uniform swing could only come about if a party's voters behaved differently, not the same, according to the constituency in which they lived: a uniform 5 per cent swing from Labour to Conservative (for example) requires Labour voters to defect at higher rates in hopeless seats than safe seats. That this tended to happen reflected the 'partisan neighbourhood' effect: the loyalty rate of Labour (Conservative) supporters increased the more Labour (Conservative) there were in the constituency. There was a parallel 'social neighbourhood' effect: the Labour (Conservative) vote among the working class (middle class) increased the more solidly working-class (middle-class) the constituency was.

These geographical factors have always operated but they were especially pronounced in the 1980s. In 1983 social neighbourhood effects were powerful enough to save the Labour party from oblivion: had national rates of class voting applied in every constituency, Labour would have been reduced to 25 seats. Since 1970 they have produced a systematic and cumulative local deviation from the national swing. Each election has been a 'two-nation' election: the Conservatives have advanced most where there was economic expansion and security and least where there was deprivation and decline. (In 1992 the pattern was partly reversed. The swing to Labour was above average in the Midlands and some parts of the South, and below average in Scotland and some parts of the North – reflecting the untypical character of the 1989–93 recession which had hit the South and Midlands earlier than elsewhere.) As the geographical axis of economic growth has tilted, so too has that of party support. Thus the long-term swing to the Conservatives has been in the South and Midlands, the suburbs, small towns and countryside, where the Conservatives have always predominated. And the long-term swing to Labour has been in the North and Scotland, the large towns, inner-city areas and outer-fringe council estates, where Labour has always predominated.

The accumulative effect has been dramatic. Between the similar elections of 1959 and 1987 Labour's share of the two-party vote fell by 6 percentage points overall, but by much more in the South – by 16 points in East Anglia, 14 in the South-West, 11 in the South-East and 12 in the East Midlands. Above the Humber–Mersey line, however, it actually increased: by 5 percentage points in the North-West (and a massive 31 points in Liverpool); by 7 points in the Northern region; and by 14 points in Scotland (29 points in Glasgow). In 1959 the northern cities of Glasgow, Edinburgh, Liverpool, Manchester, Newcastle,

Bradford, Leeds, Sheffield and Hull elected 28 Conservative MPs; in 1987 they elected a mere 5. By contrast, only 3 of the 176 seats in the South, excluding London, returned Labour MPs. Thus each party represents quite separate halves of Britain – the urban North in the case of Labour and the rural, small-town and suburban South in the case of the Conservatives – and neither has much direct contact with the other half.

The nature of these geographical effects is not entirely clear, but they reflect more than the economic conditions prevalent in each region. Contributory factors include the presence or absence of a traditional Labour culture; tactical voting; partisan patterns of migration (e.g. the tendency for Conservatives to move out of economically declining areas) and, probably most important of all, the sheer visibility of poverty in some areas and prosperity in others.

Whatever the precise cause, there has been one consequence of profound significance. The reinforcing relationship of economic growth or decline, geographical region and prior party strength has dried up the supply of marginal seats. By the standard definition the number steadily fell from 166 in 1955 to 88 in 1987 and on current trends will fall further at future elections. This means that the number of seats changing hands on a 1 percent swing has halved from 18 in 1955 to 9 in 1987, although it rose slightly to 10–11 in 1992. Thus the exaggerative properties of Britain's electoral system, which underlie its capacity to produce single-party governments, has been seriously weakened.

On balance long-term structural changes in the British electorate are helping the Conservatives and hurting Labour. The gradual contraction of the working class, particularly the 'traditional' working class, has diminished Labour's natural vote without new social bases of significance emerging in its place. The growing importance of regional and constituency factors saved the Labour party from extinction in the 1980s but, as more constituencies are created in Conservative territory, will make it more difficult for Labour to win outright victory. This does not mean, however, that 'Labour cannot win', for the weakening partisanship that has accompanied these structural changes offers each party greater rewards than before from the exploitation of short-term political opportunities. We turn next to the role of short-term factors in the voting decision.

The character of the British voter

Party systems provide the framework within which elections are contested; the actual result depends on the impact of unpredictable short-term factors on the uncommitted voter. In a typical election about 20 per cent of voters switch parties but that proportion almost doubles if movement to and from abstention is included: thus, in theory, about 13 million voters are 'up for grabs'. If all of them moved in the same direction the favoured party would win by a landslide; in reality the vote switching largely cancels out. Direct conversion from one major party to the other is exceptional (less than 0.5 per cent in either direction) and, while traffic to and from the centre parties is heavier, it rarely produces a net swing of more than 1 per cent either way. The national swing between two elections is small, therefore – the post-war average is 2.8 per cent, the post-war record 5.2 per cent – and much of it arises from differential abstention and the physical replacement of the electorate.

What kind of voters are those who switch parties and contribute to the small net swing that determines election results? Contrary to democratic myth, few of them conform to the model citizen who carefully assesses the qualities of each party by paying close attention to the news, the quality press and the party manifestos. The most avid consumers of political information tend to be party loyalists wishing to arm themselves with ammunition to defend their prejudices. The vote switchers tend to be the least interested and informed about politics.

Television's dominance of campaigns has inevitably prompted the notion that voters increasingly judge the parties on the basis of their leaders. Being a visual medium, television is prone to define the campaign in terms of the party leader's electioneering – the morning press conference, the afternoon visits and walkabouts, the evening set speech – and to cover serious issues by the device of the long set-piece interview with the leader.

The assumption that British elections are turning 'presidential' is superficially plausible, yet stubbornly resisted by hard evidence. The electorate voted Labour out of office in 1970 and again in 1979, despite preferring Wilson to Heath and Callaghan to Thatcher as Prime Ministers: popular Prime Ministers have not saved unpopular governments. A more telling test is how people vote when they prefer the policies of one party but the leader of another: in the 1980s about a fifth of all voters were in this position and their vote split by five to one in favour of the first. What counts is not who stands for the party but what the party stands for.

Voters claim to vote on the parties' policies. This can involve any of three types of judgment. The issue of unemployment serves as an example. Voters might judge the parties by their specific proposals for creating jobs ('position voting'), by their commitment to solving the problem ('priority voting') or by their record on unemployment ('performance voting').

Position voting is the old-fashioned liberal democratic ideal, and what politicians probably mean by 'voting on the issues'. But it is not what most voters, especially uncommitted voters, do: they have neither the information nor inclination to judge the parties' specific policy positions. However, they can get a feel for the parties' records and priorities. The electorate therefore prefers to conduct a post-mortem than confer a mandate, and for good reason: it makes more sense to judge parties on the hard evidence of their past record than on the flimsy speculation of their promises. Thus British elections are more likely to be lost by governments than won by oppositions.

Party electioneering is based on the assumption of priority voting. The parties rarely engage in genuine dialogue but talk past one another, each putting emphasis on its 'own issues' such as taxation, defence and law and order in the case of the Conservatives, and unemployment, pensions and the National Health Service in the case of the Labour party. On each issue British voters consistently regard one of the parties as 'better' for long periods of time and it is very rare for a party to 'capture' an issue from another. Thus election campaigns are agenda-setting competitions rather than policy debates.

In modern elections British voters put the management of the economy and their standard of living at the top of the agenda and it is on these grounds that they judge the government's record. The state of the economy in the run-up to an election is crucial to the result, but there is no simple, mechanical formula which relates inflation, unemployment or other aspects of the economy to popular support for the government. The precise relationship varies from election to election. It depends on voters' perceptions of the economy, which are influenced not only by the real economy but by the media and government. The touchstone of the economy has shifted from the balance of payments in the 1960s, to inflation in the 1970s, to unemployment in the early 1980s, to interest rates in the late 1990s. Moreover, public expectations can be altered: unacceptable levels of unemployment or inflation in the 1950s would be regarded as triumphs in the 1990s. Economic perceptions are also influenced by trends as much as levels as steeply rising unemployment frightens voters more than a high plateau and, through constant news of lay-offs, is more visible.

Whatever the form taken by issue-voting, its impact should not be overestimated. In 1983 voters overwhelmingly cited unemployment as the single most important issue and consistently chose Labour as the better party on the issue, probably on performance and priority grounds. Yet Labour went down to its worst defeat since 1918. In 1992 voters cited the Health Service, education and unemployment as the three most important issues, and said they preferred Labour to the Conservatives (by a wide margin) on each; yet the Conservatives won. In fact there was no policy or issue-based explanation for the Conservatives' victory.

For policy-based party preferences to be translated into votes, a prior condition is crucial: the party in question must be regarded as 'fit to govern'. Every government defeated at the polls since 1945 has suffered a conspicuous loss of authority and cohesion shortly before the end of its term and in that sense ceased to govern. Image, in these terms, is all-important. The ingredients of this primary judgment by the voters include party unity, a 'strong' leader (both within and outside the party), clarity of policy, the avoidance of minority positions ('extremism') and probity. Here the exaggerated importance accorded to gaffes and 'banana skins' by the media during a campaign play a role: they are used as the currency of a party's governing capacity.

Prospects and conclusion

This chapter has already noted how the Labour party's policy review and John Major's replacement of Margaret Thatcher as Conservative leader has pushed both major parties back to the pragmatic centre ground of British politics. The 1992 election was the first since 1966 to be fought by three centrist parties; arguably there were fewer policy differences between the Conservative and Labour parties than at any time this century. The centre ground has shifted, however: the new consensus is not the old post-war settlement of welfare Keynsianism within the Atlantic Alliance but a post-Thatcher settlement of the 'social market' within the European Community, in which the state's role is limited to the supply side of the economy and selective, targeted welfare. This new consensus will probably make it difficult for voters to discern major policy differences between the Conservative and Labour parties. Voters are therefore likely to judge the parties, even more than before, by their past and prospective performance, not their policies, where 'performance' means the management of the economy coupled with the provision of adequate public services. Elections will turn more than ever on the state of the economy which will increasingly depend on international economic forces beyond the control of any British government.

How effective is the British party system? As an instrument of government it is capable of providing durable and cohesive administrations which can carry their legislative programme through Parliament and which are periodically accountable to electoral judgments. Given the absence of extra parliamentary checks on government in the form of a constitutional court, or a federal structure of independent local governments, or an independent central bank, the party system concentrates very considerable formal powers in the Cabinet and Prime Minister. This is a mixed blessing: helpful for prosecuting wars such as the Falklands or for resisting entrenched interests, but capable of foisting policies on the public that are so unpopular as to be unworkable, such as statutory incomes policies or the Poll Tax.

As an instrument of representation the party system is less successful. By under-representing the Liberal Democrats, Greens and, to a lesser extent the Scottish Nationalists, it keeps important issue areas such as the constitution, individual rights, and the environment off the agenda either permanently or for too long. The dominance of the Conservative and Labour parties has effectively restricted the issues on which the public can choose to a narrow range of social and economic questions. Elections have become little more than referendums on the outgoing government's recent economic record. As a result of the growing socio-geographic polarization of party representation, politicians' direct knowledge and experience of British society is partial and selective, and this is reinforced by the marked preponderance of the upper middle classes, men and whites among MPs. For large sections of society parliamentary representation is abstract, weak and intermittent. The party system does not carry out its integrative functions either across groups or between citizens and state very effectively, to the disadvantage of effective government in the long run.

Chapter 6
Political communications
Kenneth Newton

Not so long ago few books on British politics had chapters on the media; now they are standard. Yet such is the pace of change it is no longer enough to talk just about the media – we need to examine the broader theme of political communication. The media are, of course, an important part of the political communications system – indeed, they are probably the most important single part – but the term 'political communications' covers a wider range of subjects, including political propaganda and advertising, as well as political censorship, and the management and manipulation of political news and information.

It is not possible to understand the role of the media in the British political system without also understanding something about censorship and secrecy, on the one hand, and political propaganda and political advertising, on the other. They are all part and parcel of the same thing. It is also argued that just as the political importance of the media has grown over the past thirty or forty years, so have other aspects of political communication grown during the past ten to twenty years, especially the importance of political propaganda and news manipulation.

Information control

Political analysts generally agree that Britain is one of the more secretive states in the West. One explanation for this argues that the British political system combines the two preconditions which are necessary for a high level of government secrecy, namely, a motive to keep things secret, and an opportunity to act on the motive. The motive for secrecy is based upon the degree to which central government is held directly responsible and accountable for its actions. Since it cannot easily shift political blame to other levels or branches of government, it has a strong motive to keep potentially troublesome matters secret. Lines of accountability and responsibility lead from the electorate through the political parties to Parliament, and from there to the government, the Cabinet, and the Prime Minister. Accountability and responsibility are, in turn, based upon the centralized two (or two and a half) party system, the simple majority electoral system, single-party government, collective Cabinet responsibility, and individual ministerial responsibility. Moreover, being at the centre of a unitary state, central government is directly responsible for a broad range of public functions. This, in turn, is compounded by the overlap between the executive, legislative and judiciary.

Moreover, the British government has considerable opportunity to translate its motives into action. In the absence of a written constitution and a bill of rights, with relatively new and weak freedom of information legislation, and with the principle of parliamentary sovereignty to back it up, the government has considerable power. In particular, the Official Secrets Act gives the government great powers to withhold information about national security, and these matters are broadly defined in the UK. In other words, by the standards of the Western democratic world, the elitist traditions and the centralized constitution of the British state provide both the motive and the opportunity for government secrecy and political censorship.

Although a reputation for government secrecy has been long established, the 1980s were unusually restrictive even by British standards. Indeed, there were far too many incidents and events to list here, but the more notable included: criticism of the BBC in 1982 by the Prime Minister and Conservative MPs for its reporting of the Falklands war; the arrest and trial of the civil servants, Clive Ponting and Sarah Tisdale, for leaking documents; a long series of controversies about TV programmes and attempts to censor them, including *At the Edge of the Union* and *Real Lives* (both about Northern Ireland), *Death on the Rock* (about the killing of IRA suspects), and *My Country Right or Wrong* (about the secret services); the attempt to prevent the publication of *Spycatcher*, the memoirs of the secret service agent, Peter Wright, who alleges attempts to 'de-stabilize' a previous Labour government; the admission that MI5 vetted BBC journalists; a dossier submitted by the Conservative party chairman, Norman Tebbitt, alleging BBC news bias, especially on the American bombing of Libya; the banning of a TV programme on Zircon (a spy satellite) and subsequent Special Branch raids on the homes and offices of journalists and broadcasters. In October 1990 the European Commission on Human Rights ruled that the British government had violated Article 10 of the European Convention by preventing the publication of extracts from *Spycatcher*. Before that, the BBC became so sensitive to government reaction that it set up an elaborate monitoring procedure for political programmes, with the consequent danger that in anticipating government censorship it would censor itself.

In addition the government tightened up on Official Secrets with the Act of 1989, banned the broadcasting of the voices of some politicians in Northern Ireland, passed Clause 28 of the 1988 Local Government Act, which apparently made illegal actions promoting homosexuality. The Act also placed restrictions on the publicity activities of local government. To this may be added a list of other incidents, including difficulties and delays with the publication of official figures on such things as homelessness, health and unemployment. What makes these restrictions on political communications all the more significant is the other side of the coin, which involves government advertising and propaganda.

Government advertising and party propaganda

The techniques of modern advertising and public relations are increasingly used by the politicians of most Western nations, but nowhere more enthusiastically than by the Conservative party and government of the 1980s. The services of the advertising agency Saatchi and Saatchi were used extensively by the party, and the personal appearance and speech of Mrs Thatcher, and other Cabinet members, were changed to try to make them more attractive to the public. It was increasingly said that unpopular government policies should be explained and presented more carefully – that is, not changed, but packaged more attractively.

Election campaigns *were* changed, with the unpredictability and rough-and-tumble of public meetings being replaced by carefully stage-managed press events and photo-opportunities. The Conservatives more than doubled their campaign budget between 1979 and 1987, concentrating their efforts on the Central Office, and particularly on national advertising. The advertising budget was more than doubled in real terms between 1983 and 1987. The other parties followed suit, so far as they could afford to.

This is not the whole story, or even the most important part of it, for while the government was cutting public spending, it was also increasing its own advertising budget by leaps and bounds – from £35.4m before it came to power in 1978–9 to close on £200m in 1989–90, an increase of 465 per cent. The Prime Minister's and the Cabinet Office increased spending on press, publicity and other promotions from £342,000 to £525,000 in one year (1987–8), an increase of more than 50 per cent.

Some government advertising is in the public interest and cannot possibly be described as political – the don't drink and drive campaign, the belt up campaign, information about health and safety, for example. It is also extremely difficult to say where government advertising in the public interest ends and where political and party propaganda starts – there is a very thin line between them. Nevertheless, there is concern about the size and extent of government advertising, and about its use of particular campaigns which, some argue, have stepped well over the thin line. A great deal of the money was spent on campaigns promoting privatization, which the government was most anxious should succeed, and some spending was politically controversial: an Employment Training advert stated that 'the government is investing £1.4bn in New Employment Training'; the slogan 'Action for . . .' appeared repeatedly in publicity for the Department of Employment, the Department of the Environment, the Conservative Party Conference of 1987, and the party's local election campaign.

There are regulations about government advertising, but these are rather vague and ambiguous. Even so the way the government pressed against them has caused concern (see the *Guardian*, 8.8.88, the *Sunday Times*, 4.10.88 and the

Independent, 12.8.88). Just before the 1987 election, for example, an advertising campaign for an unemployment scheme was aimed, apparently, at audiences and in regions where unemployment was relatively low, raising the suspicion that the campaign was aimed not at the unemployed, but at voters who might be concerned about unemployment. In 1989, leaked documents (not a pun!) suggested that a private £20 million 'water awareness' campaign was part of a longer term government privatization plan. A Poll Tax information leaflet was widely criticized for being party political.

It is clear that some government advertising is a legitimate and necessary part of the modern state. What has been questioned is the need for the government of the 1980s to have spent so much more on advertising than its predecessors, and whether some of this money was used, in effect, for party political propaganda.

The media

The mass media are enormously important in the political life of the nation. Most of us get the great majority of our political information not from first-hand experience or personal contact, but from the media. Consequently, the media are not merely channels of communication, but by virtue of their capacity to determine what we see and read and listen to, they have great potential influence in their own right.

Television is our most important source of political information. With about 35 million TV sets in the country, most households (97 per cent) have one, and most people get their diet of political information and opinions from its news and current affairs programmes. Newspapers are still important, though. By international standards, Britain has unusually high newspaper circulation figures, and the great majority of households (about 80 per cent) take a daily paper. A smaller proportion listen regularly to extended news and current affairs programmes on Radio 4, and many hear shorter news bulletins on other stations.

There are, however, two distinct branches of the media: first, the print media, of which the national press is most important; second, the electronic media, with television dominating. Where government and politics are concerned it is often misleading to talk of the two as if they were the same. Rather they should be carefully separated.

The print media

Three facts about the British press stand out. First, it is highly centralized in London. There are local and regional papers (notably in Scotland and Northern Ireland) but most people (75–85 per cent of the adult population) regularly see a national paper. Second, by international standards, circulation figures for British papers are generally very high. Third, the fact that it is a national market (which is capital intensive and dependent on a few, large distribution networks) means that relatively few papers compete for a few large markets. Therefore, ownership and control of the newspaper business is highly centralized in the hands of a few companies.

In fact the British press is highly stratified in so far as newspapers appeal to distinct social classes. The five broadsheets (*Times, Telegraph, Guardian, Independent*, and *Financial Times*) have a total circulation of about 2.7 million, and sell to middle- and upper-class readers. Two tabloid papers (*Express* and *Mail*) are lower middle-class, and the three others (*Mirror, Sun* and *Star*) are working-class. The five tabloids have a total circulation of almost 12 million. It has been said that the *Times* is read by people who run the country, the *Financial Times* by those who own it, the *Guardian* by those who would like to run it, and the *Sun* by those who don't know or care who owns or runs it.

The growing concentration of ownership and control of the press means that the number of newspapers in Britain has gradually declined since the turn of the century. Since 1900 the number of national daily papers has fallen from 21 to 11, and since 1923 the number of provincial and local papers fell from 134 to 99. Moreover, the remaining papers are increasingly owned by a few, very large multi-media companies.

In 1983, three newspaper owners (Murdoch, Maxwell, and Matthews) controlled 75 per cent of national daily circulation, and slightly more of national Sunday circulation. Five companies share 85 per cent of national daily, and 96 per cent of Sunday circulation, and the same five controlled more than half the provincial evening circulation, almost three-quarters of provincial morning circulation, and almost a third of the local weekly papers.

The concentration of ownership and control extends well beyond publishing to films, recording, radio, television, entertainment of all kinds, and into property, shipping, insurance, and many other business interests stretching across two or more continents:

- When he died in 1991, Robert Maxwell had newspaper sales of around 12 million in the UK (including the *Mirror* and *Sunday Mirror, Sunday People*, and *Sporting Life*), and interests in TV, books, magazines and journals, as well as computer software, transport and plastics.
- Rupert Murdoch owns newspapers and has television interests on three continents (the UK circulation of the *Sun, News of the World*, the *Times, Sunday Times*, and the Times supplements, surpasses 10 million). He has large interests in book, magazine and journal publishing, Reuters news agency, property, transport, oil and gas production.
- The Pearson Group with national and local papers, also controls Penguin, Longman Books, and *The Economist*, as well as TV, film, mining, banking and other companies.
- Associated Newspapers (Lord Rothermere) publishes the *Daily Mail*, the *Mail on Sunday*, and *Weekend*, with a total circulation of over 5 million, and its interests in Northcliffe Newspapers and other companies extend over three continents and into publishing, broadcasting, theatre, oil, transport and investment companies.

- The International Publishing Corporation controls over 200 magazine titles.

In short, a relatively small number of multi-media and multi-national companies own and control a large proportion of the mass communications market.

Although the *Independent* broke into the national market with relatively little capital, other attempts to do so have generally failed. The most publicized attempt of the 1980s was Eddy Shah, who used the latest publishing technology to launch *Today* – the first new national daily paper in decades, and the first in colour. Within weeks of the first issue he was in financial trouble, and within months the paper was bought by Lonrho, one of the larger multi-media, multi-national conglomerates. It was later bought by News International. The idea that the free market will produce a pluralist and competitive press does not seem to apply to modern Britain. We will return to this point below.

Last, mention should be made of the political weeklies, and of the fact that their circulation, with a few exceptions, has gradually declined over the past fifteen to twenty years. It used to be said with some truth that the influence on the British political elite of such weeklies as the *Spectator*, and the *New Statesman* far exceeded their relatively small sales. This is no longer true.

The electronic mass media

It might be argued that the political complexion of the national press is relatively unimportant in the television age. As a nation we spend about 45 minutes a day with the paper, but nearly 3.5 hours a day in front of the TV. Survey research shows that around 60 per cent of people say that television is their most important source of political information, and the evening news programmes regularly achieve audiences of over 20 million. Like the papers, television (and much radio) news is national, with local news following.

Television and radio news differ from the press in at least two important respects. First, it is possible in theory for anyone to set themselves up in the newspaper business, but TV and radio are limited by what is known as 'spectrum scarcity'. Since there are too few broadcasting frequencies to create a free market, and since some frequencies must be preserved for the police, ambulance, air traffic control, etc., the frequencies are regarded as public property and publicly regulated by means of broadcasting licences. This is known as market regulation. In theory the Monopolies Commission is the market regulating agency for the press, but its failure to prevent Rupert Murdoch buying *The Times* in 1981, so gaining control of a third of the national daily market, means that market regulation of the print media in Britain has been weak.

Second, because broadcasting frequencies are defined as a public asset, broadcasters are required to serve the public interest – something known as content regulation. The moral standards of television are controlled by the recently established Broadcasting Standards Council. Since 1989 there has also been a European Directive on Broadcasting dealing, among other things, with advertising (it bans TV, radio and cinema adverts for tobacco) and sponsorship. Further EC regulations concerning the press, advertising and broadcasting are under discussion. On the political front, TV and radio are required by British law to maintain a 'proper balance . . . and impartiality', are banned from political advertising and editorializing, and are required to follow a set of rules governing fair and equal treatment in election campaigns. Party political programmes are made and financed by the parties, but are broadcast free, with time allotted according to the national voting strength and number of candidates.

The free market system of the print media entails the dangers of oligopoly, and the undemocratic concentration of ownership and control. Market and content regulation of the electronic media bring with them a different danger – that of government control. Both the BBC and Independent Television Commission (the ITC replaced the Independent Broadcasting Authority in 1991) are formally and constitutionally independent of the government, and to a great extent British broadcasting is as free from direct government control as most countries in the Western world. But, like all national broadcasting systems, it has never been completely autonomous, and during the 1980s its independence has been under pressure. For example, the BBC Board of Governors is appointed by the government, although for most of the post-war period there has been a tradition of political balance. However, the government of the 1980s did not always follow this tradition. The appointment of Marmaduke Hussey as chairman in 1986 was widely regarded as an attempt to counter-balance what the government saw as a liberal-left bias in the BBC. And the climate of criticism and suspicion in the 1980s was so strong that some felt the government might 'punish' the BBC, if it was too critical, by refusing to increase the licence fee, or even by reorganizing it out of existence. The letters 'BBC', it was said, stood for 'Be Bloody Careful'.

None the less, TV news and current affairs programmes are as different as can be from the tabloid press – more balanced and fair, and trusted much more by the population. Although the figure is declining slowly, about two thirds of the electorate think that TV news is unbiased, compared with a third who believe the same of the papers. A third think that the newspapers show a political bias, compared with about 10 per cent who think the same of TV. About 10 per cent of voters think that the press coverage of election campaigns is complete, compared with 60 per cent for TV.

It is argued by some that when cable and satellite multiply the number of channels, they will produce something resembling a competitive market, at which point regulation (both market and content) should be discontinued. The Peacock Committee, set up by the government in 1985, took this view. Its Report (Cmnd 9824) said that technological developments in cable and satellite TV will probably produce something resembling a market in the mid-1990s. Meanwhile it rejected 'the commercial laissez-faire system' for BBC TV (but not for Radios 1 and 2), and recommended the continuation of the licence fee, index-linked to inflation.

Nevertheless, it is widely believed that the government's dislike of the BBC is such that it will try to commercialize it, and hence, it is feared, introduce the 'free-market' characteristics of the tabloid press. The renewal of its charter in 1996 may provide an opportunity for this, fuelled by what many Conservatives saw as its hostile coverage during the 1992 General Election campaign. Although the controversy surrounding the government's system of auctioning independent TV franchises in 1991 may delay the privatization of the BBC for a time, the BBC remains the one uncommercialized prize in the media market. It is ironic that British television, widely admired abroad, is under pressure to become more like the 'free-market' model of Fleet Street, which produces some of the worst journalism.

Media bias

News and current affairs programmes can never be free of bias, but they can try, with varying degrees of success, to treat the news as fully and fairly as possible over a period of time. Democratic theory recognizes this, and one important form of it goes on to claim that a politically informed and educated population can only be produced by a free and competitive media market in which a variety of political opinions and viewpoints are expressed. For several reasons this theory does not seem to apply very well to Britain.

First, the British press tends to oligopoly. It is not surprising, therefore, that in spite of its circulation wars, the press shows little of the political pluralism required by democratic theory. Second, since the national press is owned largely by multi-millionaires and multi-national companies, it expresses political views which are largely compatible with their values. It is no coincidence that, among the national dailies, only the *Guardian* and the *Independent* are both politically independent of the big parties, and financially independent of big business. Third, papers rely upon commercial advertising for a large proportion of their income, and they are unlikely to bite the hand that feeds them. Fourth, in countries with a local press, newspapers have to appeal to a wide range of social types and political opinion in order to achieve a market of economic size. In Britain, the national market allows papers to appeal to a particular section of the population and to express strong political views. Fifth, generations of press barons have been in the business not only for money, but also for politics and power, and have exercised direct political control over their papers – Northcliffe, Rothermere, Astor, Beaverbrook, Thompson, King, Matthews, Rowland, Maxwell and Murdoch.

Consequently, the British press as a whole is highly partisan compared with that of most other Western nations. In fact, many people have become so accustomed to the British tabloids over the years that they are no longer aware that the general tone and content of these papers is matched in few other Western countries. In terms of content, bias, cheque-book journalism, sensationalism, and general unreliability, it may be seriously doubted whether they count as newspapers at all. The Press Council did little to arrest the rapid decline of the tabloids, and the Press Complaints Commission, which replaced it in 1991, will find it difficult to improve matters.

The party politics of the national press have also become more strident and more one-sided in the past three decades. In 1945, there were four Labour national dailies, with a readership of 4.5 million, or almost 35 per cent of total sales. The Conservatives had four papers with just over half the national daily circulation. By the 1987 election, the two national dailies with Labour sympathies (the *Mirror* and the *Guardian*), had about 25 per cent of the market (3.6 million), while seven Conservative papers took almost 75 per cent (10.5 million), and the newcomer *Today*, supporting the Alliance, took 2 per cent (0.3 million). The *Mirror* is often critical of the Labour left, and four of the five mass circulation tabloids are strongly Conservative. Three of them with a circulation of over 9 million, far from providing diversity and variety, are virtually identical. The links between the Conservative party and some national papers (both tabloid and broadsheet) are believed to be regular and close, particularly during election campaigns.

The lobby system also contributes to a news bias. The 150 or so Westminster journalists who are known as 'the lobby' get special and privileged access to government information, sometimes delivered at dictation speed, and sometimes on a non-attributable basis. Critics claim that the system induces a laziness in journalists, who tend to repeat government press releases. The *Guardian*, the *Independent*, and the *Sun* have broken with the lobby system. The effects of the lobby are reinforced by the lack of a strong tradition of investigative journalism, such as one finds in some parts of the USA.

For some, the political bias of the national press is a cause for alarm. According to Hugo Young, 'Taken as a whole the press is massively biased in one direction. In the last three years it has become distinctly more so . . . detachment has been devalued and politicization increased . . . the press becomes more narrow, monolithic and doctrinaire' (*Sunday Times*, 18.3.1984). Another writer claims that 'Press bullying arises today from the dogmas of "consensus" . . . Scargill, Benn, Ken Livingstone, even the pathetic Peter Tatchell, are harassed and hounded with a venom and persistence which have no justification and no precedent' (Neil Ascherson, *London Review of Books*, 21.2.1985). Several recent books document these claims in detail.

Bias in the electronic media may be a different matter, if only because it is subject to market and content regulation, as already discussed. However, the BCC has never been wholly independent of government. During the General Strike and the Second World War the government exercized influence, if not control, over BBC reporting, and although the BBC has gained more autonomy during the post war period, Clause 13 (4) of the BBC's Licence and Agreement gives the government a formally absolute power of veto over BBC programmes. Although the government has not made public use of this power, it can still exercise influence, not least by refusing to increase the licence fee, or threatening the reorganization or abolition of the BBC.

Content regulation of both BBC and ITV has had the desired effect of producing a news coverage that is far more reliable and neutral than the tabloid press. Nevertheless, a debate rages about the impartiality of TV news and current affairs: the political left sees it as part of the conservative establishment; the right criticizes it for its soft-centre/liberal consensus bias, and some see it as a left-wing conspiracy.

Academic researchers are divided on the matter, though none see it as unduly favouring the left. Several books by the Glasgow Media Group have discerned in the BBC a systematic bias which involves 'the laying of blame for society's industrial and economic problems at the door of the workforce' (Glasgow Media Group, 1976: 267). It is said that because this bias is hidden and implicit, it is all the more insidious, especially since most people believe they are getting impartial news. Compare, for example, the meanings behind the terms 'The miners' strike' and 'The coal dispute'. Other academics have criticized the Glasgow Group's work, claiming that they have ignored evidence that contradicts their own claims, and that they have systematically misinterpreted the evidence they do discuss. The debate continues.

The influence of the media

It might be argued that the controversy about TV bias is academic, if TV (and the media as a whole) has little influence over the political attitudes and opinions of citizens. The nature and extent of media influence is difficult to study, however, for at least four reasons. First, it is exceedingly difficult to disentangle its effects from other influences such as education or social background. Second, the effects of different media may pull against each other, and cancel each other out. Third, influence between the media and their audiences almost certainly flows in two directions: people select the paper which best fits their view of the world (self-selection); and news sources tailor their politics to suit the market they supply. Fourth, exactly the same message may be interpreted in completely different ways by different people. Given these problems, it is not surprising that there are varying estimates of media influence. Three stand out, however.

First, reinforcement theory claims that the media do not create or mould public opinion, but merely reflect and reinforce it. It claims that audiences are powerfully disposed to select the messages they find most congenial, and that the media are obliged by market forces to supply what customers want. In other words, the sovereignty of the consumer means that even the press barons and the broadcasting companies are bound by the golden chains of the market. The end result is a largely powerless media, in modern democratic states at any rate.

Second, agenda-setting theory agrees with reinforcement theory so far as it claims that the media exercise rather little influence over what people think, but argues that the media help to set the political agenda – they do not determine what people think, but they do influence what people think about. There is some evidence in the research of the 1980s to support this view. It has been said, for example, that the early success of the Social Democratic party was largely a result of their media exposure. Equally, it might be said, this did not save the party from decline in the late 1980s.

Third, there is growing evidence that the papers do indeed have an independent influence over political attitudes and voting behaviour. Britain is a good test case for this research, given its national newspapers and their partisanship. Recent research finds that the papers have a significant impact on voting behaviour even after political attitudes and party identification are taken into account. In other words, even those who identify with a given party and believe in its policies are more likely to vote for another party if, over a period of time, they regularly read a paper which supports the other party. Evidence is accumulating to suggest that the political impact of the national press may not be insignificant after all. (As estimated in Chapter 5, giving the Conservative party a swing of 1 per cent at elections.)

More generally it is often argued that the mass media support and reinforce the centre-ground, middle-of-the-road, conservative establishment view of politics. This is partly because they wish to appeal to the largest markets, and partly because they are owned and operated predominantly (though not exclusively) by conservative, establishment people. These range from the great and the good on the BBC's Board of Governors, to the professionals who staff the newsrooms, and to the (often middle class) experts who are asked for their opinions. As a result, some believe that the media tend to legitimize the liberal consensus, giving minorities (political minorities, women, trade unionists, demonstrators, ethnic and sexual minorities) little time or sympathetic treatment.

General effects

Global communications are now distributed at such a high speed, and politicians and public alike can react so quickly, that the pace of political life has shifted into a higher gear. In some ways this has had a major impact on the conduct of politics, particularly international affairs. A hundred years ago, it took days or even weeks to get news from some parts of the world. Now, news events from around the globe unfold under the public gaze, with consequences both for the speed of political events and their development. In both the Falklands and the Gulf wars, politicians were concerned that news and pictures of war casualties might weaken civilian and military morale, and that the wars should be over before this could happen. In domestic affairs, stories can unfold so quickly, as comment is followed by counter-comment, that a news story can go through several different stages in a twenty-four-hour period. Politicians now have less time to consider events, and to make mistakes and correct them. Equally, news is a perishable commodity, and even news coverage of some important matters tends to be short-lived.

The mass media have also helped to alter the nature of news and political life: they concentrate on personalities and human interest stories, rather than policies and political issues; they deal in sound-bites and artificial photo-opportunities, rather than debate and analysis; elections tend to be treated as horse races devoid of political meaning – politics as entertainment, elections as spectator sport. As a result, the mass media have helped to trivialize and personalize politics, and to cast the leading actors as 'goodies and baddies'. This has been particularly true of the tabloid press, but further commercialization may create 'tabloid television' as well.

Conclusions

In some ways the political communications system changed little in Britain in the 1980s. New papers arrived on the scene, and some were lost, but the same few continued to dominate the market. Channel 4 started in November 1982, but BBC1 and ITV maintained their mass-market lead. Breakfast television started in 1982, but was merely a six-day wonder. Local and community radio proliferated, but the BBC (local or national) retained its brand leadership, and TV continued to dominate radio. Parliament was first televised on 21 November 1989, but this made little difference to the nation, and probably no more to the nature and atmosphere of 'the most exclusive club in London'. The widely publicized satellite TV war between Sky Television and British Satellite Broadcasting ended in their amalgamation to form BSkyB. Cable TV was introduced but did not spread far.

In other ways, the system took on a new, or more clearly defined shape in the 1980s, mainly under government influence. For the first time the 1983 Conservative Central Office's election campaign was run entirely by advertisers and public relations firms out of television studios and press offices – public meetings were dispensed with. The Labour party followed suit in 1987. The government spent much more on political advertising and propaganda, and so did the political parties, so far as they could afford it. At the same time the government moved into a new era in terms of news management and manipulation. On the one hand, it restricted its own information, it tightened up on the already strict Official Secrets Act, it imposed tighter limits on local government publicity, it passed Clause 28, and imposed restrictions on broadcasting some politicians in Northern Ireland. On the other hand, the 1980s saw a series of confrontations between the government and the BBC in particular, but also ITV (*Death on the Rock*). At the same time the standards and style of the tabloid press created serious worries in some quarters.

If these trends continue through the 1990s, the political communications system of the nation will continue to fall short of democratic ideals and practice. There is currently a concern that the communications system is no longer adequate as a 'watchdog of the constitution'. In the course of the next decade these concerns may well turn into alarm.

Looking ahead, it is clear that the 1990s will see profound, if not revolutionary changes, particularly in broadcasting. Cable and satellite TV are likely to expand, the new commercial Channel 5 will open, Channel 4 is due to become a commercial trust, and microwave and cable technology will make local television possible. By the mid-1990s there may be as many as fifty television channels and hundreds of radio stations. International broadcasting (mainly satellite TV) requires international regulation, and the EC is considering new codes for broadcasting and advertising. Some of its existing regulations are built into the Broadcasting Act of 1990, but it is likely to play a larger and larger part in both market and content regulation of the media. Radio will become more commercialized following the creation of the Radio Authority in 1991 and its award of the first two national commercial franchises shortly after. It is planned to make advertising and sponsorship on commercial radio unlimited. A new BBC Charter and Agreement must be written by 1996, and it may either preserve the *status quo*, or introduce commercialism, or abolish the BBC in its present form. The franchise sales system for sixteen independent television companies was introduced (along with the new Independent Television Commission, or ITC) in 1991. It is too early to say what the impact of all this will be. The Chinese curse is 'May you live in interesting times'; we are likely to live in interesting times in the 1990s.

Chapter 7

The other governments of Britain: local politics and delegated administrations

Vivien Lowndes

One of the major peculiarities of British central administration, as we have seen, is that Cabinet and Civil Service rarely implement policies at the point of delivery through their own agents. Britain has never had officials such as the French Prefects, appointed from the centre and directly responsible to it, who carry through its policies directly and in detail throughout its territory.

Instead, British government has relied on the co-operation of affected groups or on autonomous administrations at the local level. Some of these are nominated and some are elected. Of these the most important are the county and district councils.

There are long historical reasons for this state of affairs. Historically the modern British state emerged as a compromise between the central executive (the Crown), which administered certain common interests (above all defence and internal security), and independent-minded notables who ran the localities. If central government wished something done locally, it had to get the notables' agreement. When the notables were replaced by (or elected to) local governments in the nineteenth century, these inherited their position *vis-à-vis* central government. The same was true of the various nominated bodies on which notables originally served (responsible for local health, social security, buildings and roads, etc.). The notables were increasingly replaced by professionals but the latter inherited the entrenched position of their predecessors.

As government took on responsibilities incrementally, and in response to personal needs, the administrative system was never comprehensively reorganized. Even when major changes were made – for example, the institution of the National Health Service in 1948 – they co-ordinated and extended the activities of existing autonomous bodies such as hospitals and health boards rather than replacing them with a greatly extended Ministry of Health. The latter confined itself to the traditional central role of formulating requirements and preparing and interpreting legislation, leaving it to local bodies to carry these out.

The Conservative governments of the 1980s and 1990s tried to force these local bodies to accept their reforms. There was, however, a certain contradiction in their policy, which we have already noted. Seeing 'big government' as the enemy, they were committed to reducing rather than extending the scope and powers of central as well as local government (and indeed, through 'Next Steps' and 'hiving off', making many parts of it semi-autonomous). Their solution to problems of implementation at the local level was therefore not to replace local bodies with a central field administration, but to regulate and reorganize them, while still relying on their compliance for service delivery. This was far from an ideal solution to problems of co-ordination and implementation; it increased rather than diminished the fragmented nature of British policy-making.

The period from 1980 onwards has thus seen unprecedented change in sub-central government and administration. It has been the focus of fierce political battles – local government alone was the subject of more than forty pieces of legislation during the 1980s. While the Thatcher governments of 1979 and 1983 were concerned chiefly with control of spending, the 1987 administration concerned itself with reforming methods of service delivery and the internal organization of local authorities, the National Health Service and other sub-central bodies. These concerns continue to dominate debate in the 1990s. Despite being formulated at Westminster, many of the government's 'big ideas' like 'opting out' and the 'Citizen's Charter' are designed to be implemented locally – in health, transport, education, housing, social services and so on.

Sub-central government is important because of the range (and cost) of its responsibilities in relation to the British political system as a whole. This means that any central move to change the conditions of ordinary life inevitably puts it at the forefront of national politics. In this chapter we examine the new developments in decision-making and service delivery. We start by reviewing the scope of government beyond Westminster and Whitehall, and identifying the main sets of agencies which operate at a sub-central level. We go on to consider how these agencies relate to one another and to central government (and increasingly the European Community), arguing that inter-governmental relations should be conceived in terms of 'spheres' as well as 'tiers' of government. Next, we look at restructuring within the NHS and local government, focusing on two themes which have dominated policy towards sub-central government over the last decade: the attempt to control spending, and the introduction of market-style rela-tionships. We finish by considering how sub-central government is likely to change during the 1990s under the impact of renewed Conservative policies.

The scope of sub-central government

As we have seen, British central government is non-executant and fragmented. Civil servants and ministers are largely concerned with processing legislation, regulating standards and allocating funds. The implementation of policy and the day-to-day delivery of services is the responsibility of sub-central public bodies (with the exception of defence, Customs and Excise, the Inland Revenue and social security which do deliver services). The non-executant nature of central government is reflected in the fact that 90 per cent of public servants work in sub-central agencies. As well as being largely non-executant, central government is highly fragmented. Central departments may have several divisions or regional offices; and whole ministries (as in the case of the Scottish, Welsh and Northern Ireland Offices) find themselves outside the realm of central government proper. This fragmentation and disaggregation of government has led to Britain being characterized as a 'differentiated polity'.

Sub-central government is not restricted to what is commonly referred to as 'local government', i.e. elected councils and their supporting administrative and service delivery structures. Beyond central government we can identify four key sets of government institutions and agencies: territorial ministries and intermediate institutions; non-departmental public bodies (including the nationalized industries, the courts and the NHS); elected local government; and non-elected local government (see Table 7.1). These are discussed in turn below.

Table 7.1 Institutions and agencies of sub-central government

1 **Territorial ministries and intermediate institutions**
 – Scottish, Welsh and Northern Ireland Offices
 – Sub-central arms of central government departments (e.g. regional offices of the Department of the Environment)
 – 'Next Steps' executive agencies (e.g. Benefits Agency and Employment Service)

2 **Non-departmental public bodies**
 – Nationalized industries (e.g. British Rail and British Coal)
 – National Health Service
 – Single-purpose bodies (e.g. Arts Council and Commission for Racial Equality)
 – Central Law Courts

3 **Elected local government**
 – County councils (England and Wales)
 – Regional councils (Scotland)
 – District councils (England, Wales and Scotland)
 – Parish and town councils (in some areas)

4 **Non-elected local government**
 – Joint boards (e.g. for police, fire and transport services in London)
 – Local law courts (Justices of the Peace)
 – Inter-governmental forums (e.g. London and South-East Regional Planning Conference)
 – Public/private partnership organizations (e.g. local enterprise agencies)
 – User organizations (e.g. housing co-operatives)
 – Central government 'arms-length' agencies (e.g. Training and Enterprise Councils and Urban Development Corporations)

Territorial ministries and intermediate institutions

Territorial ministries occupy an ambiguous position as they are both of the centre and the locality. They act as agents of central government but, unlike most ministries, are not defined functionally but territorially. Rather than having charge of policy in a certain 'subject area' (e.g. health or employment) they are responsible for a wide range of functions as they affect a particular territory within the United Kingdom. The Scottish, Welsh and Northern Ireland Offices are located not in London but in the territories they serve, where they function as a 'mini-centre' for that territory.

Territorial ministries take responsibility for the implementation of policy in their areas and exercise a certain amount of discretion in doing so. They also perform a lobbying and 'spokesperson' role on behalf of their territories in negotiations with Westminster and Whitehall. Territorial ministries develop ways of working which reflect to some extent the particular culture and identity of the territory; they may operate in the context of distinct legal, educational and religious institutions. However, despite periodic calls for regional self-government, Britain has remained to date a unitary state in the sense that only Westminster can delegate powers to sub-central agencies, or revoke such powers. This situation may be challenged by recent developments. Pressure within Scotland for a Scottish parliament may lead to change there with consequences for the rest of the UK (Northern Ireland had such a devolved status for 50 years from 1922 to 1972). The Conservatives' limited parliamentary support in Scotland makes it increasingly difficult for the party to continue to resist such pressures.

Intermediate institutions are the sub-central arms of central departments. Their functions and characteristics are varied and their organizational pattern is highly complex. In general, sub-central structures have a managerial character, facilitating the implementation of policy and the smooth running of the department. To take an example, the Department of the Environment has a network of regional offices which are responsible for administering certain regionally based programmes (e.g. on housing investment), monitoring the operation of departmental policy in general, and representing local interests to the centre. Occupying an 'intermediate' position, sub-central offices can get caught in a cleft stick. On the one hand they are expected to convey and argue the case for departmental policy in the areas, whilst on the other hand they are required to represent the views of local actors (for instance in local authorities) back to the central department – views which may be quite at odds with central direction. Personnel in the regional offices of the Department of the Environment, for example, are classic middlemen caught in an ambivalent position.

Although intermediate institutions may have regional responsibilities, their position is very different from that of the territorial ministries. They are concerned with the implementation of policy within a particular 'subject area'; they are single-function bodies rather than territorially defined, multi-functional agencies. Intermediate institutions are likely to become of increasing importance in the light of the 'Next Steps' reform of the Civil Service (discussed in Chapter 2) which involves the devolution of managerial responsibilities to executive agencies, at 'arm's length' from Whitehall central departments.

Non-departmental public bodies

Territorial ministries and intermediate institutions could be considered more as extensions of the centre than as truly sub-central bodies. This cannot be said of non-departmental public bodies which have a much greater degree of autonomy from central government departments and ministries. The prototype of these are the law courts which regulate many important aspects of society and the economy and perform the oldest function of government – maintaining public order. So important are they that we consider them separately in the next chapter. Outside the courts, the most important non-departmental public bodies are the nationalized industries and the National Health Service (NHS).

Public corporations were created in the immediate post-war period to facilitate Keynesian-style government economic planning which aimed to promote growth through demand management and full employment. Support for privatization developed in the 1970s and 1980s in the context of poor productivity, poor industrial relations and poor customer service in many nationalized industries. Some of these problems related to their monopoly status, but a major problem was the lack of clarity concerning the relationship between government departments and the managers of public corporations. In the absence of a clear regulatory framework, confusion and political manipulation can result.

More than twenty privatizations occurred in the 1980s, including share issues in key services like British Telecom, British Gas, and the water authorities. However, the fact that many of these have remained as monopolies has reduced the possibility of efficiency gains. The privatized utilities have come under criticism for keeping prices high in a situation of limited (or no) competition and high profits. With only minimum government regulation over the operation of the new utilities, they are under little obligation to pursue 'social' objectives (such as low prices for the needy or the provision of emergency services). The Conservatives are now taking privatization further with the selling-off of remaining public corporations like British Rail and British Coal.

In 1986–7 the NHS employed nearly one and a quarter million people and spent just under £20 billion (one-eighth of all public spending). In England the NHS has a two-tier structure of 14 Regions and 192 Districts (Scotland and Wales have a single tier system). Regional Health Authorities (RHAs) and District Health Authorities (DHAs) are chiefly concerned with hospital services; there is a separate system of Family Health Service Authorities (FHSAs) which regulate primary health care (including GPs and dentists). Community Health Councils provide a forum for community representatives to exercise a 'watchdog' and advisory role. Ongoing changes to the structure, management and financing of the NHS are currently the subject of fierce debate. The restructuring of the NHS is considered in depth later in the chapter.

There exists a range of other agencies each fulfilling a single purpose, receiving public funds and operating under the supervision of a Whitehall-appointed board – the Arts Council, the University Funding Council and the Commission for Racial Equality, for instance.

Elected local government

Local councils are the element of sub-central government subject to local political control. Councils are made up of unpaid, locally elected representatives, who are usually organized in party groups. In 1991–2 local authorities spent £60 billion (roughly one-quarter of all public expenditure) and employed around 2 million full- and part-time staff in professional, administrative and technical capacities. At present, a two-tier system of elected local government operates in most of England, Scotland and Wales. Upper-tier authorities (9 regions in Scotland and 47 counties in England and Wales) are responsible for strategic planning, transport, fire, education and social services. Lower-tier authorities (53 districts in Scotland and 333 in England and Wales) have responsibility for housing, local planning, environmental health and leisure services. However, following the abolition of the metropolitan counties in 1986, there is only one tier of elected local government in England's 'metropolitan' – or large city – areas (36 metropolitan districts and 32 London boroughs plus the City of London Corporation). This tier carries out all local government functions, although 'joint boards' have been appointed in some areas where cross-city co-ordination is needed (e.g. police, fire and transport).

Like the NHS, elected local government is currently the subject of review and ongoing changes, which are discussed in full later in the chapter. A commission has been established to consider the structure and functions of local government. There is a growing consensus in favour of a change to unitary authorities, but a new model has not yet been agreed. Counties could be abolished and their functions devolved to districts, or counties could be retained and districts wound up. Some sort of compromise solution could be found which allowed for a measure of local choice, perhaps using local referenda to determine the most appropriate size and boundaries for local councils. There is also an emerging agreement on the need to re-establish some form of London-wide governing body. These changes will undoubtedly be carried through in the 1990s.

Non-elected local government

Non-elected local government refers to the myriad of local bodies that have an influence on local policy and services but all outside the direct control of elected local councils. Such bodies generally concentrate on one policy area or purpose and are run by appointed governing or management committees. We can include under this heading joint boards for police, fire and transport, various inter-governmental forums (e.g. the London and South-East Regional Planning Conference), public/private partnership organizations (e.g. local enterprise agencies), user organizations (e.g. housing co-operatives) and central government 'arm's-length' agencies (e.g. Training and Enterprise Councils and Urban Development Corporations). Perhaps the prototype of all these hybrids are the Justices of the Peace who (in England and Wales at any rate) handle local criminal and civil cases, but who until the end of the nineteenth century were the local government in the counties.

These organizations are neither fish nor fowl. They are local, but not under the direct control of local authorities. They are concerned with public policy, but involve inputs from the private and voluntary sectors. These hybrids are often referred to as 'quasi-governmental agencies' or 'quangos'. A Department of the Environment survey carried out in 1988 discovered over 500 quasi-governmental agencies, mostly operating in the spheres of economic development, tourism, arts and recreation.

Inter-governmental relations

Sub-central government is more than a set of institutions, functions and budgets; it involves a complex network of relationships. Britain's differentiated polity is sustained through 'vertical' relationships which link sub-central agencies to central government and through 'horizontal' relationships which link sub-central bodies to one another and to bodies outside the public sector. These relationships may be of a statutory nature (regulated by law), or they may involve the discretionary devolution of powers. Inter-governmental relations change over time – they are dynamic. Laws can be changed, funding regimes can be manipulated, new agencies can be created, and decentralized powers can be recentralized. In this section we will look at the variety of inter-governmental relations and the direction in which they are changing.

Vertical relations

We begin by looking at the 'vertical' relations which link different *tiers* of government. Here we are particularly concerned with relations between central and sub-central government. Many commentators on sub-central government claim that the 1980s have been a decade of political centralization in Britain. It is said that there has been a centralization of power away from sub-central government to Westminster and Whitehall. The Thatcher governments have sought to turn the agencies of sub-central government into implementing arms of the centre with no policy-making role of their own. This would indeed be a historical reversal of long-term trends, which as we have seen have operated up to now in quite another direction. It would also involve implicit constitutional change, particularly in the case of local authorities which are by law accountable to their own locally elected members. Central government legislation has attempted to specify and define the functions of local authorities and, most importantly of all, it has set limits on the level of local authority spending through the manipulation of grant funding and the 'capping' of locally raised revenues. (We return to the attempt to control spending later in this chapter.)

In the 1990s any understanding of vertical relations should be extended to include an additional tier of government – the institutions of the European Community (the European Parliament, Council of Ministers, and European Commission). Any analysis of trends in British sub-central government should be located in the European context. Centralization of power from sub-central to central government in Britain is 'out of step' with Europe, where the 1980s have typically seen a *strengthening* of the role of elected local authorities. As elements of policy-making are 'moved up' from central government to the European level, many European countries are 'moving down' other powers and responsibilities to the sub-central level. Within the wider European context, sub-central government could be set to increase in importance. One important model for the future of the European Community is that of a *Europe des régions* in which sub-central governments express regional identities and provide local services within the context of strong European-level political structures. Such a vision has not been shared by Britain. Central government has shown a reluctance to pass powers 'up' to the EC and, at the same time, has sought to reduce the autonomy of sub-central government.

However, even in the British context, sub-central bodies must increasingly look 'upwards' to the EC as well as to Westminster and Whitehall. Sub-central agencies must maximize potential grant income and meet their statutory obligations (some of which are now set and monitored by European-level bodies) through relationships with the EC. The two-tier model of central–local relations that has dominated discussion of sub-central government in Britain is rapidly becoming out of date.

Horizontal relations

In addition to 'vertical' relations between different tiers of government, 'horizontal' relations between sub-central bodies exercise an important influence over governance. The functioning of horizontal relations is well captured in the idea of 'policy networks'. Policy networks arise within fragmented government systems and cut across organizational structures. These networks are made up of personal contacts or more formalized communication channels between diverse governmental agencies. A network may have a territorial character (linking agencies inside Scotland or Wales, for example), or a professional base (linking members of the same or related professions working in different agencies), or they may develop around a particular policy area, facilitating communication and joint working between actors in a variety of sub-central and central government bodies.

Policy networks change over time, arising in response to new concerns and dwindling in importance (or even disappearing) as circumstances alter. The Conservatives' restructuring of sub-central government during the 1980s has had a significant impact on policy networks. Taking the case of education we can observe that there has been an attack on 'core values' and on the role of key players. Vocational education has been promoted over and above traditional ideas of 'personal development'. 'Parents' choice' has been elevated above the professional judgement of teachers and educational administrators. The role of central government, employers and parent representatives has increased. At the same time, teachers' lobbies have been sidelined and local education authorities bypassed as the trend to opting out and local management of schools gains pace. In a variety of different policy areas, central government in the 1980s has destabilized, bypassed and even abolished or replaced long-standing policy networks in sub-central government. Legislative change, the manipulation of funding arrangements and attempts to direct public and professional opinion are powerful tools in the making and remaking of policy networks.

As old policy networks fall into decay – perhaps simply losing their relevance or perhaps being deliberately undermined – new networks develop. The European dimension is having an effect. As the role of the EC increases there are new possibilities for policy networks which span national boundaries. In some areas closer links are being established between local authorities in neighbouring countries. The Motor Industries' Local Authorities Network, for instance, is providing a forum for local authorities in several European countries to discuss and co-ordinate their responses to economic change and development within the motor industry.

Our understanding of horizontal relations can be further developed by introducing the idea of links between bodies implementing public policy but working in different *spheres* (Bain, Benington and Russell, 1991). Most work on policy networks has, to date, concentrated on relations between agencies within the public sector. In the 1990s a wider focus is required. Increasingly the implementation of public policy involves inputs from private and voluntary sector agencies, or the setting up of partnership arrangements bringing together public, private and voluntary sector bodies.

Much recent legislation on sub-central government has involved ending (or preparing for the end) of public sector monopolies. Whether we are looking at the fate of the nationalized industries or the introduction of competition in local authorities and the NHS, we find that the old idea of a monopolistic public sector is giving way to a new picture of competing service providers in the public, private and voluntary sectors. This need not mean complete privatization. In many policy areas slimmed-down public bodies will retain overall *responsibility* for services, whilst not necessarily *providing* services themselves. They will assess needs, specify the service required and award contracts to the provider which makes the most attractive bid for the job. Figure 7.1 shows how the operation of sub-central government will increasingly involve inter-organizational relations between 'spheres' as well as 'tiers'.

Restructuring in sub-central government

Two aspects of the current restructuring of sub-central government are of particular importance in the co-ordination of public policy-making: the

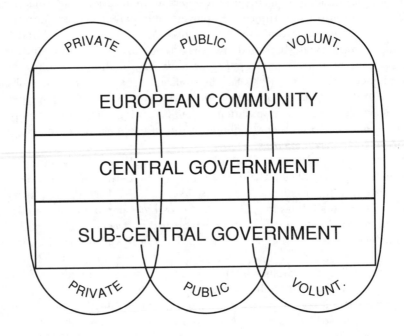

A. Model showing tiers & spheres of governance

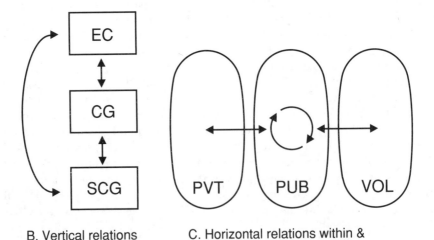

B. Vertical relations
   between tiers of
   governance

C. Horizontal relations within &
   between spheres of governance

Figure 7.1 Models of Inter-governmental Relations

attempt to control public spending and the introduction of market-style relationships. These themes became established in the 1980s but they continue to dominate debate in the 1990s. The attempt to control spending has led to a restructuring of 'vertical' relations – between central and sub-central government. Marketization has involved a re-making of 'horizontal' relations – between sub-central agencies both inside and outside the public sector. How and why did these changes emerge?

Since the mid-1970s, governments have attempted to control or curtail public expenditure. This reflects a breakdown of the 'post-war consensus' on the need for high government spending in order to stimulate demand in the economy and facilitate full employment. By the mid-1970s economic difficulties – particularly high inflation rates – were leading in new policy directions. These problems were seen as having their origins very much within the public sector: on the one hand inflation was fed by ever-increasing bills for welfare services, and on the other hand state-run services and industries had low productivity and poor industrial relations. If new economic policies were to be pursued the government would have to exercise greater control over the public sector, particularly in terms of the resources it absorbed. The difficulties in exercising such control became all too obvious in the series of public sector strikes and stoppages of the 'Winter of Discontent' (1978–9). The Conservatives took control from Labour in 1979 and promised to exercise strict control over public spending (and public sector trades unions) through 'rolling back the frontiers of the state'.

While taking care to be seen as pursuing this policy vigorously, the Conservatives have actually experienced difficulties in controlling – let alone cutting – public expenditure. Overall spending levels have remained fairly constant during their period of office (although there have been changes within and between particular spending programmes). There have been strong countervailing pressures for state spending to be maintained or increased. Among the pressures on Conservative policy have been:

(a) the rising demand for social security benefits during recessionary periods in the 1980s and 1990s;
(b) the rising proportion of elderly people in the population who make high demands on welfare services;
(c) the fact that much public spending is carried out by agencies of sub-central government which are not under the direct control of central government;
(d) the difficulty in attempting to increase productivity in services relying on face-to-face interaction (e.g. health care or social work).

This is not the place to discuss the changing structure of demand for public services and transfer payments. Instead we consider here the last two points which both relate to the functioning of sub-central government. If public expenditure was to be controlled the government had to limit the spending of sub-central agencies that were not under its direct control. This led to a focus on restructuring 'vertical' relationships – the government sought to exercise tighter control over the spending programmes of the sub-central implementing agencies. As we shall see, this turned out to be very difficult and after 1987 the government turned its attention to seeking productivity improvements within the sub-central agencies. If overall levels of spending were so 'sticky', reforms were needed to make the same amounts of money 'work harder'.

It is not easy, however, to achieve productivity gains in the service sector where work is not susceptible to mechanization or intensification. In addition, the control by professionals of many elements of service delivery limited the ability of central government to intervene in the management of day-to-day operations. A way out of this impasse was for the government to switch its attention from 'vertical' to 'horizontal' strategies. 'Horizontal' strategies involved attempts to achieve productivity improvements ('value for money') through the introduction of market-style relationships into the public sector. The relationship between *spheres* rather than *tiers* of government was the object of policy.

Marketization is more than straightforward privatization. Privatization involves a change of ownership, as in the 'selling off' of nationalized industries to private shareholders. Marketization, however, embraces the introduction of a whole range of market-style relationships in the public sector. Local authority or NHS services may be 'contracted out' to private firms or charitable groups, or they may stay inside the public sector but be supplied on a contractual basis by a 'provider' unit to a 'purchaser' unit. In either case bureaucratic methods of allocating resources are being replaced with market methods. Rather than being governed by professional judgment, rules and precedent, resource allocation involves competition, contracts and 'value for money'.

We now go on to illustrate our two themes – the attempt to control spending and the introduction of market relations – with reference to the restructuring of the NHS and local government.

Restructuring the NHS

The attempt to control spending

After the 1979 election there was growing concern in the Treasury about the funding of the NHS. From 1980 only 9 per cent of spending on the NHS was coming from national insurance contributions; the rest had to be paid by the Treasury. A Royal Commission report considered that the private health-care sector was too small and, if expanded, could 'mop up' part of the ever-increasing demand for health services. The 1980 Health Services Act reduced restrictions on private operators and introduced limited tax concessions for companies paying private health insurance premiums for their employees. The Act also legalized lotteries and voluntary fund-raising by health authorities. The growing importance of voluntary fund-raising can be seen in high-profile national campaigns such as that by Great Ormond Street Children's Hospital to raise £30m for vital capital works. Income-generation is an increasingly important part of health professionals' work; today it is not uncommon to see hospitals asking for 'fund-raising experience' when advertising staff nurse posts.

As for budget allocations to health authorities, the government tried to limit growth by setting budgets after making allowances for efficiency savings (via 'cost improvement programmes'). In addition, funds were made available subject to projected levels of inflation (which were generally under-estimated during the 1980s). Cost savings were also pursued through attempts to reduce the drugs bill by limiting the list of drugs from which doctors and hospitals could purchase (generic drugs were favoured over more expensive brand names).

Overall spending on health care did not fall in the 1980s, but there was a widespread perception of budgetary cuts. One reason for this was that a number of individual health authorities did experience cuts. This was due to the putting into place of a new needs-based resource allocation mechanism (which dated from 1977–8). In the absence of significant new resources this meant that existing resources were being redistributed away from 'well-off' areas to those with fewer facilities. Areas with many facilities therefore lost part of their budgets; they did not, however, experience a reduction in *demand* for health services and so a shortfall – or cut – was experienced.

Why then did the government fail to make cuts or hold NHS spending levels constant? This is in part because the 'post-war consensus' remains strong with regard to the NHS and its popularity makes radical change a political hot potato. It was Labour's strongest issue in the 1992 General Election and the opposition parties continue to put the government under pressure on health policy. In fact, health is the one area where the government has sought publicly to *defend* its spending record. The structure of demand has also exerted an upward pressure on spending. On the one hand the increasing proportion of elderly people in the population require more health services; on the other hand, technological developments push up costs as new 'hi-tech' treatments become available. The increasing demand for more and more expensive health care meant that, even with stable spending levels, services remained in short supply and the government was accused of 'cutting'. However, the government remained determined that it would not sign a 'blank cheque' for the NHS and thus create an upward spiral of expenditure. It therefore became increasingly important to seek productivity improvements.

The introduction of market-style relationships

Achieving productivity improvements in the NHS is not easy. Central government was faced with two key problems. First, it is much harder to increase productivity in services which rely on face-to-face interaction and are not susceptible to mechanization or intensification. Second, health care at the point of delivery was not under the control of central government but rather of medical professionals. The professional judgment of doctors, nurses and paramedics was all-important in affecting how delivery was organized; managerial concerns with cost-savings, efficiency and rationalization were sidelined. The recognition of the limited impact of 'top–down' attempts to control spending led the government to consider alternative ways of curtailing growth. Policies aimed at introducing marketization and strengthening commercial-style management were seen to be the answer. There has been intense debate as to whether such reforms constitute full-blown privatization, 'creeping privatization', 'commercialization' and so on. The fierce war of words surrounding the introduction of market-style relationships reflects concern about the extent to which the reforms are challenging the culture and values of public service. We look now at how these controversial policies are being put into practice.

The NHS is being restructured under the provisions of the 1990 NHS and Community Care Bill. The membership of RHAs and DHAs has been revised along the lines of 'boards of directors', in the style of private companies. Both the RHAs and the DHAs now have a chairperson appointed by the Secretary of State, five non-executive directors and up to five executive directors (the general manager, finance director and so on). The FHSAs also have a chair appointed by the Secretary of State plus nine non-executive directors and the general manager as the sole executive director. These reorganizations have significantly reduced the role of local authorities in nominating board members as well as limiting the participation of clinicians at board level.

As for day-to-day management arrangements, the 1983 Griffiths Report had already brought in one round of changes. The reforms aimed to transfer control from powerful professional groups to managers who were directly accountable to central government and would stress 'value for money' considerations. Consensus-style decision-making had traditionally dominated; this operated through teams of doctors, nurses and hospital managers, with doctors very much in the lead. Consensus management was to be replaced by a form of 'line management' which strengthened the hand of hospital managers. There were attempts to integrate clinicians into the new commercial-style arrangements by making consultants responsible for their own budgets. However, there was still difficulty in controlling expenditure and the government acted to strengthen 'market discipline' still further in the NHS.

The 1990 Bill (based on the White Papers 'Working for Patients' and 'Caring for People') provides for changes in the structure, finance and management of the NHS based upon the principle of 'managed competition'. Rather than the full-scale privatization of the health service, the reforms aim to create an internal market within the NHS, thus simulating the workings of a private market within the public sector. The government believes that markets are more efficient allocators of goods and services than professionalized bureaucracies and claims that the introduction of 'quasi-markets' in sub-central government will bring gains in terms of 'value for money' and 'customer service'. The language as well as the practices of the private sector are being grafted on to sub-central government.

In order to create 'managed competition', the activities of the NHS are being separated into 'purchaser' and 'provider' functions on the basis of a distinction between (a) the acts of assessing and determining health needs, and (b) the actual provision of services to meet those needs. The purchasers within the NHS (e.g. DHAs and GPs) will make contracts with the providers (e.g. hospitals). The existence of contracts means that the quantity, quality and cost of service provision can be closely monitored by purchasers. It also means, in theory at least, that purchasers can pick and choose between providers – a GP in one area might make a contract with a hospital in a different area, or even with a private clinic, to treat a patient.

For their part, providers must become self-sufficient in management terms, dealing with their own accounts, personnel and infrastructure. This form of devolved management has been taken a step further by the government with the idea of 'Trust' status. After a three-month period of consultation, 56 Trusts started operating from 1 April 1991. Hospitals (or other provider units) which 'opt out' have their own board of directors and are independent from RHA or DHA supervision, relating to purchasers solely through the contractual mechanism. Neither are Trusts expected to meet with the public, and Community Health Councils have no right of access to their meetings.

Trusts are able to acquire, own and dispose of assets; borrow money within agreed limits, create their own management structure and employ their own staff on their own conditions; and advertise their services within agreed guidelines. Trusts' income will derive from the contract they negotiate with purchasers. Trusts are expected to make a 6 per cent return on assets and to break even one year with another. Within certain limits they are able to retain surpluses made on their trading accounts. In short, providers are being encouraged by central government to operate like quasi-companies.

Comparing the 'Working for Patients' changes with the earlier Griffiths reforms, Flynn (1990) notes a change in government strategy. In our language, new attention is being paid to achieving goals through the restructuring of 'horizontal' rather than 'vertical' relationships:

Earlier managerial reforms relied on the establishment of formal authority over the doctors. The latest changes impose a form of market discipline. If doctors run the hospitals in such a way that they become too expensive, the hospitals will automatically lose resources and there is nothing the doctors can do about it.

Since the introduction of the NHS Bill the setting up of contractual mechanisms has taken precedence over encouraging competition. Restructuring the NHS is politically a highly sensitive matter, particularly when it comes to stimulating private sector provision. In its traditional form the NHS has commanded great public support and critics of the government's reform programme claim that it constitutes 'creeping privatization' and will jeopardize the founding principles of the NHS – that health care should be open to all regardless of income and free at the point of use. However, the Conservatives are determined to press on with the restructuring of 'horizontal' relations in this key area of sub-central government during the 1990s. The defeat of Labour in the 1992 General Election has served to strengthen their hand, as opposition to the changes was such a central feature of the losing Labour campaign.

Restructuring local government

The attempt to control spending

In comparison with the NHS, the spending battle really hots up in the case of elected local government. There are three reasons for this. First, the heat of the battle arises from the fact that local government accounts for such a high proportion – one-quarter – of all public expenditure. Controlling local government spending is the key to limiting overall levels of public expenditure. Second, it reflects the fact that local authorities are inherently difficult to control. Unlike many other arms of sub-central government, local authorities are not just service delivery agencies. They are also organs of government. As we have seen, local authorities are run by democratically elected representatives, who are in turn serviced by their own administrative and professional machines. Local authorities are controlled by whatever political party wins the majority of council seats. During the 1980s and 1990s there has been a higher proportion of Labour than Conservative controlled local authorities. So not only have local authorities been concerned to protect local as against central government interests, there has also been a party political dimension to the contest. Many of central government's policies with relation to local government seem to have been fuelled by a desire to reduce the power (and opposition) of local Labour parties.

Third, the stand-off between central government and the local authorities reflects the fact that local authorities are not solely dependent upon grants from central government; they have their own revenue-raising capacities. By law, local authorities have the right (and duty) to levy local taxes to finance local services. Hence central government has control only over one part of local authorities' income – that funded out of grants or loans from the centre. It has attempted to manipulate spending levels in two ways. On the one hand it used its power to allocate grants (and the right to borrow); on the other hand it pursued policies designed to reduce the power of local authorities to resist central control, either through political means or through the use of their own revenue-raising powers.

Callaghan's Labour government of 1976–9 had already acted to limit local authorities' capital spending so the new Conservative government focused on controls over revenue (recurrent) spending. (Although further changes in the control of capital expenditure did follow, our discussion will concentrate on the struggle over revenue spending.) The new government sought to change the grant system in order to deter high spending by local councils. The Conservatives inherited an 'open-ended' grant system which effectively 'rewarded' local authorities which spent over central government's assessment of their overall budget. Overspends were matched by the Department of the Environment providing an extra element of grant. In 1980 the system was changed so that a smaller proportion of grant was received on overspends. However, when this failed to deter overspending a system of penalties was introduced. Not only would there be no extra grant on overspends, but deductions would be made from the basic grant to 'punish' high-spending councils. By the mid 1980s an overspend of one pound was being punished by a grant reduction of five pounds.

The manipulation of grant-funding failed to bring down local authority spending. High-spending local authorities continued to maintain their expenditure levels in two ways: through 'creative accounting' and increasing rates. 'Financial wizardry' was used to reduce the apparent level of revenue budgets (in order to avoid grant reductions) while maintaining spending programmes: for instance, elements of revenue spending were bundled together and reclassified as capital expenditure (e.g. passing off housing repairs as capital works); alternatively, assets were sold to finance companies which then leased them back to local authorities, whilst the monies received in payment were used to finance other spending programmes.

Local authorities also maintained their spending levels through levying higher rates (local property taxes). The government had assumed that such a strategy would be electorally disastrous for the high-spending councils, and this would encourage them to keep rates low. The evidence, however, is that the electorate blamed central government for high rates (because of the reduction of grants) and was prepared to vote back into office high-spending councillors. Sheffield Council, for instance, put its rate up by 41 per cent in 1980 and 37 per cent in 1981 and still received support at the polls. (The existence of rate rebates certainly cushioned the effect of rate increases on the poorest members of the community.)

Local authorities were clearly difficult for the government to control. The grant system was not a powerful enough tool. The government moved to reduce the autonomy of local authorities by interfering with their revenue-raising rights. The 1984 Rates Act gave the Secretary of State for the Environment the power to limit the rates levied by individual local authorities. 'Rate-capping' meant that it was no longer possible for local authorities to replace lost grant with extra monies from the rates. The government published a list of 18 authorities to be rate-capped in 1985–6; all but 2 of the 18 were under Labour control. Rate-capping was seen by many to be as much about silencing Labour opposition to government polices as about 'good housekeeping'.

An anti-rate-capping campaign was launched by Labour authorities with the support of local government trade unions and many community groups across the country. A strategy of 'non-compliance' was agreed which gave councils the option of either refusing to set a rate or planning a deficit budget (e.g. a level of spending that could not be financed out of expected revenue). The campaigning authorities initially refused to set a rate for the 1985–6 financial year but after losing complex legal battles the stand collapsed with only Lambeth and Liverpool not setting a rate by March 1985. The die-hard councillors were surcharged and banned from office.

The collapse of the anti-rate-capping campaign did not end local authorities' defiance of central government attempts to restrain spending. There was a return to creative accounting strategies – capitalization, deferred purchase, lease-backs and so on. Authorities like Hammersmith and Fulham involved themselves in complicated 'swaps' on the finance markets, thus exploiting the Thatcher government's own deregulation of financial services in order to squeeze out of the spending straitjacket.

In the context of Britain's 'differentiated polity' it was proving difficult for the government to control local authorities. Central government was not the only source of political legitimacy in the country. In many cases local authorities were successful in building strong local campaigns in support of local services and the councils' defiant stand on spending. Nowhere was this more the case than with the Labour-controlled Greater London Council. The GLC had been at the forefront of the early campaigns against rate-capping and, in addition to opposing Conservative policies on spending, it had become a focus for an alternative agenda for local government. The GLC championed equal opportunities concerns and adopted policy positions on issues not traditionally of concern to local government (e.g. nuclear disarmament and apartheid in South Africa). More importantly, the GLC involved itself in economic policy in the capital under the banner of 'restructuring for labour'. The GLC was prepared to use its resources to confront the government as an alternative political voice – a voice that polls showed to command significant popular support in London at least.

The abolition of the GLC and the other six metropolitan councils (which took effect from April 1986) was justified by the government on the grounds of rationalizing the structure and functions of local government, as a means of reducing bureaucracy and waste. It can also be seen as a Conservative government attempt to stifle opposition to its policies on local government and, more generally, as a sign of increasing political centralization. Such centralization reflects a desire to reduce the differentiated nature of the British polity – to silence alternative (and antagonistic) political voices. (Serious practical problems have arisen in managing cross-London services following the end of the GLC; these are now recognized even by the Conservatives who, along with the other main parties, are considering models for a new London-wide body.)

There is one more episode of the spending saga that needs to be addressed before we go on to consider the second element of government policy, marketization. The final episode concerns the rise and fall of the Poll Tax. Thatcher had a long-standing personal commitment to the abolition of the rating system. The débâcle over local government funding, which reached its climax with the struggle over rate-capping, suggested to many ministers that a review of the rates (the local differentiated property taxes) was long overdue. There was also a reluctance on the part of the government to undertake the long-overdue revaluation of the rates for England and Wales. When revaluation took place in Scotland in 1985 there was evidence that householders most likely to vote Conservative were faced with the steepest increases. In 1981 a Green Paper was published which set out alternatives to the domestic rate, including a sales tax, a local income tax, and a poll tax. After much debate the Poll Tax emerged as the favoured option and the 1986 Green Paper 'Paying for Local Government' set out the reform package.

The domestic rates were to be replaced by the 'community charge' or Poll Tax, a flat-rate tax set by each local authority and payable by every adult. There would be full rebates only for a very small group of special cases (e.g. monks and nuns); those on low incomes (including students and the unemployed) would have to pay 20 per cent of the Poll Tax bills. At the same time, locally set business rates were to be replaced by a nationally set non-domestic rate. Central grant to 'top up' monies levied through the Poll Tax would be on the basis of Standing Spending Assessments (SSAs) which included a needs-based element designed to take into account the particular physical, social and demographic characteristics of an area. Although SSAs would vary between authorities, the aim was that each would represent the resources necessary to deliver the same standard of service in different areas. The reforms were introduced after the Conservatives gained their third term of office in 1987. The new package was brought in for Scotland from the financial year 1989–90 and in England and Wales from the year 1990–1. (It is interesting to note that the reforms were not introduced at all in Northern Ireland for fear of their impact in an already-tense political environment.)

The Conservatives argued that the new system would be fairer in that all adults (rather than householders only) would be making a contribution to local authority spending, and single householders would not be over-burdened with large rates bills. It was claimed that increased accountability would follow. Once residents could see how much local authority services cost *per head* and had to pay that amount, they would be more likely to hold their councillors to account – voting them out of office should they be seen to provide poor 'value for money'. Because business rates would now be set nationally, local authorities would not be able to shift the burden of contributions onto local businesses. The government was confident that Conservative councillors would be seen to be prudent and responsible managers of local authorities and would gain electorally as a result of the introduction of the Poll Tax. In contrast the profligacy of Labour councillors would at last be revealed and the public would respond by voting against them in local elections.

The accountability argument was always a weak one. Local authority budgets were not made up solely from Poll Tax revenues but also from central government grant and business rate contributions. In fact, the Poll Tax would account for no more than one-third of local authority revenue. Hence it was still impossible for residents to see a clear correlation between what they were paying and what they were receiving in terms of services. The correlation grew ever weaker as the government brought in subsidies such as 'transitional relief' and 'safety netting' to ease the introduction of the Poll Tax. Moreover there was evidence that such sweeteners were being allocated on a party political basis, leaving Labour authorities most likely to issue high Poll Tax demands. Charges of political bias increased when the government introduced Poll Tax-capping. Like rate-capping before it, the purpose of this new round of capping seemed mainly to be to penalize Labour-controlled councils. In 1990–1

Labour-controlled Haringey set a Poll Tax within its government target but was capped, while Conservative-controlled Newbury and Lancaster set Poll Taxes above their targets and were not penalized.

Even if residents could detect from their Poll Tax level the cost of local services, would they vote out high-spending councillors? The results of local elections in May 1990 suggested that this was not necessarily the case. Elections were not held in all areas, but the results were disappointing for the Conservatives who gained 31 per cent of the vote (against 42 per cent for Labour) – their lowest showing in a nationwide election for over 50 years. Public opinion polls showed that although many people thought their Poll Tax was too high, they blamed the high levels at least in part on central government. The Poll Tax was seen to be expensive to collect and its introduction wasteful of resources. As local authorities complained about the 'administrative nightmare' of up-dating registers and sending out hundreds of thousands of individual bills, the Conservatives' own criticism of profligacy and inefficiency was thrown back at them. Moreover, the Poll Tax was increasingly seen to be unfair – was it right that a millionaire and his secretary should both pay the same Poll Tax? Aside from local election results, the public was making its dissatisfaction with the Poll Tax known through national and local demonstrations and a campaign of non-payment.

The Poll Tax was increasingly being seen by the Conservatives as an electoral liability at a time when electoral considerations were becoming more pressing as the government moved towards the end of its term of office. Mrs Thatcher's intransigence over the Poll Tax led at least in part to her downfall as party leader and Prime Minister in November 1990. A review of the Poll Tax was ordered by her successor, John Major, who handed the 'poisoned chalice' of the Poll Tax to his defeated rival for the leadership, Michael Heseltine. Heseltine had been openly critical of the Poll Tax and now had the task of either making it acceptable to the electorate, or ditching it.

In the short term Heseltine eased the burden on local authorities and Poll Tax payers by making available a £140 subsidy on each bill. Local authorities would be compensated by central government out of revenues raised through an increase in VAT rates. (With the Poll Tax making up a yet smaller proportion of local spending, the 'accountability' argument in favour of the tax was further weakened.) In the longer term the review announced that the Poll Tax would be replaced with a 'council tax', to be introduced from the year 1993–4. The new tax, which will account for no more that 15 per cent of local spending, involves a rates/poll tax hybrid. Like the rates it will be levied on households rather than individuals and will relate to the value of their property. Like the Poll Tax it will ensure that single householders are not over-burdened, through making available a 25 per cent discount for households of only one adult. Unlike the Poll Tax, full rebates will be payable to those on low incomes.

Who won the battle over the Poll Tax? It seems that all parties lost out. The government's credibility and popularity suffered a serious blow. Mrs Thatcher was shown to have made signficant misjudgments over the introduction of the new tax and her fall from office at least in part resulted from this. The Poll

Tax had been introduced without consultation and the relationship between central government and local authorities had reached a new low. Local authorities suffered because of the expense and complexity of collecting the Poll Tax. They are now faced with another costly switch to a new tax system. Many authorities have also suffered because of lost income due to low collection rates and non-payment campaigns; cuts in services have resulted, particularly among capped authorities. As for the public, by the end of 1990 one-third of the population of Scotland were subject to legal proceedings for the enforcement of the tax; a year later a quarter of Manchester residents had followed suit and refused to pay their Poll Tax. There is now a fear among local authorities that 'Poll Tax exhaustion' among the public has led to the idea of non-payment taking root. While collection rates for the rates were close to 100 per cent, it is unclear whether this situation will be replicated for the new council tax.

Local authority spending has not fallen since 1979; in fact, it has increased slightly. The government has not given up its attempt to control spending and 1992 saw the introduction of yet more draconian 'capping' measures. Universal capping plus the effects of Poll Tax non-payment may lead to local authorities' biggest financial crisis yet. However, the battle over local government spending demonstrates the weakness of central government's 'vertical' strategies, i.e. its attempt to control spending through increasing central control over elected local authorities. Local authorities are inherently difficult to control. Yet for any government committed to 'rolling back' the state or even just holding spending steady, the need to pay attention to local government is paramount – because it spends so much of the national purse. It appears that since 1987 the government has recognized the difficulties of exercising direct 'vertical' control and has developed new 'horizontal' strategies aimed at increasing efficiency. If overall levels of spending cannot be brought down, existing monies must be made to go further. Marketization – the adjustment of relations between spheres rather than tiers of government – has been a vital element of this new approach.

The introduction of market-style relationships

Just as the NHS is being restructured in the form of a series of quasi-companies, 'marketization' is changing the shape and character of local government. The Secretary of State has floated the possibility of moving to a system of smaller, more 'business-like' councils made up of fewer councillors, who would be elected annually and perhaps even paid to work full-time on local government business. Although these proposals are no more than suggestions at present, a 'board of directors' model would accord with other changes already introduced in local government. As we have seen, the first two Thatcher governments were primarily concerned with attempts to restrain local government spending (via a restructuring of 'vertical' relations). Since 1987, however, central government has turned its attention to the internal management and operation of local authorities (via a restructuring of 'horizontal' relations).

Legislation has required the separation of 'client' and 'contractor' functions – a separation mirrored by the purchaser/provider splits now being introduced in the NHS. The government's aim is to introduce market principles into the operation of sub-central government, claiming that this will lead to greater efficiency and improved customer service. We can illustrate the application of these arguments to local government with reference to: the introduction of compulsory competitive tendering; changes in socal services, education and housing management; and the growth of non-elected local government.

Compulsory competitive tendering (CCT) had been introduced from the mid-1980s in the NHS, covering catering, laundry and domestic services. The Local Government Act of 1988 required local authorities to put specified services out to tender, including building, cleaning and refuse collection. Compulsory competitive tendering is being extended to cover further services – sports and leisure management in 1992 or 1993, and eventually a whole range of 'white-collar' clerical and professional services. Under CCT local authorities can themselves tender for the work that they had previously undertaken as a matter of course. However, to be able to tender, the authority has to separate client (purchaser) and contractor (provider) functions. The client side is responsible for specifying services, letting and monitoring contracts. The contractor side has to compete with private sector companies in tendering for work. If, as has happened in many cases, the in-house contractors are successful in their bids they have to operate as a trading company and make a specified return on investment.

CCT brings with it the possibility of higher quality services. Whether contracts are won in-house or by private firms, the local authority (client side) will have to assess need carefully and specify in detail the requirements of service provision if it is to let and monitor contracts effectively. On the other hand, the need for private firms and in-house contractors to make a return on their investment could lead to the neglect of 'social' goals in favour of maximizing productivity. At present, local authorities are required to choose between tenders on the basis of price alone; a basic quality threshold having been established. What is certain is that CCT is having a major effect on the conditions of employment of local authority staff, especially those in manual jobs. It has been estimated that around 700,000 local authority jobs are directly affected by CCT. As Stoker (1989) puts it:

> The search for increased productivity on the part of both in-house and private contractors may lead to between 15 and 30 per cent of these jobs being shed. Those workers that remain in employment will probably be operating under new conditions of employment and are faced with the prospect of competing for their jobs on a regular basis.

The management of social services, housing and education has also seen the separation of 'authorization' and 'production' functions. Under the 1992 NHS and Community Care Act local authorities are required to assess the needs of individuals in the community requiring care – the elderly, the disabled, for instance. The local authority is to design care programmes for those in need and then 'buy in' (and monitor) care packages from private and voluntary sector providers, whether for residential or community-based provision.

In housing, local authority tenants had already been given the opportunity to buy their homes at discounted prices. The popularity of this measure led to the rapid decline of the size of many local authorities' housing stocks; the best properties going first. The 1989 Local Government and Housing Act went further in seeking to end the monopoly position of local authorities as social landlords. Tenants are to be given the opportunity to 'opt out' of local authority control and have their housing managed by another landlord – a private individual or company, a housing association or their own tenants' management co-operative. The local authority retains the 'authorization' role, as the 1987 White Paper 'Housing' puts it: 'Local authorities should see themselves as enablers who ensure that everyone in their area is adequately housed; but not necessarily by them' (cited in Stoker, 1990).

Where local authorities continue to manage their own housing stocks, 'landlord' functions must be managed by a quasi-company with its own trading accounts – again, client and contractor functions within the local authority must be separated. The Housing Revenue Account is 'ring-fenced' which means that it cannot be subsidized from the local authority's general fund. This puts pressure on local councils to run their housing stock on a commercial basis, charging market rents and competing for tenants with other service providers. Critics of the government's housing policies point to the rise of homelessness and overcrowding in Britain during the 1980s, attributing this to the decline of the local authority rented sector.

The 1988 and 1992 Education Acts require local authorities to devolve managerial responsibility to provider units (schools and colleges) and act as monitors of standards and assessors of overall need. Self-managing schools are encouraged to compete for pupils and the planning capacities of local authorities have been reduced. Central government is encouraging the development of a non-local-authority-controlled sector of education providers. Such schools may be private and funded out of fees, or they may be traditional 'grant-aided' schools supported by charitable trusts and central government grants. However, this sector now includes state schools which are allowed to 'opt out' of local authority control and be funded directly by central government. The pattern is clear – just as in community care and housing (and paralleling developments in the NHS) the local authority must distinguish between its 'client' and its 'contractor' functions. Even if contracts are not yet in operation and no money changes hands, the fact that the functions of authorization and provision have been separated allows for the future development of competition between a wider range of service providers.

Non-elected local government has been of growing importance in the 1980s. In several key policy areas, central government has attempted to bypass local councils by creating new (and more malleable) implementation agencies. These new agencies have also served to open up new opportunities for the participation of private and voluntary sector interests in implementing public policy – more evidence of central government's determination to break up public sector monopolies in sub-central government. We will look briefly at two policy areas in which the role of local authorities has been reduced in favour of a privileged role for private sector actors.

Urban Development Corporations have been established in inner-city areas. UDCs aim to attract private investment to run-down areas through grant-giving and rate and planning concessions. They operate under Whitehall-appointed boards and are empowered to take over development control functions from local authorities. To take another example, a network of 100 Training and Enterprise Councils (TECs) has been established in England and Wales to take responsibility for local training initiatives and business development (a smaller group of Local Agencies has been set up in Scotland). The TECs are employer-led: two-thirds of directors are private-sector managers or entrepreneurs. In contrast to the old Area Management Boards of the Manpower Services Commission, the role of local authorities and trade unions has been significantly reduced. Critics of both the UDCs and the TECs say that without community representation via the local authority, these bodies are unable to develop a proper understanding of the needs and potential of an area and are unlikely to protect or further the needs of disadvantaged groups.

Through our examination of reforms in the NHS and local government we have focused on two key themes in the restructuring of sub-central government: the attempt to control spending and the introduction of market-style relationships. We turn in the next section to look at the wider debate on the future of government beyond Westminster and Whitehall.

The wider debate on the future of sub-central government

There are many different 'stakeholders' concerned with the future of sub-central government. First, there are those involved in policy-making: the politicians at central and local level. Second, there are those concerned with the delivery of services: the professional, administrative and manual staff employed by sub-central agencies and, increasingly, by private firms and voluntary groups. Third, there are the users of services delivered at the sub-central level: members of the public as tenants, patients, students or swimming-pool users. Between and within each group of stakeholders there are different sets of priorities and preferences for the future of sub-central government. Rather than outlining areas of conflict – many of which we have touched upon already – let us look at where, if at all, there is any agreement on the future of sub-central government.

There is agreement about the need for change. The 'bureaucratic paternalism' that dominated many areas of sub-central government in the post-war period has been subject to criticism from all quarters – from politicians of all parties, from professionals and from members of the public. Large-scale, centralized bureaucracies are widely seen as being unresponsive, inaccessible, inefficient and wasteful. The need for some form of restructuring in many areas of sub-central government is agreed.

Politicians have been frustrated about their lack of control over the functioning of sub-central agencies and have developed strategies for their reform. The Conservatives have attempted to apply the medicine of the market with the stated aim of increasing management efficiency and also consumer rights and choice (through the 'Citizen's Charter'). The Labour party at both a national and a local level has protested against marketization and defended public-sector solutions. However, in the 1990s Labour is no longer committed to full-scale re-nationalization and accepts the need for some form of restructuring in sub-central government. Labour is also concerned about centralized bureaucracy and has argued for new forms of regional government, decentralization within local government, greater emphasis on quality rather than quantity in service delivery, and a new 'user orientation'. The Liberal party has traditionally been a staunch critic of bureaucratic forms of government and an advocate of local political autonomy. Liberals share some of the Conservatives' 'anti-state' sentiment but favour a greater role for forms of 'community action' and 'collective self-help' rather than for private firms. Thus, at the start of the 1990s it is possible to detect convergences as well as divergences in party thinking.

Staff working in sub-central government have also been frustrated by bureaucratization. They have often felt alienated, trapped by 'red tape' and unable to fulfil their 'public service' goals. In the 1980s staff in many occupations have seen public sector salaries and terms and conditions deteriorate in relation to the private sector. Professional groupings have argued for decentralized, community-based service provision in many areas – in planning, housing management, social services, and even some aspects of health care. Some groups have welcomed the opportunity to work in partnership with private or voluntary sector agencies. In health care, for instance, many doctors already work in the private sector as well as the NHS and understand its modes of operation.

For some local authority managers, it makes sense that elected local government should concentrate not on day-to-day service delivery but on strategic planning, acting as the community's advocate and spokesperson. The local authority is seen as 'enabling not providing'. Among those whose jobs have been threatened by CCT, staff at the higher levels have often pre-empted the challenge though 'management buy-outs' or the setting up of new 'not for profit' agencies. (Their enthusiasm is unlikely to be shared, however, by those at the bottom of the occupational ladder who stand to lose their jobs within an uncertain economic environment.) The ending of public-sector monopolies in welfare provision would actually bring Britain more into line with the practice of many European countries, including liberal, Social Democratic nations like the Netherlands and the Scandinavian countries.

The public has been on the receiving end of bureaucratically organized sub-central government, which has involved waiting lists of many years duration for health and housing services, as well as poor quality services in some areas. Although they may be sceptical as to the likely impact of the Conservative Citizen's Charter or local authorities' 'customer care' plans, most people welcome the idea of 'putting the customer first'. Much welfare provision in the post-war period was organized on the basis that the 'professionals knew best'.

Policy disasters like high-rise housing estates or redeveloped (gutted) city centres have left many people doubtful that there is a technocratic, professional 'fix' available for all social problems.

Many individuals and communities are keen to get more involved in the management of the services they use. The 'emptying out' of local authorities could lead to new opportunities for voluntary and community groups as well as for private firms (particularly if rules on contracting are modified). Under the present government's policies, service users have a chance to develop new skills and assume new responsibilities through involvement on school governing boards and tenant management co-operatives. It is essential, however, that such opportunities are supported by professional advice, training and back-up resources (e.g. child care).

We have established, then, that the restructuring of sub-central government cannot be written off as a New Right plot. It seems that there is widespread agreement among many stakeholders in sub-central government on the need to restructure methods of service delivery, although the precise methods remain contested. The ending of public sector monopolies and a switch to more pluralistic patterns of welfare provision are perhaps inevitable in the context of resource constraints and widespread criticism of large, centralized bureaucracies. As we noted above, 'welfare pluralism' is typical of many countries within the EC. However, what is not typical among EC states is the centralization of political control in Britain during the 1980s – the attempt by the Conservatives to reduce the differentiated nature of the polity. In many other European countries the role of sub-central government is increasing, including that of elected local government. Forms of sub-central government could be the key building blocks in developing an EC in which regional and local identities can be expressed at the same time as decisions in certain areas are 'moved up' to the European level.

Chapter 8

Preserving order and administering justice: other faces of government in Britain

David Robertson

There is one aspect of 'service delivery' in Britain which we have mentioned only in passing so far: this is the activity of the police and the courts.

In many ways these form semi-autonomous jurisdictions present everywhere at local level, who perform the oldest function of government: keeping public order – that is preventing and punishing crime, resolving disputes which might provoke disorder, and also repressing illegal forms of opposition to the central government.

Several developments during the last fifteen years have underlined the political significance of these bodies. Conservative trade union legislation, for example, has made many previously legal activities of trade unionists illegal (e.g. the practice of 'secondary picketing' of firms not directly involved in a dispute). The massive co-ordination of police forces and the extension of powers of arrest during the nation-wide miners' strike of 1984–5 underlined the importance of courts and police in implementing policy in this area. Their role in controlling the urban and prison riots (not to mention terrorism in Northern Ireland) have been a feature of the 1980s and 1990s.

Courts and police do not only concern themselves with violence and criminal offences but also with the regulation of much of our day-to-day life. They guarantee the validity of the contracts which regulate our employment, rights to property, business and holiday arrangements – in short, most of what we do. Lawyers and police investigate allegations of fraud or failure to carry out contractual obligations: judges rule on disputes as to what is actually involved in an agreement.

Institutionally, the central law courts fall under the 'non-departmental public bodies' listed in Table 8.1, while the police and local courts fall under the 'non-elected local governments' listed there. Britain is unusual in Western Europe in that police and courts are not under tight central control. Why they function autonomously, and what are the consequences of this, are best explained by considering each in detail – first the police and second the courts. Both, of course, are subject to the same processes of change which we have already noted in other forms of sub-central government during the last decade, and which we may expect to continue in the 1990s.

The police: new structures

The structure, operational systems and ideology of the British police have changed more in the last ten years than in any similar period this century. Some of the changes have been produced by legislation, some by the economic theories of the governments since 1979, some by the need to cope with broad social changes over this period. Law and order in general, and the specific role of the police, have probably never been more salient as political issues since the current structure of the police system was set up in 1964. While the Conservative government returned after the 1992 election has no constitutional plans in regard to their position, they are increasingly dissatisfied with the 'value for money' aspect, as in the rest of local government – largely because of a supposed increase in crime even after major increases in police funding.

As with most other aspects of internal administration, the British situation in regard to police forces is anomalous in Western Europe. In most countries it seems obvious that there should be a national police force under central government control. In Britain, the traditional autonomy of the localities, and fears about the consequences of allowing government too much power, have led to police forces being organized (but, as we shall see, not controlled) locally.

The current structure of the police, enshrined in the 1964 Police Act, followed the report in 1962 of the Royal Commission on the Police, the first that had sat since 1919. Before the amalgamation consequent on the 1964 Act, Britain had a very large number of local police forces – over 170. Apart from the Metropolitan Police covering London, and a few forces in the other larger cities, most forces were small by today's standards, some tiny. The average size of a force was probably around 600, and some were as small as 150. The small size and small area they policed made these forces very local, and local politicians had, one way or another, a good deal of influence over them.

There was, in fact, a sharp distinction historically between two sorts of police forces, those in towns and cities called the 'borough forces', and those covering non-urban areas, the 'county forces'. The borough forces were ultimately governed by local Watch Committees, essentially committees of the town or city council, while the county forces were controlled, much more loosely, by the county's magistrates. In fact, because there was a tendency to appoint upper-class ex-army officers as the Chief Constables in the county forces, there was little need for direct control. The concerns and attitudes of the magistracy and the Chief Constables coincided to a very large degree, and county force policy represented these interests.

The borough forces were nearly all commanded by professional police chiefs who had come up through the ranks, and there were occasional tensions between these men and the Watch Committees, with the police wanting to take a more independent line. London has always been policed in a different manner, with the Metropolitan Police and the City of London Police being commanded by Commissioners, directly appointed and controlled by the Home Secretary.

By the early 1960s the sheer inefficiency of having many small forces, combined with a growing concern about lack of uniformity, led to the appointment of the Royal Commission. This immediately became the focus for an often impassioned debate about whether the entire structure should be thrown away and replaced by one national police force, accountable to Parliament, as is the model throughout the rest of Europe. The debate was often confusing, because the key issue, which was accountability to political control, could be argued in several ways. Opponents of a national police force feared political intervention and the thought of a highly partisan police under government control. At the same time many of the proponents of such a single national force argued that there was far too little democratic control in the current system, and a single force would be more democratic because of its accountability to Parliament – the Metropolitan Police, it was argued, had never been politicized, even though controlled by the Home Secretary.

The legislation that followed in 1964 was a compromise, picking up ideas from both the majority and minority reports. The number of forces was to be cut enormously by amalgamations that ran across the old county/borough distinction. This happened in several stages, and there are now only 44 police forces in England and Wales. The smallest forces have at least 1500 officers, and the average is around 3000. A few, like the West Midlands police, are much bigger than anything that existed before – its Chief Constable is on public record as saying he cannot control it. Similarly the Thames Valley Police, with nearly 5000 officers, covers three entire counties.

(The police force in Scotland is organized on roughly similar lines, with a few large forces, but the legal relationship between government and police has always been different, as indeed is the law they enforce and their links with the Scottish Office rather than the Home Office.)

Police accountability and control

The question of control of these forces became immediately, and has remained, a serious problem. The act envisaged a three-cornered control system, with political authority (and budgetary obligations) shared between the Home Office and new bodies, called 'police authorities', consisting of both local magistrates and local councillors. However the old question of how far either of these authorities could extend their control to details of police policy was left essentially as it had been in the county, rather than the borough, forces. The basic doctrine is that no one can give a Chief Constable any orders about how to carry out his job. He can be sacked for incompetence, but not directed. Even the courts have held in subsequent case law that they cannot intervene to order a police force to do anything particular in their carrying out of their functions.

In fact the police authorities have almost no powers, because they need Home Office approval to appoint a Chief Constable, they can be ordered by the Home Office to dismiss him, and because so much of the finance comes from the government, directly or otherwise, they hardly even have the power of the purse over him. (In fact it is also the Home Office which sets minimum and maximum manning levels, equipment tables and so on.) This situation became finally clear in 1988 in a major case where the Northumberland Police Authority tried to get the courts to forbid the Home Office from interfering with their own preferred policy. The case in question (R v. Home Secretary, *ex parte* Northumbria Police Authority [1988] 2 WLR) is probably the most significant legal ruling on police and politics this century, and although it is a little technical, it is worth some discussion.

What happed is this. The Home Office decided that it would authorize the acquisition of plastic bullets (technically 'baton rounds') for use by police forces, and hold these centrally for distribution to any force who had convinced the Home Office Inspectors of Constabulary that they might need them. The Chief Constable of Northumbria did decide that he might have a need for such weapons, but his police authority took the policy decision that he should not have them, and refused to authorize his purchase of plastic bullets out of funds he was granted. The Home Office authorized him to have them. The police authority, outraged that their view of what was acceptable in Northumbria had been flouted, went to court, asking for an order to quash the Home Office decision. The court held that the Home Office did have the power to provide weapons to a police force against the wish of that force's own police authority. Even more, they held that the Home Office had this power not because of the 1964 Police Act, but under the 'Royal Prerogative'. What this means is that the central government has an automatic right to fix local police policy, whether or not Parliament has specifically given it this right! The only control on weaponry, and probably on any policy question where a Chief Constable wants something is, therefore, the central government. The powers of the police authority are simple – they are entitled to one yearly report by the Chief Constable on the activities of the force. They are also entitled to ask for other reports on specific matters, *but the Chief Constable can refuse to make these reports if he feels he should not give them!* In contrast, the Home Office can demand any report or investigation it likes, and the Chief Constable must then report.

So the situation is that police forces are entirely under the control of the Chief Constable, subject to the Home Office. There are only 41 Chief Constables of English and Welsh forces. There are about a dozen Inspectors of Constabulary, and perhaps 50 policy level civil servants controlling the use of police power throughout the UK. This is a significant level of elite power. The question is whether or not this also constitutes a move towards a national police force. The debate on a national force has never been properly resolved. Most Chief Constables themselves do not wish one, and no government has ever suggested its creation. But it is often suggested that a *de facto* national force exists, and some critics have even argued that the government prefers to have a system which operates effectively as one force but with the formal trappings of a series of separate forces. This way, it is argued, parliamentary control is avoided, making the police force even more independent of democratic control than it would otherwise be.

There are two basic arguments behind the thesis that Britain has a *de facto* national force. The first is the existence of a small national police elite from whom all senior police officers are recruited. Apart from Chief Constables themselves, there are two other ranks – Deputy Chief Constable and Assistant Chief Constables – who make up the membership of an extremely powerful pressure group, the Association of Chief Police Officers, usually known as 'ACPO'. These people, and more junior officers aspiring to membership, share a closely integrated set of experiences. They have all been on senior officers' courses at the Police College in Bramshill; they all have some sort of national experience, for example, being a Staff Officer to an Inspector of Constabulary or being seconded to the Home Office; and they have all served in several forces, almost certainly including a stint in 'the Met.'. Their career patterns are interesting. Although they have all started as constables, and will usually have taken seven or eight years to become sergeants, they will have gone through the next five ranks, to Assistant Chief Constable, at the rate of about two years per rank – they are high flyers, and the need to move from force to force in order to fly so fast leads to a much more national outlook. As with any small elite, these officers know each other well, have attended endless courses and seminars together, and have formed their ideas and attitudes in concert. Most important of all, they are members of ACPO. (ACPO membership is open to those of Assistant Chief Constable rank upwards and equivalent rank in the Met.)

As is typical in Britain, ACPO is not an official governmental organization, and technically is simply the professional organization of senior policemen, part trade union, part club, part official spokesman for professional views – something like, say, the British Medical Association. However it is funded by the Home Office, and it is ACPO who selects delegates to Home Office conferences and committees. The importance of ACPO finally became completely clear during the 1984–5 miners' strike. The problems of policing the picket lines were beyond the capacity of any one force, so ACPO set up the National Reporting Centre (NRC) to co-ordinate demands for support from heavily embattled forces and the supply of such support. Although technically Chief Constables could refuse to co-operate with other forces, the Home Office made it quite clear that they would use legal powers to enforce co-operation if the NRC did not work. The felt need to co-operate was intense, and at least in terms of manpower supply the British police became effectively a national force, under ACPO control, for over a year.

Nor was it merely a matter of delivering manpower to the right spot. A nationally co-ordinated policy of putting up road blocks, to stop convoys of pickets rushing to particular mines from all over the country, was put in place. Effectively this meant that operational decisions in some areas far from the crisis points were being made in the light of operational needs hundreds of miles away. (The policy was, incidentally, of very dubious legality.) The Chief Constables themselves deny that ACPO and the NRC constituted a national force. But significantly, what they argue is that if they had not organized themselves unofficially to *act* like a national force, the government would, during or after the strike, have created one. It is unclear that saying there is no *de jure* national force because there is a *de facto* one means very much. This combination of independence from local control, dependence on the Home Office, a small national elite of common-minded professionals, and ACPO's co-ordinating role adds up effectively to a national force. Other factors, like the increasing importance of specialized units, nearly all run by the Met., and a serious concern for a uniform position to be taken in Europe after the frontiers go down, further this.

Police procedures and the individual

There have been two crucial changes enforced by legislation in the last decade that have materially affected police work. The most important was the passing of the 1984 Police and Criminal Evidence Act, known universally as 'PACE', which was partially based on the report of the Royal Commission on Criminal Procedure published in 1981. This Act is hard to assess objectively because it managed to offend both civil libertarians and the police. Civil libertarians object, for example, to the general power the Act gave to stop and search people or vehicles where an officer has reasonable grounds for suspecting stolen or prohibited objects. In fact to a large extent this part of the Act just generalized and tidied up a mass of separate stop and search powers and has probably not changed police procedure very much. Civil libertarians are in part suspicious of the act because ACPO's evidence to the Royal Commission stressed the need for new legal powers for the police, but now very few police officers think they need them – they got what they wanted in PACE. However they also got a lot they did not want.

What PACE has done is change enormously the procedures for questioning suspects and for taking down what they say and any statements they make. Police are unanimous that they are seriously hampered by the need to tape record all interviews, and to have a complete *and contemporaneous* account of the entire interview process. Second, the rights to have a solicitor present, and to say absolutely nothing to the police, mean that police on the whole cannot risk detaining and interrogating anyone until they already have enough evidence to win a committal in a magistrates' court. In other words, reliance on getting a confession because the police do not have enough evidence otherwise has had to be abandoned. (There is still pressure to make a conviction impossible merely on the basis of a confession, which is already the law in Scotland.)

In fact PACE has merely formalized rights that existed in judges' rules before, but putting them in a formal statute has made them very much more effective. In the words of one expert, 'the old informal procedures for crime control, based on fabricating evidence, have had to go'. It is interesting to note that the recent rash of acquittals in the Court of Appeal of people wrongfully convicted years earlier, all stem from the days before PACE.

PACE has had an interesting side effect on statistical measures of police effectiveness. The 'clear-up rate' for crime has declined substantially. In part this is because, before PACE, a detective could often persuade an offender to confess to a series of other crimes which he would ask to be 'taken into consideration' in court. Criminals are very much less willing to co-operate with police in this way now, and 'TIC' clear-up has dropped considerably. The fact that police were so dependent on these admissions, and the question of just how people were persuaded to co-operate in this way (against their interest, because a court was likely to increase the sentence if there were a number of TICs) suggest PACE was very much needed.

The secondary statutory restriction on the police to come out of the 1981 Royal Commission was the creation of the Crown Prosecution Service (CPS) by the Prosecution of Offences Act 1986. This is, constitutionally, a more radical change than PACE, which (at least in theory) simply gave statutory recognition to received practice. Before the setting up of the CPS England and Wales had a system quite unlike that in any other Western democracy. Everywhere else in the world there was a sharp distinction between the job of detecting crime and the task of deciding whether or not to prosecute and handling the prosecution. In continental Europe the decision to prosecute (as well as the supervision of much of the investigation) was in the hands of a member of the judiciary called an Examining Magistrate. In Scotland an official rather like the Examining Magistrate, the Procurator Fiscal played this role. In the USA these decisions are taken by an elected district attorney (or a politically appointed one in the case of federal jurisdiction).

But in England and Wales the police themselves decided whether or not to prosecute. In the magistrates' court they themselves handled the prosecution, in higher courts they instructed counsel themselves. Now all such decisions are made by solicitors who are full-time salaried officers of an independent service, organized regionally but under the ultimate control of the Director of Public Prosecutions, a central government officer who had always had this power for certain very serious crimes.

The previous fusion of responsibilities mattered principally because there is always a considerable element of discretion involved in the decision to prosecute, and in what evidence will be used by the prosecution. Discretion covered both which crimes to prosecute, and when to prosecute any particular offender. There may be some value in discretion in the first sense, because community standards on, say, pornography, do vary. In fact the police can still exercise some discretion in this area by simply refusing to investigate crimes they don't want prosecuted, given that the police authority cannot order them to act. The police also used their discretion to prosecute cases which were simply not worth taking to court because it was a minor offence which would lead to an extremely light sentence, or a complete discharge for someone who barely deserved to be picked out for a minor offence.

This use of discretion was effectively using court appearances as a method of social control, as a policing activity, rather than as a legal consequence of clear guilt. For example, police very often merely caution, or simply talk to young offenders guilty of minor affrays or disturbances of the peace. But if there were complaints about behaviour on a certain housing estate they would suddenly start to prosecute instead. It was an inappropriate use of the discretion to prosecute. The CPS is much more likely to use objective, nationally determined guidelines in this sort of case.

Discretion on when to prosecute really depends on how high a probability of conviction there should be before a prosecution is launched. The rate of conviction in a jury trial where there is no plea of guilty often surprises people, because it is only around 70 per cent. As the cost and suffering of going to trial can be devastating even for those acquitted, no prosecution should be launched lightly, however certain the police may be in their own minds that they have the right person. There is no doubt that the Crown Prosecution Service demands a significantly higher probability of conviction before they will prosecute than the police used to expect. Finally, the CPS will inevitably be much keener to check that evidence is reliable and all police procedures watertight, thus further enforcing civil rights against police enthusiasm. The CPS has not yet won widespread approval in any sector, because it has been seriously under-funded and under-staffed, and there are doubts by some about its administrative competence, but the change in constitutional control over the police may ultimately be more important than any other likely or previous reform.

Police effectiveness and 'value for money'

Finally, it is worth considering just how effective the police are, because in recent years the adequacy of government policy concerning law and order has become more and more politically sensitive. The increase in salience has come about largely because the Conservative party has always presented itself as much more concerned on this issue than Labour, and the governments since 1979 have considerably increased resources for crime control.

It is necessary first to get some sense of scale in this problem. The British police force has a total of 128,000 officers (20,000 in the Met.) with perhaps 40,000 civilian employers. This makes it roughly half the size of the French police, and not much more than a third of the size of the Italian forces – that is, Britain has roughly one police officer for every 450 inhabitants, France one for every 250.

Second, unlike European counterparts, the British police is a general duty and entirely civilian force, handling every aspect of policing. Elsewhere in Europe the police are more functionally specialized, usually with a para-military organization like the French Gendarmerie or the Italian Caribinieri who are primarily responsible for public order. It is, as everyone knows, a predominantly (though decreasingly) unarmed force, and one which has always tried to police consensually.

In this latter respect the British police have probably improved since the severe criticisms of heavy-handed policy tactics in the 1981 Scarman Report. Usually senior officers will avoid using serious force to contain rioting in case it exacerbates the situation, though this has not been the policy in industrial disputes like the miners' strike and disputes at the News International plant at Wapping in the period 1986–8. On the whole this policy has paid off, and public order policing is fairly effective without being too oppressive. The other sense of use of force, the use of deadly force with firearms, is currently less impressive, with a notable rise in the number of criminals or simply disturbed people shot to death by the police in recent years. But the total numbers are too small to constitute a significant rise.

Assessing how effective the police are in detecting and 'clearing up' crime other than public-order offences is a methodological nightmare. Crime statistics are widely regarded as the most unreliable social indicators published by any government in any policy area. Taking an entirely uncritical view, there has been a major increase in crime in Britain over the last few years. The total of all reported crimes hit 5.3 million in 1991, an increase of 16 per cent over the previous year, almost double the rate for the early 1980s. From 1981 to the mid-1980s crime increased at around 8 per cent per year. It levelled off for two or three years, and then started a very sharp increase from 1988, at about 15–17 per cent per year.

Over this period police manpower increased by an average of 8 per cent in most forces and by much more in the Met. The cost of the police force increased even more sharply because of major pay rises in the early 1980s. The detection rate, however, remains very low – roughly one-third of crimes are cleared up, with the rate dropping marginally every year.

It should immediately be noted that, even were these figures reliable, they do not represent quite the epidemic of horror some politicians use them to indicate. Ninety-six per cent of all crime is crime against property, and the overwhelming bulk of that is very minor – where the cost of the stolen or damaged property is less than £200, and often very much lower. For example, though the overall change for 1990–1 was 16 per cent, the rate of increase in sexual offences was only 1 per cent, and in violence against the person it was only 3 per cent. In face 'violent crime' accounts for only 5 per cent of all crime, and annual increases fluctuate randomly.

But these data cannot be taken at face value. For example, criminal damage is only recorded if the property is worth more than a set figure. In 1972 this figure was set at £20. The figure is still set at £20, though to avoid a spurious increase in crime, it should now only be recorded for property worth around £200. Another example – the greatest increase in crime in recent years has been in car-related crime. These crimes are always reported, because they cover insured objects, and the insurers will not recompense unless the theft is reported. Rape has increased – but so have efforts to make it easier and less 'shaming' to report rape, and the concept of 'date rape' has become legally recognized.

More than all of this, crime is reported, in part, according to how easy it is to report it, and what the police do to encourage the report of particular crimes. There almost certainly has been some increase in property crimes, especially opportunistic minor property crimes – roughly along the lines one would expect from increased unemployment and a rising debt burden on the less well-off. How exactly the police are supposed to prevent a rise in such crime is unclear, but it is certainly not a matter of increasing the detection rate.

One example of the arbitrariness of the detection rate was reported in March 1991. One single criminal, in prison, confessed to a prison visitor that he was responsible for 3000 unsolved shop-lifting cases. This accounted for 25 per cent of the clearing up of crime in his county in 1991! Yet most of these crimes would never have been reported in the first place – undetected shop-lifting never is. None the less the force in question was able statistically to demonstrate an increase in crime detection over the previous year.

Concentration on the detection rate, as opposed to crime prevention and deterrence measures, has always been misplaced. Roughly 30 per cent of police manpower is in the CID, yet the huge bulk of crime is not detectable. It is of some interest that the clear-up rate has varied very little for several decades – the obvious point is that dealing with crime after it has happened, except for a few major crimes against the person, is neither easy nor cost-effective. However the government and opposition are equally unhappy with the police – the Conservative government wants better value for money, and the Labour party wants local accountability. Plans are afoot which will almost certainly mean a decrease in the autonomy of the police in future years.

Dealing with criminals

This brings us to an intermediate point between an account of the police system and the description of the courts in the UK: both have in common that they deal with crime. Policy in this area needs to be considered before going on to a general assessment of their work.

The biggest problem, intellectual and practical, about crime, is what should be done after the detection and arraignment of a criminal. In the last twenty years it has become ever more clear that orthodox penalties imposed by courts have an entirely negligible impact on crime, either by deterring criminal behaviour or by reforming those convicted and imprisoned. This world-wide criminological finding is often known as the 'Nothing Works' thesis. Research in many countries has shown that recidivism, the probability that someone once convicted will offend again, is completely uncorrelated with the sentences imposed. If there is any pattern, it is a social-psychological pattern related to the offenders' age and sex: most crime is committed by males aged between 18 and 30. 'Nothing Works' is a very strong finding, and it rubs against the 'common sense' assumptions of many people, and of most Conservative politicians.

In particular, research shows that lengthy prison sentences have only one effect – to increase the probability that a prisoner will re-offend, because he will have been further socialized into a criminal life-style. This general idea has been accepted by the Home Office for some years, and for a decade or more efforts have been made to reduce the rate of imprisonment and substitute other sentences. Community Service Orders, for example, have been operative in Britain since the mid-1970s, and have been copied in most other common-law countries. Probation services have been expanded and encouraged to find more sophisticated ways of dealing with criminals.

Though such sentences are doubtless preferable on humanitarian grounds than prison, research again suggests no real impact. Community service recidivism is simply neither better not worse than recidivism from any other sentence.

All of this has long been accepted by professional criminologists, including those in the Home Office. Combined with other concerns about prison over-population, it has led to an increased effort to reduce the use of prison sentences. These have all come to nothing, with prison populations rising inexorably year after year, and the recidivism rate staying constant.

The first effort was the idea of a suspended prison sentence. This simply increased the imprisonment rate, because so many re-offended that they ended up serving both the new sentence and the suspended sentence. Community service was introduced to replace prison at the 'lower end' of imprisonable crimes. The courts used such orders for people who would not have gone to prison anyway, and happily continued sending down everyone they would have done before.

Britain continues to have the highest *per capita* prison population of any major Western democracy except the United States. Why do these reforms fail in the face of indubitable evidence that prison does not work? Because the criminal justice system, once it gets to the courts, is completely out of the government's control – the judges simply *will* not take on board the government's, or anybody's, belief that imprisonment is useless in the vast majority of cases.

To the judiciary sentences must follow, and only follow, the seriousness of the crime, not the utility of the sentence. The most recent attempt by the government to restrict prison sentences and replace them with 'community correction', the 1991 Criminal Justice Act, is likely to be fairly ineffective because it plays into the judges' hands by making 'seriousness' the test of what sentence is appropriate. It is drafted so loosely that no judge who wants to send someone to prison could possibly be prevented.

How can this come about? This is where we turn to the other side of law and order in the UK, the structure and functioning of the legal system. This is the most extreme case of the institutional autonomy and fragmented policy-making which we have found to be so typical of British administration.

Court structure

The court structure of England and Wales (it differs in Scotland and Northern Ireland) is always changing in detail as governments try to find ways of dealing with the flow of business. But the basics have not changed since a major reorganization in 1972. They are summarized in Table 8.1. At the bottom, in the localities, are the Magistrates' Courts, staffed by part-time, unpaid laypersons. These are local worthies, appointed by secret committees nominated by the Lord Chancellor – there are over 28,000 magistrates, known as Justices of the Peace (JPs). Though sometimes described as 'the peoples' courts', they are in no sense representative of the populations in their areas, and no direct public participation in their selection occurs. They deal with most minor crime. Though the crimes are minor, they have, and very much use, the power to imprison for up to six months. Though they are aided by legally trained Clerks to the Justices, the biggest problem about the Magistrates' Courts is the enormous variation from area to area, and indeed between benches in the same area, of their sentencing practices.

England and Wales are the only jurisdictions in the world to rely on this fourteenth-century relic, which has enormous power because it handles so much of the work. Magistrates only handle minor crime, but the huge bulk of crime *is* minor. Two million cases a year – 96 per cent of all criminal cases – start and end with magistrates.

A peculiar anomaly of English law makes the fact that one can appeal from a magistrates' decision almost irrelevant. This is because a convicted person sentenced to prison starts his sentence immediately, even if he is appealing. The slowness of appeal means that anyone serving a sentence of a month or six weeks, the most common sentence, will have served at least half before the appeal is heard. And as Crown Court judges often increase the magistrates' sentence, it is seldom rational to appeal, however innocent one feels.

Above the Magistrates' Courts come two sorts of professionally staffed courts – the Crown Courts for criminal law and the County Courts for civil law. There are 94 Crown Court centres in England and Wales, and about 270 County Courts. These are staffed, for most trials, by the most junior rank of judge, the Circuit judges. There are about 400 of these, drawn from the legal profession, most being barristers. Though solicitors can be appointed, only 10 per cent of Circuit judges do come from that branch of the profession, though solicitors outnumber barristers by ten to one. (Barristers are lawyers, mostly concentrated in London, who specialize in court appearances, and have more prestige than solicitors who do the bulk of legal work. Although the situation is changing, historically the barrister side of the profession has been seen as both socially and intellectually the superior, and until 1977 it was officially known as 'the senior branch'.)

Crown and County Courts are the workhorse courts for non-minor crime, and for the overwhelming bulk of civil cases. What restrictions exist on civil cases that can appear in the County Courts are to be abolished by common consent before long. In criminal law the Crown Courts try all serious offences; the more serious, the more senior the judge, but almost all crime will end at that level. Of the criminal cases dealt with in the Crown Courts, about 120,000 per annum, only 34,000 fail to plead guilty and have to be fully tried. Only 8,000 of those found guilty appeal, and the bulk of appeals are about the severity of sentence, not the verdict itself.

Above these courts we enter the world of the real legal elite. The first step is the High Court. This is a very complex institution, but it can be summarized by saying it handles all complex or financially serious civil cases, but deals with criminal cases only peripherally. It is also the nearest the UK comes to having a constitutional or administrative law court, in a subdivision of one division – the Divisional Court of the Queen's Bench Division. The other divisions are Chancery, which mainly handles financial, inheritance and tax problems, and the Family Division, dealing with divorce, adoption and allied matters. All one really needs to know is that the High Court consists of 86 judges (of whom only one is a woman, predictably in the Family Division); nearly all are upper middle-class, public-school and Oxbridge; and all have worked for about twenty years as barristers, reaching the rank of Queen's Counsel after about fifteen years (these are the most senior barristers). They are not only conservative, with both a small and large C; the bulk are judged, by one of themselves, to be Thatcherite Conservatives.

Above the High Court are the two tiers of appellate courts. Probably the more important, though not technically the higher, is the Court of Appeals, thirty of England's most able lawyers, entitled as 'Lord Justice of Appeal', who sit in benches of three to hear appeals mainly from the High Court in civil matters – personal injury cases, contract and land law, taxation, company law, libel, the entire range of law where either a very large amount of money is at stake, or a very complicated legal problem arises. (There is currently only one woman on the Court of Appeal.) Interestingly, and perhaps typically, when the Court of Appeal deals with criminal law it sits as the Court of Appeal (Criminal Division), and only one or two of the members will actually be Lords Justice of Appeal – the others will be High Court judges borrowed for the day. Only about 1,500 cases get to the Court of Appeal (Civil Division) each year. About 8,000 go to its Criminal Division, nearly all being appeals against severity of sentence, not against the guilty verdict itself.

Most jurisdictions satisfy themselves with one level of appeal court. Britain has two. Above the Court of Appeal there is the House of Lords, a different entity from the Parliamentary House of Lords. The judicial House of Lords consists of around twelve specially created Life Peers – the Law Lords (technically, Lords of Appeal in Ordinary) who have reached the summit of the English and Scottish legal profession. By convention, two of the Law Lords will come from Scotland, and the court is the ultimate Court of Appeal on Scottish law, but only on civil matters. For Scottish criminal law the Court of Sessions in Edinburgh is the ultimate appeal court.

The judicial House of Lords is very senior indeed. It handles less than 200 cases each year, and there is no automatic right of appeal to it – the right to appeal has to be given by either the Lords themselves, or the Court of Appeal. The doctrine is that it will only handle cases which have far-reaching implications for the impact of law on the whole society, and not simply cases where the individuals involved in the actual case have major interest. Not surprisingly therefore it hears very few criminal law cases, and rather a lot of tax law cases.

Judicial policy-making?

The entire legal elite in the higher courts numbers less than 130 people, drawn from the Barrister's branch of the legal profession, or, rather, drawn from the senior section of that, the Queen's Counsel. There are only 650 QCs practising at any one time. (Practising barristers number only about 5000.) One becomes a Queen's Counsel only if the Lord Chancellor and a committee of senior judges and other Queen's Counsel agree. There can be very few more

Table 8.1 The modern English court system in outline

Court	Functions Criminal	Civil	Number of courts	Annual case load	Composition	Additional comments
Magistrates' court	Petty crime	Very limited	Several hundred	Vast	Part-time lay JPs	Apart from trying minor crime, these courts vet all prosecutions in remand hearings
County Courts	None	Extensive case load for all civil law cases subject to financial limits	Over 100	Nearly 2 million cases started each year; less than 5% come to trial	Circuit judges and Recorders (more than 500)	Most civil cases start and finish here, and much of the work is small claims business
Crown Courts	All	Some limited areas	Technically one court, with 97 centres	Approximately 60,000 cases put down for hearing	High Court and Circuit judges and Recorders	This is the main criminal court. It has three tiers; in the first High Court judges sit to try the most serious crimes, in others circuit judges try more minor offences. It also hears appeals from magistrates' courts and passes sentences on certain cases where conviction has taken place before magistrates
The High Court A: Chancery Division	None	Trusts, wills, tax law, company law, property, etc.		Approximately 700 trials	12 High Court judges under the Vice-Chancellor	
B: Family Division	None	Family law in general		2/3,000 defended cases	17, under the President	All divorce cases start in the County courts but defended ones may come here, as with adoption procedures
C: Queen's	Some appeals, mainly in public law from tribunals and	All civil law not dealt with elsewhere, especially		1,500/2,000 full trials	44 judges under the Lord Chief Justice	

Court				
Court of Appeal A: Criminal Division	Most criminal appeals	None	6/7,000	It consists usually of one or two judges from the Court of Appeal sitting with judges from Queen's Bench Division in a bench of three
B: Civil Division	None	Most appeals from anywhere which are not strictly criminal law	c. 1,500	The Master of the Rolls and 16 Lord Justices of Appeal. Usually operates in 3 man benches
The House of Lords		Appeals from any court in England and Wales on any matter, and from Scotland and Northern Ireland in many cases. Most of the work consists of civil appeals from the Court of Appeal	50/60	Between 10 and 12 Lords of Appeal, under the Lord Chancellor (who will very rarely sit). Usually works in five-man benches
The Judicial Committee of the Privy Council		Basically this is a group of Law Lords acting as a Supreme Court of Appeal from some parts of the Commonwealth		

Note A.   Case loads are very difficult to estimate because the bulk of civil cases are resolved either before coming to trial at all, or before the trial is over. The figures given are rough estimates of the number of cases that actually do come to trial, whether they are actually brought to judgment or not.

Note B.   The various divisions of the High Court all play some appellate role over cases in their areas from lower courts and from tribunals. This is particularly so for the QBD which has an overall responsibility to supervise all inferior courts and tribunals.

exclusive political elites in the world than Britain's higher judiciary. (Though in practice a person can be promoted from the rank of Circuit judge, very few are – the senior jobs go to successful QCs who would not dream of going off and trying ordinary cases in a small provincial town for – at the most – a third of their private practice salary.)

It is no surprise that these people are socially very exclusive. Until recently one needed a private income to get through the first few years at the bar. Thus the age cohort from which judges are drawn is almost entirely middle- and upper-middle-class, public-school educated and, at least in 80 per cent of cases, from Oxbridge. This social exclusiveness is combined with having lived in a very narrow world of lawyers. The entire London based bar is only 4000, constituting almost a face-to-face society. The very practice of law tends towards conservatism in attitude, and everything about a judge's previous life reinforces this.

Calling this group a *political* elite, rather than merely a social elite raises the fundamental question – why should one care who the judges are? There are two levels of response to that question, and both involve an understanding of how law works. To most people not involved with the law, there is some basic idea of a book of rules which the judge looks up, and then announces a decision. In truth laws are very 'open-textured', leaving enormous scope for discretionary judgments.

One level of judicial discretion is simply whether or not a particular defendant or plaintiff has, in fact, done something the law requires or forbids. In criminal trials this matter is left to the jury, but only after the judge has decided what evidence is acceptable and how the case should be explained to them. In civil cases there is usually no jury (the exception is libel), so the judge himself decides how the evidence fits the law. This whole area of discretion is not, perhaps, theoretically important, but the unrepresentative nature of the judiciary means that all the marginal decisions are made in a way that may well conflict with the life-style of the typical defendant or plaintiff.

In some areas, notably family law, the discretion is even broader, because the law will say something as basic as 'the child's interests are paramount', leaving it entirely to the judge to decide what is in the interest of a child. In a Law Lords' decision a few years ago on whether a gay father could refuse to allow his son to be adopted by his mother's new husband, it was announced flatly that the father had to understand that a homosexual could have nothing to give a son.

The more important area of discretion, which really only applies to the Court of Appeal and the House of Lords, occurs where a statute is vague, unclear, or simply fails to cover some problem. This area is known as 'statutory interpretation'. Here the judges literally make the law by defining the statute as they think it should be, and unless Parliament passes a corrective act, as it has done very occasionally, the judge's reading becomes the full law. This is where the real power of the judiciary comes into play. British courts do not have the power of judicial review of legislation that is enjoyed by the Supreme Courts of the United States, Canada, Australia,

Germany or Italy, where a court can rule an act of the legislature invalid on constitutional grounds. This has led to a tendency to assume they are politically powerless. But those who take this view vastly over-estimate how often foreign Supreme Courts do use the power of judicial review, rather than the powers, shared with English courts, of *interpreting* statute.

There are several factors interacting here. First, Parliament is now so busy, passing so much legislation in highly technical fields, that it can really not hope to do much more than write down the outline of laws. The details are left for administration and the courts to work out. Second, this work pressure on Parliament means that it is no easy thing to pass an act amending a previous one to get round a judicial interpretation that Parliament finds offensive. (Quite apart from possible party divisions over the policy it defines.) Third, though an act may be passed by one parliament, the courts may not deal with it for some time, by which the parliament will have changed in membership, there can be a government of another party, and there may be no particular desire to overturn the court's discretion. We will give examples shortly.

The other area in which judicial discretion makes the judiciary very much a political rather than merely a social elite is in what is usually called 'Administrative Law'. Because of the outline nature of modern legislation, much power is left to Cabinet ministers to issue orders and regulations to fill in details, or to make discretionary judgments to apply the acts, as with planning permission, for example. Or power is delegated to quasi-governmental bodies like the Civil Aeronautics Board (CAB) which regulates airlines. (As we have seen, this is a general tendency in British administration.)

All of these activities *do* come under judicial vetting, through what is confusingly also called 'Judicial Review', where someone who feels he has been disadvantaged by an action of a minister or public body can ask the courts to judge whether or not the decision maker really did have the power to act as he has done.

Similarly almost all actions of local authorities, because they will be acting under powers delegated by Parliament, can be challenged in the courts. So we are really saying two similar but different things. First, that the judgment of whether someone has really made out his case under the law will be interpreted by a judge, and second that just what the law actually says will be interpreted by judges, and there is precious little anyone can do to stop them.

A good case to start with, because it underlies just how independent the courts can be, comes from 1969, and is known as Anisminic v. Foreign Compensation Commission. The Foreign Compensation Commission was set up by an act in 1950 when the then Labour government was trying to reduce the power of the courts. The Commission's job is to distribute money to compensate people of firms who have been harmed by an act of a foreign state. This was seen as very much a political act, and something which should not become an English legal matter. Consequently the law specified that there could not be any appeal to any court from whatever the Commission decided. None the less Anisminic, which was a trading firm, did appeal against the Commission. The courts, by very tortuous logic, agreed they could consider the case and granted them their appeal. The government was furious, and passed a bill making even clearer that the courts should leave this matter alone (these are called 'ouster clauses'). The bill, however, failed in the Lords, and the government gave up. There have, in fact, only been two or three successful attempts to re-pass legislation that the courts have interpreted in a way the government did not like, and 'ouster clauses' have proved so ineffective that Parliament has largely ceased to attempt them.

Even when Acts are re-passed, it can take a long time. Thus the 1965 and 1968 Race Relations Acts were seriously weakened by decisions of the Law Lords not to apply them to social clubs, for example. These have now been reversed, but the new Act was passed only in 1976. (Note that the first two Acts were passed by a Labour government, and the Act was not changed until Labour was returned to power after 1974.)

During the 1970s and early 1980s there were a series of major cases in which the courts interpreted legislation in a distinctly conservative manner. These applied particularly to industrial relations. Throughout the century in fact, courts have been seen as systematically biased against the trade union movement. This latter charge may, in some ways, be unfair. The unions have tended to blame the courts whenever they have lost, even when the legislation was crystal clear and the courts could have had no choice. So, for example, cases relating to picketing during the long-drawn-out industrial conflict with News International at Wapping were always found against the rights of picketers. However, the legislation, drawn up by the early Thatcher governments, was quite intentionally anti-union.

In fact, it is always hard to find clear-cut evidence of political bias in judgments, because the senior judges are extremely subtle in their arguments. Despite this there seems to be a clear pattern. Two cases will have to suffice. The first is Secretary of State for Education v. Tameside Metropolitan Borough Council, in 1977. Here a Labour council which had almost implemented a plan to scrap grammar schools lost power in an election, and the incoming Conservative council immediately altered the plans, even though most people thought they were far too far along to be satisfactorily changed. The Secretary of State for the Labour government used his powers under Section 68 of the 1944 Education Act to stop these last-minute changes, as he is empowered to do if the local education authority is acting unreasonably. None the less the Law Lords ruled that it was the Secretary of State who was acting unreasonably, in an entirely novel interpretation of the law, and allowed the Conservative council to go ahead. In the last of the major 'political cases' to come up, the 1982 case Bromley London Borough Council v. Greater London Council, we find essentially the same sort of argument, but this time in favour of the (Conservative) borough council against the (Labour) GLC.

In Bromley what was at stake was the GLC's use of its discretionary powers to subsidise London Transport to carry out a manifesto promise to cut fares by 25 per cent. In order to do this they levied an extra rate demand on the separate boroughs. Bromley challenged this in the courts. By a complicated argument the Law Lords read into the relevant legislation a series of rules, quite new to English law, which required the GLC to operate London Transport on ordinary business principles, thus making the subsidies illegal. It is particularly interesting here that they completely denied that the manifesto commitment on which Labour had won the GLC elections could have any force in law at all.

These are only a few cases out of dozens over the last twenty years where major changes have been made to the policies elected politicians wanted to pursue, but they are illustrative of a general point. The point is that modern legislation *has* to grant discretion to ministers and governmental bodies, but as soon as it does this it opens up chances for judges to decide that the discretion has been improperly exercised. (Cases like this go back at least to the early 1960s – before then the courts had been more quiescent or restrained.) There have not, however, been any important cases since Bromley (except for the trade union cases mentioned above). One is tempted to the theory that courts will only be active when Conservative challenges are brought against Labour administrations. But it might be fairer to say that when the middle class are upset they think of going to court, and when the working class are upset they go on to the street. Thus the police have been more active in public order control under the Tories, and the courts, in a different sense of public order, under Labour.

Limiting judicial discretion

In fact judges are not Conservative in any very straightforward partisan sense. They are 'small c' conservative, by training, socialization, and by the very nature of the law, and many of them would accept this and simply say that law is *supposed* to be a restraining force. These arguments are true to some extent, but they do not explain decisions like Tameside and Bromley which were widely treated as bad law by other lawyers.

However, judges are, above all, law-abiding, and if legislation is drafted tightly enough, they will enforce it. The relevance of this could become extreme if a written constitution and bill of rights are introduced, as they may well be in the next decade. We cannot really know how British judges would react to a written bill of rights. Certainly most of them have refused to treat the European Declaration on Human Rights, of which Britain is a signatory, as having any force in English law.

One piece of evidence we do have comes from another role the Law Lords play. Wearing other hats, as Privy Councillors, they make up the Judicial Committee of the Privy Council, which hears appeals from some of the remnants of the British Empire, especially from West Indian members of the Commonwealth. These countries all do have written constitutions. Time after time one finds in the Privy Council rulings an extremely strict adherence to the letter of the constitution. These cases, especially those relating to the death penalty, have been such that the strict construction of the constitution favours the government. But everything about the rulings suggests that the judges would have been equally adamant on strict construction if the constitution had favoured the defendants. We also know that British judges have been good, and much better than French judges, in accepting the rulings of the European Court of Justice (ECJ). Under the Treaty of Rome and Britain's accession to it, directives of the European Commission, or rulings of the ECJ itself, take precedence in some areas over British statute law. The English courts have gone out of their way to accept this superior jurisdiction, in a way that surprised many observers at first.

The lesson is fairly obvious. Statutes must be drafted with much more of an eye to making them 'judge-proof', and any written constitution must be written with a very clear idea of how judges might interpret it. There is no way that one can avoid judicial interpretation, and wherever the balance of interpretation can favour a conservative result, it will. Thus, for example, the decisions of Employment Appeals Tribunals against unfair dismissal, or the Immigration Appeal Tribunal against deportation orders are always, at the margin, going to favour employers and the Immigration Service. This sort of discretion can be dealt with only by changing the make-up of the Bench itself, not by constitutional tinkering.

However, the prospects for change in the legal profession and consequently in the selection of judges during the 1990s are very limited. Why this is so is illustrated by an episode which also demonstrates the limits of effectiveness of the central government in relation to vested interests and to the autonomously organized bodies on which it depends for service delivery.

In 1989–90 Mrs Thatcher and her reformist Lord Chancellor, Lord Mackay (significantly a Scottish lawyer) put forward proposals for the most far-reaching reform of the legal profession since the nineteenth century. This involved effectively abolishing the distinction between barristers and solicitors, simplifying court procedures and throwing open the selection of judges to the whole of the legal profession.

The proposals, though they had the support of solicitors representing the vast majority of lawyers, were fought tooth and nail by judges and the barristers' associations. They were diluted more and more until only minor changes remain. Legal reform changed direction, in sympathy with the government's value-for-money concerns, with cutting down on legal aid (which assists persons of up to middling incomes with the high legal costs of any court action) and expanding administrative discretion in such areas as appeals by immigrants against deportation. Sentencing, which involves enormous prison costs, remained unaffected.

The changes the government made in the end thus adversely affected solicitors rather than barristers and made no difference to judges.

It is a sign of its entrenched power that the Bar managed to fight off nearly all proposed legal reform during the 1980s and seems well able to continue its successful resistance over the next decade.

Chapter 9

A third level of government: Britain in the European Community

Emil Kirchner

The complexity of British politics/administration has been increased over the last twenty years by the country's entry into the European Community and the increasing influence of European legislation and decisions on what is done internally in Britain. As we have noted, local councils and other bodies not only look directly to the Community for financial assistance but try to influence its decisions, and even form horizontal links with similar bodies in other countries. The European Court of Justice has probably had more success in getting British judges to comply with their rulings than British governments have had. The Community's adoption of the principle of 'subsidiarity' (having things done at the level of government appropriate to it) may well have important implications for central–local relations in Britain.

There is a paradox, however. While many aspects of life in Britain in the 1990s will be profoundly affected by Community directives and policies, British governments themselves have often been awkward partners within the Community. This has been attributed to a reluctance, unparalleled among the other Community members, to forego aspects of national sovereignty (i.e. the power of making decisions autonomously within its own national boundaries). Traditionally an overseas and imperial power, Britain has found it difficult psychologically to commit itself to support Community policy which has constantly had to compete with alternatives such as re-establishing national strength, promoting relations with the USA, seeking global rather than regional measures and, as of late, stressing pan-European collaboration over deeper Community integration. Government emphases have more often been on how to minimize change in the British system rather than how to move forward with other members of the Community in a 'give and take' fashion.

Undoubtedly, generational change and leadership styles are significant. Public opinion polls have consistently shown that the majority of the British population, especially the younger generation, is pro-EC. Public opinion might therefore be seen as being out of step with official government policy, especially when during the 1980s Mrs Thatcher's confrontational stance in negotiations, strident defence of national sovereignty, and deep-seated distrust/dislike of Germany and the 'Brussels bureaucracy' held sway. This was clearly enunciated in her speech at Bruges in September 1988, in which she warned of the dangers of federalism and its threat to British sovereignty. Mrs Thatcher achieved certain concessions for Britain, notably over British contributions to the EC budget and on agricultural reforms. Significantly, she also signed the EC single market programme in February 1986, which in turn unleashed integrationist forces, particularly with regard to Economic and Monetary Union (EMU), a single currency and a European Central Bank. However, at the end of 1990 it was her uncompromising, if not anachronistic attitude over German unification and EC integration which unseated her, just as much as internal mistakes.

One of the most important consequences of German unification, from an EC point of view, has been a need to reappraise the EC and its future direction. Because of fears over German unpredictability or dominance, several EC member states (but not Britain) felt it necessary to accelerate the process of European integration via the Intergovernmental Conference on Political Union. This complemented efforts to establish EMU and a single market. A powerful Germany within the EC framework appeared more attractive to many EC countries than a powerful Germany outside it. Equally, it was felt that making use of a strong German economy could strengthen the EC internally and externally. The Gulf conflict, the Yugoslav crisis and the Soviet upheavals of August 1991 further reinforced the trend towards further integration.

John Major, in keeping with his generally conciliatory style, was aware of the need for Britain to respond constructively to EC developments. He announced that, 'Britain's place was to be at the heart of Europe.' However, the Conservative party was divided over the EC and in 1991 the government was forced into an impossible balancing act of getting a deal in the negotiations on Economic and Monetary Union, and on Political Union, which would be acceptable both to its EC partners and to the Thatcherite Conservative wing. The latter called for a referendum over whether Britain should adhere to a single European currency, an independent European Central Bank and, most importantly, greater EC federalism.

Labour completely reversed its previous anti-EC stance in the later 1980s. It began to advocate co-operation with EC partners, to accept the general principles of a single currency and a European Central Bank, and support greater powers for the European Parliament. Most importantly, it attacked the government for being alone in failing to sign the European Social Charter – which stipulates provisions on a minimum wage, the length of working time and annual holidays, and worker participation in company decisions – and tried to capitalize on the internal frictions within the Conservative party.

In this chapter we will examine the main EC institutions and their roles, consider the substantive areas of policy and analyse the process of decision-making. We will also look at how British interests are safeguarded or promoted within the community structures and review how EC policies are implemented in Britain, as they increasingly are, whatever the rhetoric of the party in power.

Community institutions

We should note at the outset that the Community itself is not a single institution. At least four separate bodies are involved in relationships with British governments. The best known is the European Commission, a body of seventeen technocrats located in Brussels; two nominated by each of the five big countries in the Community (Britain, France, Italy, Spain and Germany) and one nominated by each of the smaller countries (Denmark, Ireland, Netherlands, Belgium, Luxembourg, Portugal and Greece). The job of the Commission is to initiate all Community legislation, and send its policy proposals for decision by the Council of Ministers (which we describe below). In making proposals, the Commission consults with the various national governments, interest groups, etc. It also mediates Council decisions. In addition, the Commission has the task of implementing numerous regulations emanating from the Treaty of Rome (the original agreement which set up the Community) and from previous Council decisions. The Commission sees that the Treaty is observed by member states, and any infringements may be reported to the Court of Justice of the European Communities, the second major community body which affects Britain and which sits in Luxembourg. The Court, consisting of one judge from each state, ensures the observance of Community laws. Its decisions are made by majority verdict, and are binding on members.

The Commission is often viewed as the Community institution most likely to interfere in British affairs. It is certainly true that in the implementation of policy it is vested with authority that is independent of national governments. But the Commission is still tied by decisions made by the Council of Ministers. The more significant development is the supreme authority of the Court over British courts and over Parliament. Traditionally, courts in Britain have seen themselves as merely interpreting Acts of Parliament.

The explicit task of the European Court, however, is to ensure that the acts of national parliaments or governments do not conflict with the founding agreements of the Community embodied in the Treaty of Rome. For the first time Britain has in this Treaty a written constitution that limits the supremacy of Parliament, a fact that renders the position of the Court very important.

The third major Community body is the Council of Ministers, which again meets in Brussels. The Council consists of a General Affairs Council and various technical councils. The foreign ministers of member states meet in the General Affairs Council, while ministers for particular policy areas such as agriculture meet in the technical councils. Associated with the ministerial councils is the Committee of Permanent Representatives (COREPER in Community jargon). COREPER I 'shadows' the Foreign Ministers and consists of the national ambassadors to the Community. COREPER II consists of the deputy ambassadors. Associated with it are numerous committees and working parties of appropriately qualified national civil servants. All these bodies carry out detailed preparatory work for the meetings of corresponding ministers.

The single-chamber European Parliament (whose members were first directly elected for 'Euro-constituencies' in June 1979; the UK has eighty-one such constituencies) is the fourth major Community body. It meets in Strasbourg, but holds most of its committee meetings in Brussels. It does a great deal of its work in specialized committees like the Select Committees of the British Parliament. Although its members belong to seven major party groups (Socialist, Christian Democrat, Liberal, Conservative, Greens, Unitarian Left, and Progressive Democrat) and some small groups, party divisions do not dominate its proceedings as they do in the House of Commons. This is partly because its competence is limited, so there is little as yet to divide over. None the less, the Single European Act increased EP powers by introducing both the 'co-operation procedure' (whereby on the bulk of internal market provisions EP amendments have more far-reaching decision-making implications than in other EC policy areas where mere consultation prevails) and the 'assent procedure' (which gives the EP a co-decision right in the ratification of treaties the EC undertakes in the external field). The EP power to dismiss the Commission and reject the budget can be wielded only with a two-thirds majority.

Another main EP influence is through publicity and investigation where the EP has extensive and increasing scope, particularly in regard to the Commission. Apart from the Parliament, the main representative body is the Economic and Social Committee, but this is merely a consultative meeting of primarily business and union interests, with no formal powers. Figure 9.1 outlines relationships between the European bodies.

The outcomes of Community deliberations are expressed in directives, regulations, opinions and resolutions emanating from the Council of Ministers, and in judgments and opinions of the European Court. How far do these curtail the freedom of British governments to act independently or take the internal initiatives required, for example, by the need for economic regeneration? At the root of most British opposition to the Community (which divided both Conservatives and Labour quite bitterly since entry into the EC) is concern over the political and/or constitutional implications of EC membership. The main issue has been the loss of sovereignty by national political institutions to the European Community and this has been extremely visible in, for example, the 1975 referendum on membership, the resignation of Mrs Thatcher as Prime Minister in November 1990, and the manifest difficulties of John Major over negotiations on Economic and Monetary Union, and on a Political Union. Discussion is too often superficial and couched in political rhetoric. Very often it involves sterile debates among the three leading political parties which accuse each other of shortcomings without addressing either what Britain wants in Europe or what Europe's future should be.

The European Communities and British governments

In acceding to the Treaty of Rome in January 1973, Britain was accepting a body of law which formally committed governments to certain common

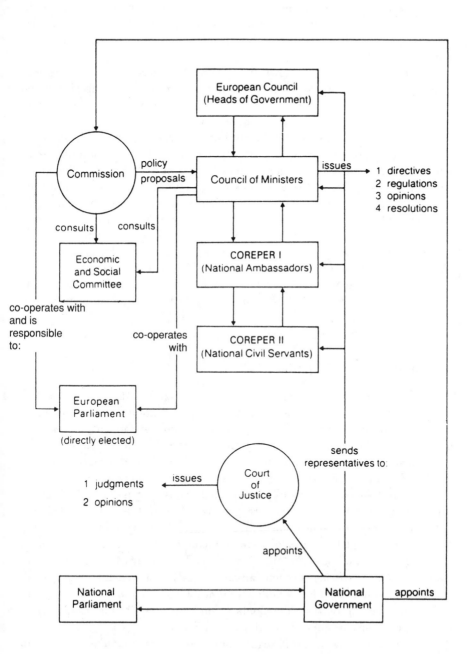

Figure 9.1 European Community institutions and their relationships with each other and with national bodies.

European policies, and to defined procedures for reaching decisions on these policies and enforcing their implementation. The Treaty of Rome, however, cannot always be taken at face value. Like many national constitutions, it often deals with prescriptions and intentions rather than hard realities. It is, too, a document that is subject to various interpretations, at least in areas where the European Court has not been asked to pronounce. Now it has also been supplemented by the Single European Act (1986) and the Accords of Maastricht (1991).

It is difficult, then, to pin down the precise characteristics of the European Community and the ways in which Community membership affects national governments. The EC is an evolving organization, moving when it can into new policy areas or those areas of common action designated by the Treaty of Rome, SEA and Maastricht Accords but not yet implemented. In some policy areas the progress has been smooth and straightforward; in other areas innumerable setbacks to common action have occurred. Equally difficult to describe generally are the decision-making structures. Sometimes, it is all too easy to point to the dominance of national governments in the making of common policies. But there are certainly instances in which Community institutions such as the Commission and the Court of Justice exercise considerable authority. Despite these problems in generalizing about the characteristics of the European Community, it is useful to examine the effects of the EC on British governments in terms of (a) substantive areas of EC policy and action; (b) the EC policy-making process; and (c) implementation of EC policies.

Substantive areas of EC policy

The EC has moved with varying degrees of success towards the creation of a customs union, then a common market, the harmonization of social, monetary and economic policies and finally the co-ordination of foreign and security policy. The final stage implies full political union. It is in the creation of a customs union and a common market that EC policies have been notably successful. Under the terms of the Treaty, the British government ceded its authority to fix quotas or taxes on imported goods (tariffs) and to subsidize exports independently. The General Agreement on Tariffs and Trade (GATT) is the international organization under which tariffs and trading agreements are fixed. But GATT negotiations are now conducted by the Commission on behalf of Britain and other EC member states. Thus what was once an area of national competence has become an area of EC competence. The British government is not excluded completely from taking action on tariffs. But that action must be approved by the Commission and fit within the framework of GATT provisions negotiated by the Commission.

Governments ignoring tariff regulations and taking unilateral action can soon find themselves at odds with the Community and legally bound to pursue policies in accordance with the Rome Treaty. Where governments have in fact ignored Community directives, as in the case of France in the 1975 'wine war' with Italy and the 1980 surcharge on British lamb imports, there is strong Community pressure on the recalcitrant state to bring policies into line with common practice.

While the EC is firmly established as a customs union, progress has been slower in the building of a common market. A common market implies a higher state of co-operation than a customs union. It involves the free movement of labour and capital and the elimination of barriers to competition. The Treaty of Rome is quite clear in setting out the various provisions for the creation of a common market. But these provisions had been enforced quite haphazardly until the signing of the Single European Act which envisages the completion of an internal market by the end of 1992. The internal market programme calls for the free movement of goods, services, capital and people throughout the Community. By the end of 1991, the majority of the 285 detailed provisions of this programme had been adopted by the Council of Ministers and a considerable proportion of these implemented nationally. In particular, progress had been made on measures relating to the harmonization of technical standards, where the Council of Ministers could act by qualified majority voting and where the principle of 'mutual recognition' of national standards had become common practice. Progress was also made on liberalizing public procurement (public sector contracts), freeing capital movement, and removing barriers to free trade in services. The stumbling blocks which remain for the completion of the internal market programme relate to removing physical frontier controls between member states, veterinary checks on agricultural products, excise duties, and harmonizing rates of indirect taxation.

Fiscal harmonization has proceeded to the point where there is a common turnover tax (VAT) throughout the European Community. But the British government, like other EC governments, has still retained its prerogatives in many other areas of taxation, such as income tax. Community control of certain discriminatory taxation policies has been more evident. British whisky producers, for instance, were pleased to see the European Court's outlawing of discriminatory taxation on certain kinds of alcoholic spirits. In some EC member states, such as Denmark and Italy, it had been government practice to impose lower duties (taxes) on home-produced spirits than on those produced elsewhere.

Other areas of competition policy also show uneven development. The granting of subsidies by national governments, for instance, is illegal under EC competition rules, except within the (officially defined) less developed regions. In Britain, these regions consist of Scotland, Wales, Northern Ireland and much of the northern part of England.

The trade and industrial policies reviewed above represent only some of the directions in which the EC has moved in order to develop a common market within Europe. In the industrial sector, as we have seen, the process is by no means complete. There is a dual problem: first, that of reaching agreement on common policies, and then in enforcing those common policies. In the commercial sector of the economy, there has been still less advance. It is primarily in the agricultural sector that the EC has made major progress towards the creation of a common market, through the Common Agricultural Policy (CAP). In this case, the common market has been achieved by an EC price support system covering most agricultural products. Prices are fixed at the Community level.

The CAP represents one of the few instances of the successful harmonization of national policies at the European level. It has been criticized in Britain because of the effect of the price support system in raising consumer food prices. None the less it provides, or is intended to provide, basic income security for large numbers of poor agricultural producers throughout western Europe. Britain is unusual in having the smallest agricultural population in Western Europe. The tiny inefficient farms found in many parts of continental Europe and Ireland are rare in Britain. Thus Britain gains little from the redistributive impact of the CAP. Since the early 1970s, the EC has been keen to promote other redistributive policies. On the initiative of Willi Brandt, then Chancellor of the German Federal Republic, the October 1972 summit of the EC heads of government in Paris called for vigorous Community action in the social field. The summit demanded a programme of action on employment training, work conditions, workers' participation, consumer protection and regional development. In 1974 a programme was approved signalling a more interventionist phase in the Community's development. Since then, further grants have been available for the restructuring of industry and the development of infrastructure, channelled through such bodies as the European Regional Development Fund and the various funds of the European Coal and Steel Community. Loans at preferential interest rates have also been made available through the European Investment Bank and similar facilities.

The supporters of these new initiatives hoped that the EC would cease to be identified merely as an organization facilitating trade and investment for European businessmen. They hoped also that agriculture would cease to be the only major area into which EC resources were channelled. With the passage of the Single European Act by the European and national Parliaments in 1986–7, coupled with the budget crisis as expenditures outgrew the tax base, some of these hopes came closer to being realized. The budget crisis prompted demands for more taxes to be raised for the Community through an extension of VAT, but also involved heavy cuts in farm subsidies, with diversion of revenues to social programmes and the promotion of new technology.

A major breakthrough occurred in February 1988 when the EC adopted comprehensive reforms in the fields of agriculture (introducing price stabilizers), finance (restructuring budgetary revenues) and regional development (substantially increasing regional aid). The Single European Act of 1986 had thus established the base for a more efficient Community; it gave increased powers to Commission and Parliament; provided for more majority voting on the Council of Ministers; endorsed new policies in the social, environment and research fields; made a formal commitment to abolish trade barriers by 1992; provided a more stable basis for Community co-operation on foreign policy, including a small new political secretariat operating in Brussels;

and called for more economic and social cohesion within the Community. The Act showed that the structure of the Community could be modified in a more federalist direction, in spite of the apathy or downright hostility of some national governments, and that Community-wide initiatives could be taken on some of the more pressing economic problems, such as the development of information technology.

The dynamics of the single market are also a factor in promoting structural and political change. By 1988, European Economic and Monetary Union was increasingly seen as a natural counterpart of the single market by political and business elites in several EC countries. They argued that for Europe's countries to retain separate currencies would itself amount to a barrier to trade. These arguments were forcefully articulated at the Hanover European Council in June 1988 where it was agreed to set up a committee of central bankers, under the chairmanship of the President of the Commission, Jacques Delors. The report of this committee, which called for a three-stage plan towards EMU, was adopted by the June 1989 European Council meeting in Madrid. Strong reservations were expressed by Mrs Thatcher about both the means and the ends outlined in the report, and in September 1989 the British revealed that they would be presenting an alternative plan, which they eventually introduced in the summer of 1990. This plan involved developing the European Currency Unit (ECU) as a parallel currency to national currencies. Britain joined the European Exchange Rate Mechanism in October 1990, eleven years after it had come into being, and a year later Britain indicated that under certain conditions it could accept a single currency and a European Central Bank.

The development of Community initiatives is still spasmodic and uncertain however. In very few areas have EC policies effectively replaced national ones. There have been interminable delays in formulating common lines of action, and also inconsistencies in their enforcement once they have been agreed. As far as British government is concerned, there are some areas of policy, such as tariffs and agriculture, which were once dealt with at national level and are now almost exclusively handled at Community level. This means that government departments like MAFF (Ministry of Agriculture, Fisheries and Food) have a very important European dimension to their work. But such has been the range of EC initiatives that there is hardly a government department that is not in some way involved in EC activity. Certainly, departments such as those of Trade and Industry are affected by EC membership; both are concerned with tariff policy, and must clearly bear in mind EC legislation when considering, for example, policies involving government aid to industry. A case in point was the Rover takeover, where the Commission asked the UK authorities to reinstate the terms of sale as presented to the Commission at the time of the sale (July 1988). The Commission also asked that the UK authorities recover from the recipients the sum of ECU 61 million granted unlawfully after Rover was sold.

Even the Home Office is affected. As the department responsible for the issue of visas and work permits, it has been very much affected by the policy on the free movement of labour within the member states. Treasury policies are affected by policies on spending and fiscal harmonization, etc. The list can go on. The Foreign and Commonwealth Office (FCO) is also heavily involved as the harmonization of foreign policies has been an unexpected and spectacular success of the Community. It also acts as the main liaison between national ministries and the EC organizations.

In terms of substantive policies, there can be little argument that Britain has become deeply enmeshed in the European Community. Though the depth of involvement differs among various policy areas, it none the less covers an extremely wide range of government activity. How, though, has the *process* of British government been affected by EC membership? To answer this question, let us now look at how policies are made in the Community.

The EC policy-making process and British politics

One of the persisting doubts (among the doubters) about British membership of the EC concerns the extent to which the British government has ceded its authority in important areas of national policy to a *supranational* organization. When Britain joined the EC, she was already a member of several other international organizations: the United Nations, the North Atlantic Treaty Organisation (NATO), the Organization for Economic Co-operation and Development (OECD), the International Monetary Fund (IMF), etc. All these organizations involved, to some extent, an international commitment by the British government, even to the point of declaring war. The perceived difference, however, between the latter organizations and the EC is that they are *inter-governmental*. Decisions within these international organizations are made by agreement among national representatives. No government is obliged to agree to a policy that it does not want to accept. The British government, therefore, could not be told what to do and be obliged to comply. In the EC, it could be told what to do. In principle, the EC has authority over the British government.

A supranational authority was exactly what the original founders of the EC had wanted. In practice, however, the way in which policy is made in the Community shows that national governments have lost very little of their authority. The EC's founding fathers had envisaged that the *Commission*, which is the executive body, would share authority with the *Council of Ministers*, which is the decision-making body representing the various member states. One of the jobs of the Commission is to initiate all EC legislation. It formulates various policy proposals by consulting with national governments and interest groups, and then submits these proposals for consideration by the Council.

As noted above, the Council consists of a General Affairs Council and various technical councils. The foreign ministers of the various member states meet as the General Affairs Council, while ministers for particular policy areas, such as agriculture, trade, social security, etc., meet in the technical councils. The decisions of the Council are issued in the form of regulations, directives, recommendations, and resolutions. Regulations have the immediate force of Community law. Directives, on the other hand, though binding on member states, leave national governments free to determine the means of carrying out the policies concerned. Thus the Community directive on direct elections to the European Parliament necessitated the British government putting its own Bill on the elections through Parliament and adopting the single-constituency, simple-plurality method of election as opposed to the PR systems used by its partners.

Though the above outline approximates to the formal procedures for EC policy-making, it conceals the developments since 1966 which have brought about a considerable increase in the power and authority of the Council. The Rome Treaty neither provides for the effective voting system used in the Council, nor for the growth of two important institutions linked to the Council: COREPER (the Committee of Permanent Representatives) and the European Council.

Under the terms of the Rome Treaty, a weighted voting system is used in Council decision-making, which allows policies to be determined by majority decision. In practice, however, ever since the Luxembourg Compromise in 1966, which ended a French boycott of Community institutions, any member state has been able to exercise a technical veto on a policy which it feels will threaten its vital national interests. In such cases the veto works simply by not putting the proposal to a vote. The veto powers enjoyed by each member state are extremely broad for there is no precise definition as to what constitutes vital national interests. Few governments would presume to define the vital national interests of another, or be prepared to have others judge their own. On more than one occasion the British government has successfully argued that the mesh size of fishing nets is a matter of vital national interest to Britain.

The only occasion when the Luxembourg compromise has broken down and 'vital national interests' have apparently been ignored was during the May 1982 meeting of Community agricultural ministers. The British government was the last one to hold out on the 1982 farm price increases, already agreed by the other nine community members. Amidst growing frustration with British intransigence, the farm deal was put to the vote by the Belgian president of the Council, receiving the support of all but the British, Danish and Greek representatives. Accordingly, the price increases were approved by qualified majority. This practice has become more common since the introduction of the Single European Act described above.

On the whole, the particular way in which decisions are made within the Council has meant that Britain and the other member states have increasingly viewed Community decision-making as a bargaining process. It has been in the interests of the British government to define its national interests carefully and then engage in horse-trading both within and across policy areas. The result has been an enormous expansion of the number of bodies in which trading takes place. When a Commission proposal arrives at the Council, it is immediately sent to one of the committees or working parties attached to COREPER. These committees and working parties consist of civil servants representing each member state. Some are permanent, such as the Article 113 Committee which assists the Commission in trade and tariff negotiations, and the standing committees on agriculture and employment. Many of the working parties, however, are set up on an *ad hoc* basis; on average there are approximately two hundred in operation. It is in these committees and working parties of national civil servants that the major part of Council business is handled.

It is only when a proposal cannot be agreed at the level of COREPER's working parties that it is passed up for negotiation at a higher level. In such cases, the function of the working parties will be to determine the major points at issue between the various parties. From the working parties, the proposals go first to Part II of COREPER, consisting of the deputy permanent representatives of the member states (i.e. the deputy ambassadors). If necessary, it will go to Part I of COREPER, consisting of the full permanent representatives. It is only when a matter has not been agreed at this level that it will go for discussion in the full session of the Council of Ministers.

It is in the nature of EC bargaining that disputes between parties tend to involve trade-offs across a whole range of issues. Such bargains can be struck most effectively by those at the centre of the policy-making process. It was a natural progression, therefore, that the European Council should have been set up in the 1970s. The European Council is the bi-yearly meeting of the European heads of government. Each member state takes its turn in hosting the meeting. Though having no formal basis in the Treaty of Rome, the European Council is the forum in which agreement can best be reached on the most intractable issues within the Community. It is rarely concerned with the fine details of an issue. These are left to the various technical councils and the working parties of COREPER: the council instead seeks to influence the broad direction of EC policy and to iron out disputes among the member states. It was the natural forum in which the countries like Italy, which were most anxious to see progress towards more integration, could get agreement to initiate the process leading on the Single European Act – substantially watering down the proposals, however, to get the agreement of more reluctant federalists like Britain. A typical meeting will trade concessions in one area for progress in another. For example, in February 1988, far-reaching reforms in the agricultural, budgetary and regional aid field were discussed, and eventually a bargain was struck which involved these three major areas of policy.

As things stand, there is little doubt that the Council of Ministers and the other institutions representing member states dominate the EC decision-making process. Though the Commission has been eager to take initiatives on common policies, it has usually found itself playing a mediating role. The Commission has been obliged to accept a much more gradualist view of European integration than the one it had adopted in the early days of the Community. As studies of EC policy-making have indicated, the formulation of common policy has depended far more on the strength of support among national governments for a particular policy than upon the activities of the Commission. Even where strong support is forthcoming, determined opposition from another member state can effectively stifle the legislative process. It is for this reason that we are likely to see a continuation of existing constitutional practices within the Council of Ministers.

The direct election of the European Parliament (the first elections were held in June 1979, a second set in 1984) has also made little difference to the policy-making dominance of the Council of Ministers and its associated organizations. Like the appointed European parliament before it, the present parliament has few powers with which to challenge the authority of the Council, though it has become more assertive in recent years in delaying approval of the Community budget and in putting pressure on the Council of Ministers through the 'co-operation' and 'assent' procedure.

What consequences, overall, has the EC policy-making process had for the processes of British government? First, it is clear that the *executive* branch of British government is very closely involved with the Community decision-making process, at all stages. It is consulted by the Commission when the latter formulates its policy proposals; it is also, with the executives of the other member states, at the centre of the Council decision-making process. As a consequence, British government ministers and civil servants now make frequent trips to Brussels, engaging in meetings both with the Community and their counterparts from other member states. Prime Ministers meet in the European Council, ministers in the Council and its technical councils, and civil servants in working parties of COREPER and other committees.

Besides the home civil servants making frequent trips to Brussels, there are also significant numbers based for longer periods at the United Kingdom Permanent Representation to the European Communities. Though this office is headed by officials from the Foreign and Commonwealth Office, approximately two-thirds of its staff consist of home civil servants from other government departments. In its own way, the Permanent Representation is a mini-Whitehall, and is thus quite different from the usual British embassy abroad. The home civil servants are seconded for approximately two-year periods. They make up many of the regular staff of COREPER's working parties. Though formally accountable to the FCO, they maintain close liaison with their home ministries.

The close involvement of the executive branch of British government in the EC policy-making process stems, of course, from the fact that policy is determined by a process of bargaining between national governments. These circumstances in turn affect the way Britain's EC policy is formulated. Clearly, in many areas of policy, British officials do not think of their role in terms of formulating a bargaining position. Relationships between the British government and the EC are very much an ongoing process, day by day and minute by minute. In this way, relationships between department civil servants and their opposite numbers in Community secretariats are rather like those they had in the past with some domestic interest groups.

From the British point of view, much EC legislation and activity is entirely non-controversial. However, the fact that policy is decided through negotiations between national governments and that there are, on occasion, questions which arouse considerable controversy, pervades the entire policy-formulation process. The British government thus tends to define and defend its interests in relation to the Community as a whole and the other member states. The simple result of these perceptions is that the Foreign and Commonwealth Office, which traditionally represents British interests abroad, has become the central co-ordinating ministry for EC policy. It organizes the UK Permanent Representation in Brussels and acts as the link between the home civil servants based in Brussels and their counterparts in the Whitehall ministries. The European Communities Section in the FCO is responsible for most of the co-ordinating work; it consists of several desk-men covering different EC policy areas.

Though the FCO plays a co-ordinating role in formulating Britain's EC policy, it does not have the technical competence to determine that policy by itself: in discussing, for instance, the specifications of an industrial product, it is hardly within its competence to make an effective contribution. Thus there is considerable reliance on the functional ministries which do possess such expertise. Departments closely involved in formulating British EC policy in their areas of competence are the Treasury, MAFF (Agriculture and Fisheries), DoE (Environment), Trade and Industry and Energy. Most of these departments have EC sections co-ordinating their involvement with the Community. Departmental representatives liaise with the FCO, but also participate directly in meetings of specialists held under the aegis of the Commission; in the working parties and associated committees of COREPER; and also in *ad hoc* committees shadowing Council and European Council meetings. The functional departments also play a major role in the preparation of briefs for Council meetings.

Co-ordination of British policy is achieved for the most part through a series of informal telephone contacts among officials from interested government departments. But there is also a committee system through which EC policy can be discussed. At a basic level, there are a series of interdepartmental committees in the major policy areas. There is also considerable scope for the creation of *ad hoc* committees, bringing together the people most immediately concerned with a particular policy issue. Usually, these *ad hoc* committees are organized at the instigation of one of the functional departments. Its composition might vary widely. A committee meeting on shipbuilding subsidies, for instance, would be chaired by a representative from the Department of Industry, and include officials from the Treasury, the Department of Employment, the FCO, and possibly the Welsh, Scottish or Northern Irish Offices. Only the FCO would be represented on every committee. Above the specialist policy committees is a European Communities Committee that oversees the preparation of briefs for the Permanent Representation and the Council meetings, and is generally responsible for the co-ordination of Britain's EC policy.

In its capacity as a central co-ordinating body, the Cabinet Office also plays a significant role in the formulation of Britain's EC policy. Officials from the Cabinet Office attend the regular committee meetings on the EC, and are very closely involved in the more controversial Community issues. They also play a mediating role in ironing out differences between government departments;

such a mediating role is especially important in the Community context, where the government tries to present its views in Council meetings in terms of a national consensus.

Besides all the interdepartmental civil service committees concerned in formulating Britain's EC policies there are, too, political interministerial committees. These include a Cabinet Committee composed of the ministers most affected by EC activities, which regularly discusses EC issues and which is chaired by the Foreign Secretary.

Many of these arrangements for co-ordinating policy form an extension of inter-departmental committees and negotiating sessions already described in Chapter 2. What is new is the central co-ordinating role of the Foreign and Commonwealth Office, and the opportunities for civil servants from different ministries to work closely within the same organization in Brussels, at the British Permanent Representation. With the additional complexity of the Community bureaucracy to contend with, we might have expected the existing fragmentation of British administration to increase. In fact, the negotiation of additional Common Market agreements seems to have been assimilated into the existing structure with considerable ease.

This may of course stem from the ability of a loose-jointed structure to adapt comfortably, but still loose-jointedly, where a tighter-knit organization might have had to recast its entire procedures. And as we have seen, change towards greater co-ordination in British administration might have been no bad thing. It is typical that Community membership has not strengthened the hands of the Treasury, the traditional co-ordinating department; nor has it produced a notable expansion in the role of the Cabinet Office, which might have been expected to plan centrally for all the activities of government. Instead a third co-ordinator has arisen in this specialized area, one without much technical expertise and with a traditional, rather cautious, attitude. With this development the fragmentation at lower levels of British government is also reflected among the co-ordinating agencies.

The Community structure also adds substantially to the points at which agreements from other parties have to be obtained in the process of making policy. This increases the already large number of bodies with inherent blocking abilities which already exist inside Britain. The greater the number of decision points, the less likely is a policy to be agreed and implemented – though conversely the more extended opportunities are for affected interests to make their views heard. In light of the much greater complexity of the Community structure it is surprising and reassuring that British administrative processes have adapted to it with relative efficiency. While membership has done nothing to reduce fragmentation in British government, it has not notably increased it.

One reason for this lies in the tendency of British interest groups to work directly with departments in London rather than negotiating at one remove with Community agencies in Brussels. It is certainly true that such groups, whether employers' associations, trade unions or others, have developed links with European organizations representing their respective interests, but co-operation still seems minimal. Some interest group representatives are formally involved in EC organizations through their membership of such bodies as the European Economic and Social Committee. The latter, however, has only consultative functions. Other British interest groups have sent delegations to the Commission and the European Parliament when they have wanted to have their say on a particular issue. The problem is that policy is made in the Council through the process of bargaining between member states. Thus interest groups have found it to their advantage to focus their attention on their own national government and, indeed, on the particular government department responsible for their own policy area. The National Union of Farmers therefore seeks to influence the Common Agricultural Policy through the Ministry of Agriculture. At best, the Commission or the European MPs will be viewed as an important ally in obtaining the desired outcome. There is no doubt, though, that in the ordering of priorities the Whitehall department most immediately concerned is the first group that needs to be convinced of a particular policy. The focus of interest group activity, then, has changed little since Britain joined the Community. (However, we have noted in Chapter 7 the emergence of direct contacts between local authorities in Britain and elsewhere.)

The general picture that emerges from our analysis of British involvement in EC policy-making is one of the dominance of the national government. For the British Parliament, the picture is not so satisfactory. Indeed, it could be argued that one of the major consequences of EC membership has been the burgeoning power of the British executive. There has certainly been a problem in exercising public control over decisions made by national governments in the Council of Ministers. From the point of view of the British Parliament, the mere fact that decisions having the immediate force of law can be made in the Council of Ministers means that Parliament is no longer the supreme law-making body in all areas.

The best that Parliament can hope for in controlling EC legislation is to exert control over the British government's negotiating position within the Council, the European Council, or COREPER. In practice, the experience of Parliament in trying to exert this control has been less than happy. When Britain joined the European Community, the Foster Committee in the House of Commons and the Maybray-King Committee in the House of Lords were set up to report on appropriate methods of scrutiny. In the Commons, the Committee on European Secondary Legislation was formed in May 1974; it consisted of sixteen members. From the beginning, it was clear that the Committee would be hard pressed to fulfil its functions of scrutiny. The Committee has a right to examine draft proposals submitted by the Commission to the Council of Ministers. These documents are supplied by the relevant Whitehall departments. However, the Committee has extremely limited powers once it has received the documents. It is *not* empowered to debate the merits or demerits of a Commission proposal; all it may do is to recommend that a particular one be referred for debate to a standing committee or, in certain important cases, to the House as a whole. With thirty to forty documents arriving at the Committee every day, there are few that either merit or can be given further consideration.

Once an issue has been earmarked for debate, there still remains the problem of how Parliament is to influence the government's Council negotiating position. No specific amendments are allowed to be made to the Commission proposals, and the House or Standing Committee may only debate on a 'take note' motion. Additional problems arise from the fact that a maximum of ninety minutes is allowed for a debate, and even this small amount of time is not made available until two hours before midnight.

From 1974 to 1976 the government was prepared to listen to the views of Parliament on EC legislation, though it would not submit its own views to scrutiny. By 1976, however, the government was no longer prepared to grant even this meagre concession in all circumstances. Michael Foot, then Leader of the House, stated on behalf of the government:

Ministers will not give agreement to any legislative proposal recommended by the Scrutiny Committee for further consideration by the House before the House has given it that consideration, unless the Committee has indicated that agreement need not be withheld, or *the Minister concerned is satisfied that agreement should not be withheld for reasons which he will at the first opportunity explain to the House.*

The italic type emphasizes the considerable freedom of action which the British government has been able to reserve for itself. The Committee faces further scrutiny problems when the Commons is in recess. No debate can be called and the Committee cannot even meet. The chairman cannot act on his own initiative to scrutinize legislation. The fact that the parliamentary timetable is not co-ordinated with the timetable of the Council of Ministers means that the Committee is often in a position where it cannot carry out its functions. When an instrument is adopted in Council before it reaches the Committee, the limit of the government's obligation is 'that the Committee should be informed, by deposit of the relevant document and by submission of an explanatory memorandum, of instances where fast-moving documents go for adoption before scrutiny can take place.'

In view of the unfavourable procedures for adequate Commons supervision of EC legislation, it is hardly surprising that there is little rush among MPs to serve on the Scrutiny Committee. There have also been persistent calls by those serving on the Committee for an improvement in the scrutiny procedures.

The House of Lords provides a far more successful example of parliamentary scrutiny of EC legislation. Like the Commons Committee, the Select Committee on the European Community in the House of Lords was set up in 1974. It has 23 members on the main committee, and some 80 peers who are involved with the 7 specialist sub-committees. Unlike the Commons Committee, the Lords Committee is able to call expert witnesses and debate the merits of the proposal before it. The chairman can decide which issues to put before the Committee, and in addition the various sub-committees allow the Committee time to deal with the more important business. As in the Commons, however, debates held in the Lords on Commission proposals are limited to 'take note' motions.

The limited influence of Parliament over EC legislation cannot be laid entirely at the door of the European Community. To be sure, the fact that ministers go to Brussels to bargain in the Council of Ministers means that it is difficult to tie them down to a particular line. The policy that emerges in the Council will almost certainly be a compromise, and Parliament cannot anticipate precisely what it will be.

Denmark, in contrast, provides an interesting example of a national parliament (the Folketing) exerting considerable authority over EC legislation. The Folketing secured its position during the debate on EC membership. Under the Danish Act of Accession, the government is required to make an annual report to the Folketing and keep Parliament informed of Council business. General debates on the EC are held at regular intervals, and special debates also take place. The main mechanism, however, by which the Folketing controls the government's negotiating position in the Council of Ministers is through the Market Relations Committee. The committee system is extremely well developed within the Folketing, and committees enjoy considerable authority. The Market Relations Committee is the most authoritative of all the Folketing's committees. It is also the most prestigious. Its seventeen members, elected proportionately from the various political parties, include many former Cabinet ministers. Under the rules of procedure, the government is committed to consult with the Market Relations Committee on all Council business. The Committee meets weekly and may question ministers and civil servants involved in EC policy. The government is obliged to seek mandates from the Committee before important Council decisions. In many Council sessions, Danish ministers have had extremely narrow mandates, and have, on some occasions, had to seek new mandates from the Committee before reaching agreement on a particular issue.

In the light of Danish experience, the inability of the British Parliament to control its government's negotiating position should perhaps be put down to the more general decline discussed in Chapter 4, and attributable to the dominance of a single party in government at any one time, government control of the parliamentary agenda, and the poor access of parliamentarians to information. What seems also to be the case, however, is that in Britain EC membership has allowed the executive even greater licence to escape legislative scrutiny. It seems unlikely that Parliament will be able to regain its authority. In the case of EC legislation, the European Parliament will possibly inherit it. Already, that body is a growing thorn in the side of the Council of Ministers as it attempts to exert authority over the Community budget and legislation and to take popular initiatives.

As things stand at the moment, there is neither European parliamentary control nor British parliamentary control over the EC policy-making process – a situation which has been described as a 'democratic deficit'. As a result, British EC membership has resulted in a considerable increase in executive power. It might even be said that the increase has been in bureaucratic power.

It is surely significant that the only British representatives permanently based in Brussels are civil servants.

The implementation of EC policies

The last of the ways EC membership has affected British government is in regard to the implementation of policy.

Once the Council of Ministers has made a decision, it may issue a regulation or a directive. The matter then passes out of the hands of the Council. In its capacity as guardian of the Treaty, it is now the Commission's task to ensure that Community law is observed, and that national governments carry out the obligations agreed in Council. Where a directive has been issued, the Commission may find itself in the position of having to cajole a government into enacting the necessary national legislation. This happened with regard to a 1976 Council directive on the use of tachographs in the cabs of long-distance lorries. Faced with British unwillingness to enact the directive, the Commission took the British government to the European Court which ordered the British government to comply.

In enforcing the observance of Community laws, therefore, the Commission can call for a judgment from the European Court. It also has the power to impose sanctions directly on firms that violate EC competition laws – for example, Pioneer was fined $6.2 million for operating a discriminatory pricing policy within the European Community. This fine amounted to 4 per cent of the company's turnover. This powerfully illustrates the points made above, about the legal enforcement of policies inside Britain.

It is, indeed, the role of the European Court that may be of most significance for domestic politics. In acceding to the Treaty of Rome, EC law immediately became supreme over domestic laws. For Britain, this change was particularly dramatic. Britain has never had a written constitution and Parliament has always been regarded as the supreme law-making body. There were no British courts formally empowered to consider the 'constitutionality' of a law passed by Parliament. As part of the EC, Britain is subject to the rulings of the European Court which has the authority to determine the 'constitutionality' of a British Act of Parliament (although paradoxically an Act abrogating British adherence to the Treaty would not be subject to review).

The supremacy of the European Court has made it an important influence on social and political change in the member states (including Britain). In the case of Smith v. Macarthy a Mrs Wendy Smith, employed by a pharmaceutical company, brought a case against her employers who were paying her £10.00 less than a man who had previously been employed in the same job. The firm was found in violation of article 119 of the Treaty of Rome. No doubt the firm would also have been in violation of the EC's 1975 directive on equal pay. An interesting aspect of the case was the claim by the advocate-general that a woman should be paid the same as a man even where only a hypothetical comparison could be made. As was noted at the time, a finding of this type would go further than Britain's own equal pay act. Not just on equal pay but also on consumer and environmental protection, action in the European Court may well represent a route whereby individuals and special interest groups can effect change. Accordingly, the European Court, in a similar way to the Supreme Court in the United States, is well able to take an important part in British politics. The slowness of the decision-making process within the Council of Ministers may actually push it into doing so.

Conclusion

The dynamics of the internal market programme, developments in Eastern Europe, German reunification, and the conclusions of the December 1991 Maastricht summit have accelerated the process of EC integration. Though Mr Major extracted important concessions from his counterparts at the Maastricht meeting, notably on social policy and entry terms to the proposed single currency, progress was made in both policy and institutional terms. This is unlikely to be stopped by difficulties in the complex ratification process. Member states and EC institutions are now tied more closely together. There is agreement on the introduction of a single currency (between 1997 and 1999) (with Britain having the right to opt in or out at a time of its choosing), increased co-operation on foreign, security and immigration matters, new policies in the field of environment, research, health and transport, and a strengthening of EP powers. Social policy had been the main item of disagreement, with Britain forcing the other eleven to pursue their aims 'outside' the Treaty confinements.

Thus, the outcome at Maastricht demonstrated, once again, that EC activities do not entail a one-way transfer of competences from the national states to EC institutions, like the Commission or the European Parliament. Rather they involve the notion of 'joint tasks', the 'pooling' of sovereignties, and a system of checks and balances. This reflects the fact that the EC works by voluntary rather than coercive methods. Consultations, deliberations and negotiations are the hallmark of EC decision-making and compromises are reached on calculations of costs and benefits, trade-offs and package deals among the major actors (governments and EC institutions) involved.

To be effective in such a process requires active intervention, vision and leadership. Britain, having for a long time played a minimalist 'wait-and-see' strategy in EC developments, and having obtained the reputation as an awkward partner in negotiations has some way to go towards becoming both an effective and constructive actor in EC affairs. It needs to do so because of the effects of Community policies on its own internal affairs.

By 1992, however, other member states were beginning to display uneasiness about the Maastricht agreement, as was shown by the Danish referendum rejecting the treaty, and the uncertainty over the outcome of the French referendum.

Chapter 10

Relations with outside governments: foreign and military policy
David Sanders

The other national governments of the EC, and the Community itself, represent only some of the foreign bodies whose decisions may affect British government policy, and with which it has to deal in a more or less continuing fashion. 'National sovereignty' is affected not only by processes of integration inside Europe but by military and power realities in the rest of the world. In particular Britain has continuing relationships with the United States which have affected internal and external policies as much, if not more, than membership of the Community. Indeed, British policy-makers' inability to decide on their priorities as between Europe and the rest of the world, have been responsible for many of the problems highlighted in the last chapter.

Shortly after the Second World War, Winston Churchill observed that Britain's international interests lay in three interlocking 'circles': in Europe, in the Empire and in the 'special relationship' across the Atlantic. For two decades after 1945, successive governments pursued a foreign policy strategy that sought to preserve British power and influence in all three. However, as the decolonizing 'wind of change' blew through the Third World during the 1950s, London's grip on its imperial possessions weakened. Partly as a result of these pressures, British policy started to focus rather less on the Empire and rather more on Europe, leading in 1973 to Britain's accession to the European Community. The British government's subsequent commitment to 'Europe', as we have noted, often appeared less than enthusiastic. Instead of embracing its 'European destiny', London attempted not only to preserve its distinctive links with Washington but also to retain a special position with the old Empire 'circle'. Indeed, even after decolonization and Britain's withdrawal from 'east of Suez', the UK continued to pursue the sort of 'three circle' strategy – albeit in modified form – that Churchill had anticipated in 1945. Although the EC was accorded top priority in economic matters, the Anglo-American connection still appeared to be paramount in the security sphere; and there was still evidence of London's continued desire to project a 'world role' amid the residues of the Empire. The result was that, by the early 1990s, Dean Acheson's thirty-year-old aphorism – that Britain had 'lost an Empire but not yet found a role' – remained remarkably apt. Worse still, given the progressive diminution of Britain's relative economic position throughout the post-war years, its foreign policy commitments still appeared to be overextended: given its straitened economic circumstances, the United Kingdom was simply trying to do too much in too many theatres around the world. Both of these problems seem likely, given the attitudes of the Conservative government, to continue through the 1990s.

This chapter reviews post-war developments in each of Churchill's three 'circles'. It shows how the balance of emphasis accorded to them has changed over time and how the requirements of one circle have frequently conflicted with those of another. The first section examines the 'special relationship' between London and Washington and reviews the implications for the relationship of the 1991 UN-sponsored 'police action' against Iraq (the 'Gulf War'). The second section analyses the retreat from Empire and demonstrates how the continued pursuit of a residual imperial role has inhibited the development of a foreign policy more in keeping with Britain's loss of status as a great world power. The third section reviews Britain's increasing involvement in the European circle and examines the way in which its Atlantic and imperial commitments have continued to impair its ability to act as a 'genuine partner in Europe'. The final section examines some of the main features and difficulties of Britain's contemporary defence policy, focusing particularly on the problems stemming from the collapse of Soviet power in eastern Europe.

The Atlantic 'special relationship'

The 'special relationship' with the United States – the centrepiece of Britain's post-war defence policy – was of obvious importance both during the Second World War and at the 'post-war settlement' conferences at Yalta and Potsdam in 1945. Even in the wake of victory, however, there were significant tensions between Britain and the United States: the British were outraged by the ending of collaboration in atomic research engendered by the McMahon Act of 1946; the Americans were wary that British imperialism might enjoy the same sort of post-war revival that it had experienced after 1918. The tensions were soon overcome, however, by the emergence of a greater external threat. During 1947 and 1948 Stalin tightened Moscow's grip on Eastern Europe by ensuring that favourably disposed regimes achieved power in Poland, Hungary, Bulgaria, Romania and Czechoslovakia. The electoral successes of the French and Italian Communists and the growth of Marxist-inspired insurgencies in Greece and Turkey suggested a worrying increase in Communist influence inside the Western camp itself. And the Berlin blockade of 1948 hinted that Stalin might be contemplating overt aggression against the West. All these developments served to reinforce the growing perception inside British and American foreign policy-making circles that the security interests of the two countries strongly converged. The result was an increase in Anglo-American political and military collaboration, both in the Third World and – primarily – inside Europe.

Anglo-American military collaboration in the Third World

In the context of the Third World, the Truman Doctrine – that the USA would support any 'free people' struggling against Communism – was the symbolic acknowledgment that the United States was prepared to assume the role of primary protector of the global interests of Western capitalism, with Britain henceforward taking a secondary, supporting role. The doctrine was never as all-embracing as it sounded, but it did lead directly to the United States taking over from Britain responsibility for the survival of the non-Communist regimes in Greece and Turkey. It also produced, in the late 1940s, an informal Anglo-American agreement to pursue 'parallel policies' in the Middle East in order to defend and promote Western oil interests in the region.

The Korean War of 1950–3 was the first major test of the special relationship as a counter to the global encroachment of Communism and, although the costs involved were considerable, the Western powers were in the event broadly successful in containing Communist expansionism within their preferred defence perimeter. However, despite both the collaboration in Korea and the pursuit of 'parallel policies' towards the Middle Eastern oil-producing states in the early 1950s, the special relationship – at least as far as the Third World was concerned – suffered a serious blow with the 1956 Suez crisis, when American diplomatic and financial pressure effected a rapid and ignominious withdrawal of the British Expeditionary Force. Thereafter, a greater degree of cynicism and suspicion entered into British and American assessments of each other's Third World entanglements. Even though the Wilson government provided token military assistance to the Americans during the Vietnam War in the 1960s, the equivocal character of British support did little to restore the notion that the special relationship had any real meaning in the context of British or American dealings with the Third World. Indeed, during the 1970s, the whole idea of a 'special relationship' between London and Washington with respect to the Third World seemed increasingly irrelevant.

With the electoral victories of Margaret Thatcher (in 1979) and Ronald Reagan (in 1980), a greater degree of correspondence between British and American Third World policies re-emerged. At the root of this policy convergence was the similarity of 'world-view' shared by Reagan and Thatcher. Both believed that certain states opposed to the international *status quo* – states which were frequently backed by the Soviet Union – constituted a profound threat to the global interests of Western capitalism. And both were convinced that this threat should be pre-empted where possible and directly confronted where necessary. Notwithstanding this, however, policy convergence between London and Washington frequently appeared to consist largely in the British following wherever the Americans had already decided to go: thus, Britain's diplomatic acquiescence to the US invasion of Grenada in 1983; its continued reluctance to apply economic sanctions against South Africa; its active connivance in the American 'reprisal' raid against Libya in April 1986; and its material assistance in support of US efforts to prevent an escalation of the Iran–Iraq War in 1987–8. Yet, even with this degree of Anglo-American policy consensus, in the late 1980s it still seemed unlikely that the British and Americans would find themselves fighting side by side in some Third World theatre, as they had in Korea. Such a conclusion, however, reckoned without the ambitions of Saddam Hussein.

The Iraqi invasion and annexation of Kuwait, in August 1990, met with an angry response from much of the international community. Saddam's invasion was in clear violation of the UN principle of 'non-intervention' and there was widespread, though not universal, agreement that his unprovoked and unjustified aggression against another, weaker sovereign state could not be tolerated. What differentiated Saddam's position from those of other aggressive Third World tyrants, however, was that his assault on Kuwait came at a time when the two superpowers were emerging from forty years of Cold War. On previous occasions when one minor power had sought either to subvert or to appropriate the resources of another, any attempt to support the victim by one superpower had risked provoking the other superpower into backing the putative aggressor. In the new climate of international co-operation, Saddam found himself opposed not only by the Western powers (which was only to be expected) but also by his former military and diplomatic sponsors in Moscow. The result was that the UN Security Council, for so long rendered impotent by the divisions of the Cold War, was able to take decisive action aimed at forcing Saddam to withdraw from Kuwait. The Americans were undoubtedly the prime movers behind the series of Security Council resolutions that first initiated economic sanctions against Iraq and subsequently provided for a 28-nation force to be assembled with the purpose of re-taking Kuwait. It is also clear, however, that Britain's diplomatic efforts in support of Washington's aims, both inside and outside the Security Council, were extremely important in the difficult process of building a broadly-based military coalition against Saddam. And the unequivocal commitment of British troops to the multi-national force – even after John Major took over as premier in November 1990 – played a decisive role in persuading other Western and Arab states that the action against Kuwait was not simply a device for furthering US ambitions and interests in the region.

In any event, the actual military campaign against Saddam's forces turned out to be both successful and short. Within six weeks of the first moves against Iraqi positions in Kuwait, in March 1991, the Iraqi forces had been routed and Kuwait liberated. Under the terms of the appropriate UN resolutions, however, the US-dominated UN forces were restricted solely to ensuring an Iraqi withdrawal from the territories they had occupied since August 1990: they were not mandated to secure the removal of Saddam Hussein from office. As a result, within weeks of their decisive victory the UN forces began to withdraw from Iraq. Although the withdrawal was put into temporary reverse during the early summer of 1991, when British and American troops sought to provide 'safe havens' for the persecuted Kurdish minority in northern Iraq, it was completed by the late summer. Some UN forces remained in Kuwait and northern Saudi Arabia as a warning to the Iraqis against a resurgence of their claims to other states' territories. But inside Iraq itself, Saddam remained in power, struggling to reassert his domestic authority and, presumably, plotting revenge against his erstwhile conquerors. It was possible that American and British troops would again be required to confront Iraqi aggression in the Gulf. None the less, given the precedent of Kuwait, the chances of future UN 'police action' in the Third World – involving, *inter alia*, both British and American forces – were higher than at any time since Korea.

Anglo-American military collaboration in Europe: NATO and an independent deterrent

If the degree of military collaboration between London and Washington over Third World issues fluctuated quite considerably during the post-war years, the same could not be said of Anglo-American co-operation in the European theatre. The NATO alliance, the West's device for deterring Soviet aggression in Europe, was a continuing focus for the 'special relationship' throughout the Cold War period. NATO had been created in 1949, in the wake of the Berlin crisis, because of the conviction shared by policy-makers in London, Washington and Paris that the West Europeans were incapable of defending themselves without American assistance. Once US participation in Europe's defence had been secured, however, the British – as the leading European advocates of American involvement – were obliged to make a disproportionately large contribution to NATO's military forces in order to demonstrate to Washington that the Europeans were indeed prepared to contribute seriously to their own defence. In 1950, when Britain still ranked as one of the world's richest countries, such a disproportionate contribution could reasonably be justified; as Britain slowly descended the economic league table, however, the commitment gradually made less sense. Of course, Britain benefited from the additional security that its extra contribution provided, but while the benefits of 'additional security' could not be gauged, the costs of making that contribution – in terms of resources not devoted to domestic industrial or social investment – were considerable. In order to keep the Americans in Europe, however, it was a price that successive British governments were prepared to pay.

But whatever the implications of Britain's disproportionate contribution to European defence, the closeness of Anglo-American relations within the NATO context was undoubtedly strengthened by the 'nuclear sharing' which Washington and London resumed after the repeal of the McMahon Act in 1958. Britain had maintained its own nuclear weapons programme throughout the years after 1945 and, by the mid-1950s, had developed a nuclear bomb that could in principle be delivered to targets in the Soviet Union by the RAF. By the late 1950s, however, missile technology had advanced sufficiently to suggest that aircraft-delivered bombs would soon be obsolete, a development which threatened to render the embryonic British 'independent deterrent' irrelevant. At this point, the Eisenhower administration stepped in with an offer to supply Britain with its own 'Skybolt' air-launched missile system: London could avoid all of the development costs of such a programme and purchase its 'independent deterrent' from Washington. Although by 1962 it had become clear that the Skybolt system was technically unfeasible, the

Americans proposed the submarine-launched 'Polaris' system as a substitute: an offer which the Macmillan government accepted enthusiastically. The crucial feature of both the Skybolt and Polaris deals, however, was their exclusiveness. Britain was alone in being given the chance to purchase US nuclear weapons technology. No other nation was trusted by Washington sufficiently to merit such preferential treatment. The result was that London was able to maintain a credible 'independent deterrent' relatively cheaply.

The public justification for the British independent deterrent was that, over and above the effects of the American 'nuclear umbrella' that covered all of Western Europe, it constituted a necessary additional device for deterring Soviet conventional or nuclear aggression in Europe. The Soviets might not find American threats to use nuclear weapons in Europe credible, given the inter-continental nuclear exchanges that would be bound to follow: Moscow might be more convinced by the existence of an independent nuclear-capable decision-centre in Western Europe itself. This public explanation, however, masked a rather more curious, political motive behind the acquisition and maintenance of Britain's bomb. This is simply that first Attlee, then Churchill – and every British Prime Minister thereafter – seemed to regard the possession of nuclear weapons as a *necessary* condition for Great Power status in the post-war world. It was thus argued that, in order to make its counsel heard in the international corridors of power, London had to possess nuclear weapons, with all the attendant costs – above those of maintaining credible conventional forces – that were thereby incurred. What is particularly disconcerting about this view is that the possession of nuclear weapons was also seen as a *sufficient* condition for Great Power status. Notwithstanding Britain's continued position as one of the five permanent members of the UN Security Council, the country's sustained relative economic decline during the post-war era eroded any claim it might have had to such a status. The irony is that in their attempts first to acquire a nuclear deterrent, and subsequently to maintain its technical credibility, successive British governments pursued a resource allocation strategy that may in some measure have contributed to the very economic decline that rendered the possession of the deterrent superfluous.

All this is not to deny, however, that the independent deterrent may have been necessary for other reasons. It is possible that, by maintaining its nuclear forces, Britain demonstrated a degree of commitment to the defence of Western democracy that was essential if the United States itself was to remain committed to NATO. There was always a strand of American strategic opinion that advocated a primarily European defence for Europe; there was thus always the concomitant danger that if the Europeans – and especially the British, given their historical role within NATO – seemed unprepared to shoulder their share of the defence burden, the Americans would effectively withdraw from NATO and leave the Europeans to face the Soviet threat alone.

The ending of the Cold War has left Anglo-American relations – and NATO – in a somewhat confused state. The NATO allies have reaffirmed their determination to maintain NATO as the primary device for their collective defence. Yet the Soviet threat to Western security which underpinned the 'special relationship' has all but disappeared, and the Americans have announced their intention to halve the number of US troops in Europe by the mid-1990s. What these developments suggest, together with the renewed interest in joint 'out-of-area' operations that was implied by the allied action against Iraq, is that the 'special relationship' between London and Washington in the 1990s and beyond – if it survives at all – may be rather different from the one that was embodied in the NATO alliance between 1949 and 1990. After Korea, the closeness of Anglo-American relations derived largely from the exigencies of the European situation: co-operation between London and Washington in Third World theatres was very much a secondary matter, if indeed such co-operation existed at all. With the ending of the Cold War, this position has in effect been reversed. Although the USA clearly wishes to preserve NATO as its only formal institutional link with Europe at a time when the EC is undergoing a renewed phase of 'broadening and deepening', the need for a specific *Anglo-American* collaboration in the European context has diminished considerably. In the Third World context, however, given the UK's prominent (if anachronistic) position within the Security Council, the demise of the Cold War has opened up the possibility of greater Anglo-American collaboration in pursuit of a 'new world order'. How successful any such effort is likely to be remains a matter for speculation. None the less, given the alacrity with which London backed Washington during the Kuwait crisis in 1990–1, it seems probable that further joint 'out-of-area' operations will be undertaken in the years ahead: the 'special relationship', albeit in amended form, looks set to continue.

The Empire-cum-Commonwealth

The problem of 'over-extension' in Britain's post-war foreign policy is probably most evident in relation to the Empire and Commonwealth. Consider the position in the early 1950s. Although London had divested itself of responsibility in India (in 1947) and in Palestine (in 1948), the British Army of the Rhine was busily protecting West Germany from a Soviet conventional assault; the RAF was assembling a nuclear strike force capable of providing an independent deterrent against a possible Soviet attack; a large expeditionary force was fighting in Korea in support of the US policy of 'containment'; guerrilla insurgencies (or, depending on point of view, liberation struggles) were being suppressed in Kenya and Malaya; British garrisons in Suez, Aden and Cyprus – stationed there to protect British 'strategic interests' – were coming under increasing indigenous pressure to leave; colonial administrators throughout the Caribbean and British Africa were finding it increasingly difficult to subdue local nationalist pressures for constitutional change; and the Royal Navy still operated a *Pax Brittanica* in the Persian Gulf and the Indian Ocean. For a Great Power, recently victorious in a world war, such widespread commitments and responsibilities seemed entirely acceptable. For a small European power, which had been obliged to sell off virtually all its overseas assets in order to finance that war; which, since 1946, had been able to pay its way only in virtue of an enormous American loan; which was experiencing endemic balance of payments crises; whose protected imperial markets were crumbling in the face of foreign competition; and whose economic growth rate was lagging behind its competitors, the commitments – with hindsight – were ludicrous.

Yet it was only after the Suez crisis in 1956 (when Britain, with France and Israel, took over the Canal Zone in order to topple the Nasser regime in Egypt) that a serious strategic reappraisal of Britain's global over-commitment was undertaken. The fact that Britain, together with France, was obliged abruptly to withdraw its militarily successful expeditionary force as a result of American diplomatic and financial pressure marked a watershed in Britain's foreign policy. After Suez, politicians of all political persuasions came to recognize that Britain was no longer quite the Great Power that it had been at Yalta: Britain could no longer compete with the two superpowers in the race for global influence.

The response of the newly installed Macmillan government was to encourage (or at least acquiesce to) the indigenous wind of change that was already sweeping through the Empire. Beginning with Ghana in 1957, the long-established pretence of 'preparing indigenous populations for self-government before we can grant independence' was abandoned. A series of acts of decolonization – in Africa, the Caribbean and the Far East – followed, so that by 1970 all that remained of the Empire were a few small dependencies scattered around the globe. (Even Rhodesia – the illegal creation of a small minority of recalcitrant white settlers – was satisfactorily disposed of after the Lancaster House agreement on Zimbabwe in 1980.) The final part of the retreat from Empire was completed following the 1967 decision of the Wilson government to withdraw British forces from east of Suez. The decision, taken primarily on the grounds of essential cost-cutting, was not reversed by the incoming Heath government and by the end of 1971, British forces had withdrawn from both Aden and Singapore; the Indian Ocean was left to the Soviets and the Americans, the Persian Gulf to Iran.

Given that it had taken Britain over two centuries to assemble its imperial possessions, the dismemberment of the Empire was accomplished with remarkable rapidity. For Britain, however, the fifteen years of 'over-extended' expenditure between Suez (when it was recognized that the global role could not be sustained) and the withdrawal from east of Suez (when the global role was effectively suspended) still represented a significant additional drain on the Exchequer, at a time when Britain's relative industrial decline was continuing apace. The drain was compounded, moreover, by the costs imposed upon the domestic economy by the sustained attempts between 1945 and 1968 to maintain the Overseas Sterling Area and the reserve role of sterling. The whole idea of the preservation of sterling as a reserve currency was always bound up with Britain's supposed 'Great Power' status: it was consistently assumed that as a Great (capitalist) Power, Britain must have a high-status currency commensurate with its dominant international political role. From the point of view of the domestic economy, however, it was most unfortunate that successive Prime Ministers through to Harold Wilson (in his first period in office at least) felt impelled to pose as leaders of a still-great power. The attempt to preserve sterling's international value and status was a major contributory factor to Britain's continuing balance of payments crises of the 1950s and 1960s; crises that provoked domestic 'stop-go' economic policies that were inimical to the long-term health of the British economy (see Chapter 11).

During the 1970s, Britain's involvement in the Empire 'circle' was commendably limited. The Commonwealth, although composed largely of regimes sympathetic towards Britain (the colonial administrators had always taken care to leave the right people in charge at the time of decolonization) had never become the sort of surrogate empire for which the more ardent imperialists had hoped; becoming instead a vehicle through which the 'new' Commonwealth could claim special aid concessions from the old imperial country. The aid thus provided, however, was by no means burdensome: Britain's strategic involvement in the Empire-cum-Commonwealth had been trimmed down to match its reduced capability. In addition, by way of a replacement, the construction of a new European role for Britain seemed to be well under way.

This cosy state of affairs, however, was not to last. In 1982, the Thatcher government – in defence of the principle of sovereignty – launched its South Atlantic campaign. Whatever the rights and wrongs of the conflict, two features of it were abundantly clear. First, the military campaign was brilliantly conceived and executed: the repossession of the Falkland Islands – like decolonization and the withdrawal from east of Suez – was a considerable 'tactical success'. Second – and more disturbing – it meant that the UK embarked on a long-term (and long-distance) military and financial commitment which it could not really afford. Britain had ceased to maintain a presence in the Indian Ocean in the late 1960s because it could not justify the expense in the face of competing defence and social welfare demands. It was decidedly odd that, almost twenty years later, a small and increasingly impoverished West European power was prepared to allocate a significant proportion of its limited financial resources to the preservation of the rump of its imperial possessions. This predilection to reassert Britain's former world role, moreover, was further strengthened in the late 1980s as a result of the 'American connection'. In September 1987 a contingent of Royal Navy mine-sweepers was despatched to the Straits of Hormuz in support of efforts by the US Navy aimed at protecting Western shipping in the Persian Gulf. And, as noted above, in the early spring of 1991, the British played a very active support role in the US-led coalition which forced Saddam Hussein's withdrawal from Kuwait, a former British protectorate. In the 1980s and early 1990s, over-extension in the old empire circle had reared its ugly head once more.

The shift towards (Western) Europe

After Suez, it was increasingly recognized that the strategy of maintaining Britain's influence in all three of Churchill's 'circles' was impossible to sustain given Britain's diminished and diminishing resource base. As Britain's involvement in the Empire gradually declined with decolonization, so its interest in the European circle grew, beginning with Macmillan's unsuccessful attempt to join the EEC in 1961–3 and culminating in Britain's membership of the Community in 1973. What created considerable difficulties with this strategic shift, however, was that successive governments simultaneously attempted both to maintain the 'special relationship' and to retain some sort of foothold in the Empire/Commonwealth circle. While the shift to Europe tended to reduce the problem of over extension, the retention of the Atlantic and imperial connections at the same time damaged Britain's relationship with Europe and prevented it from effectively performing the predominantly European role which successive governments after Macmillan's attempted to pursue. Before assessing the extent of this damage, however, it is necessary to examine the three major factors that underpinned the shift towards Europe.

Given the continuing strength of the 'special relationship', a necessary, though by no means sufficient, condition for Britain's entry into Europe was always American approval. Indeed, immediately after the war, the Truman administration encouraged Foreign Secretary Bevin to take a leading role in stimulating political and economic co-operation and integration in Europe: in 1945, a strong, united Western Europe that would act as a bulwark against Communist expansionism was inconceivable without British participation. What the Americans failed to appreciate fully, however, was that Britain could not simultaneously lead European unification and maintain its imperial links. In the aftermath of the war, the imperial bonds were far too important emotionally to permit their dilution with European entanglements. As a result, the British did not participate in the 1950 Schuman Plan and the process of functionalist integration in Western Europe proceeded swiftly – and successfully – without British involvement. The United States, however, remained favourably disposed to British entry into Europe throughout the post-war period. It regarded Britain's economic integration with the rest of Western Europe as the natural corollary to Britain's military role in the European wing of NATO.

A second reason behind Britain's shift towards Europe was that during the 1950s it became increasingly clear that the Commonwealth was not an effective instrument for maintaining British influence around the world. Suez itself had seriously damaged Britain's relation with the 'new' Commonwealth. Indeed, the Indian Prime Minister Nehru was so outraged by the British action that, in tandem with Ghana's Nkrumah, he began a series of diplomatic negotiations that were to culminate, in 1963, in the creation of the Non-Aligned Movement. After 1960 the position worsened further. In 1961, in the face of strong British resistance, South Africa was expelled from the Commonwealth. In 1965, Ian Smith's UDI created an illegal and racist regime in Rhodesia which the British government did little – effectively – to undermine. And in the same year the Immigration Act introduced strict controls on the entry of 'new Commonwealth' – that is, black – citizens into the UK. All of these developments steadily eroded Britain's standing in the eyes of 'new' Commonwealth leaders and in consequence British politicians saw less point in allowing Commonwealth ties to act as a brake on the increasing British desire to achieve an accommodation with Europe.

A third, and perhaps the major, reason underlying the strategic shift to Europe was the apparently autonomous change in the pattern of Britain's overseas trade which occurred during the post-war years. As Figure 10.1 indicates, UK exports to EC countries increased secularly over this period, while exports to the 'Sterling Area' – in effect, the old Empire circle – declined commensurately. (Exports to the United States also increased, though more gradually, over the same period.) Crucially, the process began long before Britain's membership of the EC, though it clearly continued after 1973. Given that Britain's main trading interests were becoming more concentrated there, it is entirely understandable that, during the 1960s and 1970s, the leaders of all three major parties began to stress Britain's role as a primarily European power: increasingly, this was where Britain's main material interests were located. Combined with the promise of higher growth rates which the Six had achieved during the 1950s and 1960s, the economic logic of closer British co-operation with Europe pointed strongly towards a determined effort to enter the EC.

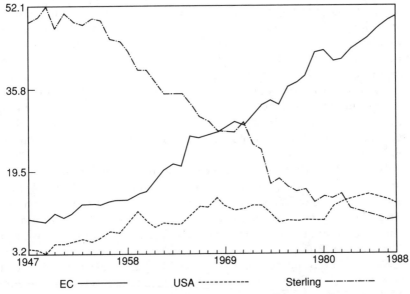

Figure 10.1 UK exports to the EC, the USA and the sterling area: all as a percentage of total UK exports, 1947–88

Yet, somehow, British leaders (with the notable exception of Edward Heath) never appeared to be really committed Europeans. In part, this was the consequence of purely domestic pressures inside Britain: the retrospective referendum on EC membership in 1975 was Harold Wilson's device for appeasing the left wing of the Labour party; the repeated efforts to 're-negotiate the terms of British membership' in the late 1970s, and the megaphone haggling over the size of Britain's contribution to the EC budget in the early 1980s both reflected inter- and intra-party squabbles at home. However, much more serious both for the Community itself and for Britain's position within it were the confounding effects of the continuing Atlantic and Imperial commitments. Three examples serve to illustrate the problems thus encountered.

The first of these concerns the circumstances surrounding Britain's application to join the EEC in 1961–3. De Gaulle's attempts after 1958 to inhibit the supranational momentum of the Community, and to keep it more as an association of sovereign states, squared very well with Macmillan's conception of what European co-operation should be about. As a result, in October 1961 Macmillan entered a series of negotiations aimed at securing Britain's entry into the new, more 'Gaullist' community; approaches which were welcomed by De Gaulle who was hopeful of building a genuinely European security community independent of the United States, as well as a less supranational economic one more to his liking. Negotiations continued for over a year – with apparent success – but, in late 1962, the 'special relationship' interposed itself with the cancellation of Skybolt. De Gaulle apparently regarded the cancellation as a great opportunity to develop Anglo-French nuclear collaboration and for the UK to reduce its military dependence on Washington. The British, however, failed to seize the opportunity. De Gaulle's hopes were dashed when, in December 1962, Macmillan accepted Kennedy's offer of Polaris. It is possible that Macmillan's acceptance was simply the excuse for which De Gaulle had been waiting in order to veto the British application. It is more likely, however, that the decision to accept Polaris convinced De Gaulle that Britain's Atlantic ties were stronger than any emergent commitment London might have had to Europe. In any event, the special relationship had for the time being succeeded in preventing Britain from moving in the European direction now favoured publicly by its leadership.

A second, more recent area in which the Atlantic relationship confounded Britain's relations with the rest of Europe was London's strong support for the American bombing of Libyan cities in April 1986, after the discovery of links between the Libyan government and terrorist attacks on American troops in Europe. This drove a further wedge between Britain's Middle Eastern position and that of her European partners. Considered in isolation, this particular divergence of European opinion over the Middle East might not have been too serious. What is important, however, is that it provided yet another example of Britain's determination to pursue an independent foreign policy – regardless of the consequences – at a time when EC leaders were desperately trying to use the development of a common European foreign policy to stimulate further integration.

It is in this context that a third example of the way that Britain's extra-European commitments prevented her from effective 'Europeanization' assumes relevance. In addition to her Atlantic ties, Britain's residual imperial pretensions and responsibilities also had a damaging effect on the construction of a common EC foreign policy. Britain's continuing insistence that *it* knew what was best for its former imperial possessions created difficulties in the negotiations over Lome II, the trade and aid package negotiated in the late 1970s between the EC and the ACP group of Third World countries. Similarly, the Falklands campaign – undertaken without formal consultation with the rest of Europe, yet demanding their formal acquiescence – caused some resentment in the Community as a result of the tensions which it created between the Nine and their Latin American trading partners. Finally, the decision by European foreign ministers in 1980 to recognize the PLO as the legitimate representative of the Palestinian people – an essential step if they were to act effectively as mediators in the Arab-Israeli conflict – was unilaterally reversed by Foreign Secretary Howe in October 1986 when two PLO negotiators (having earlier been expressly invited to talks in London as part of a wider Community initiative) were refused entry to Britain.

It is hardly surprising that these demonstrations of British 'independence' met with considerable disapproval in Europe. The British consistently affected to be 'genuine Europeans', but they were unprepared to compromise their freedom of action if either Atlantic or residual-imperial commitments made competing demands. In the late 1980s, these problems were compounded by fears in Britain that the projected 'deepening' of the EC threatened to erode Parliamentary sovereignty to an unacceptable degree. The Single European Act of 1985 had been broadly welcomed by the Thatcher government because of its promise to complete the free internal market in goods, capital and labour by 1992. EC plans for 'Economic and Monetary Union', however, were treated in London with rather more scepticism. Most Community members had joined the Exchange Rate Mechanism of the European Monetary System at its inception in 1978. But it was not until October 1990, after much prevarication, that the British government finally allowed sterling to join the ERM, only to withdraw from it in September 1992. London was even more hesitant about the Community's plans for the introduction of a common EC currency. Although a compromise, of sorts, was cobbled together at Maastricht in December 1991, the general British reluctance to commit itself to the continuing process of building a democratically accountable political and economic Community continued to cause considerable irritation in other European capitals. Indeed, such was the extent of British recalcitrance that by early 1992 the notion of a two-tiered Community – with Britain probably alone in the second, peripheral tier – was being seriously debated in EC circles. Although John Major was widely recognized as being far more pro-European than his predecessor, the continued opposition to further moves towards European integration from the Conservative right appeared to preclude the possibility of his making an unambiguous commitment to further integration.

Defence policy

The underlying aim of defence policy is to provide the domestic population of a state with a realistic sense of security. From 1949 onwards, this aim was satisfied in Britain principally through NATO, a defensive alliance based partly on the *punishment* threat inherent in the American (and later, the

British) nuclear deterrent, and partly on the *denial deterrent* represented by NATO's conventional forces stationed in Western Europe. In spite of the success that NATO enjoyed for over four decades, the management of British defence policy was always complicated by the need to devise an overall political strategy which simultaneously encouraged the Americans to remain committed to the defence of Western Europe yet which also prepared for the possibility that the USA, for whatever reason, might withdraw in the future. Successive governments resolved this dilemma by making a wide-ranging series of NATO-designated military commitments in the European theatre: the Royal Navy played a crucial role in NATO's contingency plans for protecting the eastern Atlantic in the event of future hostilities in Western Europe; the 55,000-strong British Army of the Rhine constituted a central pillar in NATO's plans to prevent the Soviet bloc from making easy territorial gains in Germany; and Britain allowed the Americans to use bases in the UK, without which Washington would have been unable to support its conventional and nuclear forces in Europe. In addition to these NATO-centred commitments, Britain also possessed a nuclear 'insurance policy' in the form of Polaris and conventional forces capable both of defending the homeland itself and of participating in limited out-of-area operations (such as the re-taking of the Falklands and the Armilla patrol in the Persian Gulf throughout the 1980s) where such action was deemed necessary.

The central tenet of NATO's military strategy from its inception was the preparedness to employ nuclear weapons against an aggressor in the event of either a conventional or a nuclear attack on any of the signatory nations. During the 1950s and early 1960s the guiding principle in this context was *massive retaliation*: an incursion by Soviet-bloc countries into, say, the Federal Republic of Germany would be met with an all-out nuclear attack on the aggressor's population centre and military installations. The doctrine was intended to signal to the Soviet Union and its allies that any attempt by the Warsaw Treaty Organization to take advantage of its clear numerical superiority over NATO in conventional forces would be suicidal. While 'massive retaliation' had the considerable advantage of being relatively low cost (NATO did not need to build up its more expensive conventional forces to match those of the WTO), doubts about its credibility gradually increased. Would the Americans really engage in a massive strike against the Soviet Union – and thereby invite a commensurate Soviet attack on the US itself – merely because the WTO had engaged in a conventional assault on West Germany?

Increasingly unconvinced that the threat of massive retaliation was credible in Soviet eyes, NATO leaders, in December 1967, formally shifted the basis of their strategy to *flexible response*. With this new doctrine, NATO effectively declared that its response to any future aggression would depend upon the exigencies of the situation at hand. A conventional attack might be met with a conventional response, but equally it might elicit the use by NATO of battlefield nuclear weapons, or even provoke a limited strike against the aggressor's population centres. Although it was implied that NATO would endeavour to ensure that its response to aggression would not provoke an escalation into all-out nuclear confrontation, the doctrine was also intended to introduce into Soviet calculations an unacceptably high degree of uncertainty as to what the West would actually do if the Soviet Union did decide to use force in order to achieve its presumed goal of dominating Western Europe. However, while the introduction of flexible response undoubtedly improved the credibility of NATO's deterrent by maximizing Soviet uncertainty, it also led to an increase in the range of hardware that NATO had to acquire in order to maintain that improved credibility. A graduated, minimally escalatory response to Soviet aggression was only possible if there were several gradations of response available to NATO decision-makers: unfortunately, 'gradations' meant more and different types of weapon system, which in turn meant higher costs.

The doctrine of flexible response was certainly more credible and less dangerous than massive retaliation. It was consistently criticized, however, on the grounds that it increased the chances of a gradual escalation into all-out nuclear war: A attacks B with conventional forces; B responds with a tactical nuclear offensive against A's conventional forces; A responds with a nuclear strike against B's military bases; B engages in selected strikes on A's cities; and so on. The danger, it was argued, is that flexible response increases the chances that the nuclear threshold will be crossed, and once it is crossed, an escalation into an all-out nuclear exchange rapidly follows. Accordingly, it was suggested that NATO should move to a 'no *first* use' position in which nuclear weapons would only be employed if a NATO signatory nation had already been subject to a nuclear attack. This option was rejected on the grounds that it would have obliged the NATO powers to devote considerably more resources to strengthening their conventional ground forces in Europe. And unless member states' defence budgets had been increased substantially, such an allocation of resources could only have been achieved at the expense of other elements in NATO's overall strategy. Not surprisingly, therefore, 'no first use' – in spite of its attractions as a conciliatory gesture – was never formally adopted, though great stress was placed on NATO's commitment to a modified version of the doctrine: no early first use.

Of course, all of this debate about NATO's strategy was predicated on one key assumption: the continued existence during the Cold War of 'the Soviet threat' to Western security. What no one actually knew was whether this threat was real or illusory. The left in Europe always argued that it was the diversionary creation of capitalist elites who needed to distract the attention of their domestic populations away from the true class enemy within. Advocates of European nuclear disarmament in the 1980s also argued that, while Soviet adventurism in the immediate post-war period had been possible because the lines of partition between East and West were at that time uncertain and relatively fluid, the hardening of those lines of partition in the intervening years had enormously increased the costs of Soviet aggression and had accordingly reduced its probability. From the opposite perspective, those strategists who believed in the existence of the Soviet threat acknowledged that there was no *direct* evidence of Soviet aggressive intent (there wouldn't be, would there?) but at the same time pointed out that this was so precisely because of the firmness of NATO's deterrent posture. There was, they argued, abundant *indirect* evidence that, wherever the costs of aggression had been relatively low, the Soviets had been quite prepared to use the military instrument in order to defend or expand their sphere of influence: thus Hungary in 1956, Czechoslovakia in 1968 and Afghanistan in 1979. If the Soviets did not have long-term aggressive intentions towards the West, asked NATO's proponents, why did the Warsaw Pact need three times as many tanks as NATO in the European theatre? Why did the Soviet Navy massively expand its presence in the Indian and Pacific Oceans in the years after 1970? Why did Moscow provide overt or covert support to almost any insurgent group that opposed the incumbent regime in any Third World country that was inside the Western sphere of influence?

These questions were not only deliberately rhetorical; they were also in large measure unanswerable empirically. NATO's strategic planners obviously had to assume that there was a Soviet threat, but they had no objective way of *knowing* whether it was NATO's existence that had deterred Soviet adventurism or whether Soviet inactivity in Western Europe had been the result of either self-restraint or lack of interest. During the late 1980s and 1990s, however, East–West relations changed so fundamentally as to render most of these debates academic. Mikhail Gorbachev's installation as General Secretary of the CPSU in 1985 heralded a new era in Soviet domestic and foreign policies which recognized the huge economic and political failures of the past. Almost immediately, Moscow began to adopt a more conciliatory approach towards the West. Moves to withdraw Soviet forces from the quagmire of Afghanistan were set in motion. Gorbachev visited all the major Western capitals. By the end of 1987 he had signed the so-called Intermediate Nuclear Forces Treaty with President Reagan, making significant cuts in medium-range nuclear weapons in Europe. In 1988 he announced unilateral cuts in Soviet force deployments in Europe. And crucially, in early 1988 he declared Moscow's intention *not* to intervene in the internal affairs of other Warsaw Pact countries: a clear indication to Poland, Czechoslovakia and the rest that, if they continued to reject Communism and move towards democracy, they could do so without fear of risking Soviet reprisals. This declaration enabled radical forces throughout Eastern Europe to press their claims for reform with renewed vigour. Democratic revolutions swept through Eastern Europe during the course of 1989 and 1990; by the end of 1990 Germany had been re-unified, with the East effectively incorporated into the West. By 1991, the reform process was proceeding apace inside the Soviet Union itself. The role of the Communist party in policy-making was enormously reduced and several of the constituent republics, inside which the party played no policy-making role whatsoever, declared their independence from the Soviet Union. The Union of Soviet Socialist Republics was even renamed as the Commonwealth of Independent States. By the end of 1991, all that remained of the previously ubiquitous Soviet threat was the danger that one or two of its former constituent republics might still possess some of the nuclear weapons which the authorities in Moscow had been unable to relocate inside the Russian republics. Even if this were the case, however, the direct threat to the security of Europe that the Soviet Union had appeared to pose since 1946 had effectively disappeared.

All of this, inevitably, required NATO to engage in a profound re-appraisal of its nature and role. In July 1990, after a lengthy process of consultation, the NATO governments announced, in the London Declaration, that the countries of the disintegrating Warsaw Pact would no longer be regarded as NATO's adversaries; that the Cold War was over. In November 1991, alliance leaders – noting that Poland, Czechoslovakia and Hungary had all expressed an interest in joining NATO – proposed the establishment of a North Atlantic Co-operation Council which would meet for regular consultations between existing NATO members and members of the former Warsaw Pact. By the end of 1991, debates about NATO's military strategy were being couched less in terms of how to deter counter-thrusts into European territory, and more in terms of the creation of some sort of out-of-area 'Rapid Reaction Force' which could be despatched at short notice to any part of the world where Western interests were seriously threatened.

As far as Britain was concerned, the changes in Eastern Europe and the Soviet Union after 1989 offered the welcome prospect of reducing defence commitments and costs. Although the West German government had, through certain 'offset' arrangements, helped to finance the British Army of the Rhine since the late 1950s, the 'continental commitment' engendered by BAOR was something that successive governments could well have done without. Equipping this force – as well as the RAF squadrons stationed in West Germany – to the required standards was extremely expensive and the result was that, even after Britain's withdrawal from east of Suez in the early 1970s, the British government still allocated a significantly higher proportion of GDP to defence than any of its European allies. (In 1979, for example, London spent 4.7 per cent of GDP on defence whereas Bonn spent 3.9 per cent; figures that had not changed substantially by the late 1980s.) During the course of 1990 it became clear that the government was engaging in a serious review of its defence needs and priorities and, in October 1991, only days after President Gorbachev had announced that the Soviet armed forces were to be halved by the mid-1990s, Defence Secretary Tom King announced the government's plans for cuts. Britain's commitments, he argued, would be reduced over the next decade: the ceding of Hong Kong to China would mean that it would no longer be necessary to station a garrison there; the unification of Germany had rendered the Berlin Brigade irrelevant and the BAOR far less important than before. Accordingly, the Army was to be reduced from 156,000 to 116,000 troops, involving a reduction in the number of infantry battalions from 55 to 38; and the RAF's capacity to deliver free-fall bombs would be reduced. So that Britain could retain its independent deterrent, however, the Royal Navy's plans to replace Polaris with Trident by the mid-1990s would go ahead as scheduled.

The planned cuts were attacked from the right as being inappropriate in what was still, as the Kuwait crisis demonstrated, a potentially unstable and dangerous world. The left argued with equal vigour that, with the Soviet threat demonstrably diminished, the cuts did not go far enough. But whatever the merits of these critiques, the real problem of security policy both for Britain and for NATO in the early 1990s was the dispute among the European allies as to the relationship between NATO and the EC. There was a marked division of opinion between, on the one hand, the French and the Germans and, on the other, the British and the Italians. Paris (which had left NATO's military wing in 1966) and Bonn, fervently wished to see the EC develop a distinct *defence* role that would complement the *economic and social* harmonization that the EC had already achieved and the *foreign policy* harmonization that the process of European Political Co-operation was trying to establish. London and Rome, however, were rather more hesitant. They feared that the development of an EC-based 'European defence identity' would necessarily exclude the Americans: indeed, they suspected that an American military withdrawal from Europe was precisely what the French in particular were aiming for. As far as the British government was concerned, anything that weakened the defence ties between Europe and the United States (and Canada) was to be studiously avoided. The disappearance of the Soviet threat did not in any sense diminish the community of interest that Europe and America had in preserving both global stability and a liberal world trade regime. There was still a future for NATO in which Washington participated just as fully as before. To be sure, the changed conditions of the post-Cold War era meant that military contingency plans had to focus less on Europe itself and more on out-of-area operations. But the need for joint Euro-American action was just as strong as it had always been, and if that meant that the EC could not easily extend its sphere of competence into defence matters, then so be it. In defence matters, Britain's attachment to NATO and to Washington was more important than any involvement it might have with the European Community: the traditional British preference for the 'special relationship' still overrode its commitment to Europe.

Summary and conclusions

British foreign policy in the immediate post-war years was predicated on the assumption that Britain was still a Great Power which possessed both the capability and the responsibility to undertake a major role in world affairs. Although the over-extended foreign policy strategy that was consequently pursued did not prevent successive governments from achieving a string of tactical successes in very difficult circumstances, it undoubtedly diluted the strength of an already weakening economy. However, with the strategic reappraisal that followed Suez, the extent of Britain's over-commitment was reduced through decolonization and the withdrawal from east of Suez. And with the end of the Cold War, Britain's military over-extension in the European theatre was also reduced. The main problem that remained as Britain approached the twenty-first century was that, even following the demise of its empire, its commitment to Europe still seemed distinctly half-hearted. While Britain's overall foreign policy in the post-war era had certainly shifted *towards* the European circle, Britain had still not fully moved *into* it. Yet, in the long run, it is as a European power – acting in concert with the rest of Europe – that Britain is most likely to find a role commensurate with its material interests and capabilities.

Chapter 11

Turning Britain around?
Ian Budge and David McKay

Delusions of grandeur, over-extended commitments, internal conflicts, disarticulation (or even uncontrolled fragmentation) of decision processes, economic crisis – all are features of British politics which have emerged in the foregoing chapters. On the other hand we have in the 1990s a Conservative government now in its fourth term of office and the opposition parties have generally failed to provide voters with a convincing alternative. This chapter tries to characterize the overall British political situation by considering all of its aspects together and examining the Conservative claims to have turned things around. To carry through such an evaluation we have to begin with the historical developments which have produced the present situation and which provide us with a context in which to locate present government policies. These go back to the development of an industrial society and of a modern state in the eighteenth and nineteenth centuries.

The historical development of the British state

Briefly put, British governments and their administrative apparatus have, historically, played a more limited role in relation to their economy and society than have governments in comparable countries. As a result they have been poorly equipped to engage in the kind of highly positive interventions followed by most other governments in the European Community. The large amount of goods and services contributed and produced by the public sector (over 40 per cent of gross domestic product) does not contradict this point. Public sector spending is only one indicator of the extent of government influence and power. Others include the extent to which, historically, the agents of central government have managed, coerced and influenced economic and social forces. The processes in Britain, which seem to have drastically limited their role, can be summarized as follows:

1. The eighteenth and nineteenth centuries saw an implicit division of powers

between the 'high politics' of defence and foreign policy, centred in London, and the 'low politics' of the localities (health, welfare, transport, maintenance of order) which were very much in the hands of self-nominated notables. The emergence of a strong national executive and a unitary system of government in London masked the realities of the dispersed system of power. The prestige and unity of the London-based elites produced the impression of a strong centralized state, especially as for most of this period economic liberalism was proving so successful and the society was unusually homogeneous and secure from outside threats. Not only did the national governments find it unnecessary to establish strong linkages with economic and other groups in society, but the nature of the political settlement and division of labour with the localities actually forbade it. There was thus no need nor occasion for the centre to ally with economic or social groups to overcome regional resistance or to impose a centralized administration, as occurred in France both before and after the Revolution or in Germany and Italy with national unification. Where linkages were established it was on an *ad hoc*, functionally fragmented basis, lacking co-ordination or general policy direction.

2. The relative independence (or autonomy) of local government, unions, business, police, courts, and so on, can be traced to this period. When industrialization produced a more reformist Liberal party and a new socialist party, they too took on the attitudes to governing of the established elites. Hence neither the politicians (old or new), nor the civil servants, perceived any need to move into society to negotiate support, to build a consensus, to create hierarchical relationships incorporating economic interests (in particular) into decision-making structures.

3. The advent of total war, the emergence of a powerful labour movement and serious economic dislocation in an increasingly changing and unpredictable world did, of course, force governments to intervene more and more in economic and social life. Chapters 2 and 7 especially have documented the extensive nature of such intervention, involving close contacts between affected interests, lower authorities and central government. However, intervention took on particular forms which in the past has limited and continues to limit its effectiveness:

   (a) It often consists of *ad hoc*, unco-ordinated action inspired by a particular problem or policy.

   (b) Intervention is also functionally differentiated and fragmented (e.g. individual firms have access to the Department of Trade and Industry on a piecemeal rather than a systematic basis).

   (c) Individual local governments often have strong links with Whitehall, but few horizontal links at the grass roots. Corresponding horizontal links at the central level are (historically) also weak. Home Office/ police/judicial relations are similarly fragmented.

   (d) Underlying this lack of contact and strengthened by it is an active distaste among elected politicians and administrators for systematic and detailed intervention. Hence great discretion is accorded lower-level authorities – whether they be police, army, judges, local authorities, agencies, various organized interests, or corporations – to implement policy in functionally distinct areas.

(e) The distaste for detailed intervention has both produced and been justified by an adherence to simple, general solutions to economic and social problems. Such solutions have been patterned on the free trade and non-interventionist policies which worked so successfully in the nineteenth century. The most obvious successor was Keynesian macro-economic planning. Precisely because this rested on central manipulation of finances without any detailed follow-up, it was universally accepted for thirty years. The universalistic principles on which the welfare state was built are also compatible with this tradition. Providing benefits for all rather than discriminating between recipients according to means-tested criteria reduced the state role to a minimum. Contemporary restriction of public expenditures without detailed follow-up, and comprehensive privatization, are in the same tradition.

(f) Hence, as pressures have increased, successive governments have found themselves obliged to confront individual lower-level groups and authorities, often in ways leading to serious conflict, especially as the political opposition tends to back those resisting central direction. Examples are the confrontations with both unions and local governments in the early and mid-1980s. Governments lack both the central co-ordinating structures and institutions and the vertical authority structures which more corporatist relationships could provide.

Developments in the post-war period

Against this background post-war developments fall into an entirely understandable pattern. With the first limited attempts by governments to manage aspects of social change on a permanent basis during the 1930s and 1940s a fragile consensus with the leading economic and political actors of society was established. The Labour triumph of 1945 precipitated a flood of social and economic reforms which led to a greatly enhanced role for government at all levels.

Crucially, however, amid the frenzy of activity associated with the Second World War and its aftermath, little in the way of permanent or fundamental changes in the role of the state occurred. The machinery of government remained virtually unchanged. Vertical linkages between central officials and the leading economic and social groups in society remained weak. And when new linkages were forged they tended to be between central government and business and labour elites who often had little contact with or control over their own members. The institutions of the state itself remained fragmented. The judiciary was fiercely independent; the police remained largely under local control. Local governments, in spite of being given vast new responsibilities, were controlled indirectly by statute and through the purse-strings. Central government did not impose its own agents (such as prefects in France) on the system. Finally, important divisions within central government, and particularly between the Treasury and the spending departments, persisted.

So, in spite of greatly increased public expenditures (and the higher public expectations of government which they brought), British politicians continued to depend on remarkably undeveloped institutions of co-ordination and control. It was almost as if the pulling of levers in Whitehall and Westminster was all that was needed to operate the new system. Keynesian demand management, with its emphasis on macro-economic policy, almost certainly reinforced such views. To reform the economy, detailed micro-intervention was unnecessary. All that was needed was a change in public expenditure or in fiscal and monetary policy and 'all would be well'.

At least until the 1960s, Labour governments were as prone to see the world in general terms as were Conservatives. In the context of relative economic prosperity and a broad acceptance of the traditional view of the constitution and party system, it is perhaps not surprising that politicians of all shades broadly agreed that the system worked. Why, after all, propose a stronger state, more planning, co-ordination and control when Britain was widely recognized as stable, efficient and politically mature?

When perceptions of Britain's reduced international role provoked attempts to reverse it, notably through economic development in the 1960s, the inherited machinery of government proved increasingly ineffective for the kind of detailed societal intervention and indicative planning that was felt to be required. To take one telling example: in the late 1970s the government invested close to £100 million to set up a car-manufacturing firm (de Lorean) in Belfast. Having done this, total operational control was left in the hands of the American founder, so sponsoring ministries were taken totally by surprise by his bankruptcy and eventual disgrace in the 1980s. The firm had not been monitored even to the extent that the civil servants knew of its month-by-month economic prospects. Within the British administrative tradition there was of course no reason why they should: their job was to dispense money in terms of general criteria, not follow through delivery in detail.

The increasingly active role of government exposed the shortcomings of the system and led to a number of alternative strategies or paths which governments could follow. Most of these involved ways whereby governments might increase supervision or accommodate the interests of societal groups.

(a) The technocratic answer

Assuming economic intervention was necessary along the lines detailed in Chapter 1, one answer was to reform the traditional machinery of government. Attempts to do this dominated the 1960s and the early 1970s. The mood was predominantly technocratic. Little was wrong with the party and electoral system or with the actual policies of governments. It was assumed that the welfare state and Keynesian demand management were inviolable foundations upon which policy was based. What apparently was defective was the linkage between these and society at large. Thus the Civil Service was branded as old-fashioned and unresponsive. The Treasury, in particular, was considered unable to take the longer view which planning required. Local governments were too small to operate with necessary economies of scale and required amalgamation into larger units. Industry and the unions were basically sound but needed the aid and guidance of a reformed governmental system intent on economic growth. Such assumptions led successive governments to embark on a series of reforms and reorganizations (for details see Chapters 1 and 2). Experience of these showed that reforms were often very difficult to achieve, even internally – witness the weakening of the Fulton recommendations (1968–9) on reform of the Civil Service, or the compromises forced on local government reorganization in 1974.

But more importantly, the reforms revealed the fundamental weakness of British governments when they attempted to influence, persuade, cajole or coerce the main economic and political actors in British society. Incomes policies foundered on the rocks of trade union resistance. Price controls were often opposed by industry. Individual firms shied away from anything but a voluntary or highly flexible industrial policy. The Treasury was constantly suspicious of long-term planning or any agency established to promote it. Many local governments showed a marked reluctance to accept central government's *diktats*.

Of course, in theory, British central governments could do virtually anything. Party discipline, Cabinet and unitary government should ensure this. Perhaps successive governments' reliance on administrative reforms shows that they too believed the myth. More fundamental changes in polity and society were considered unnecessary. But as the individual chapters of this volume have shown, both British government and British society are much more fragmented than either the traditional view or the technocratic critique would have us believe. Administrative reform was piecemeal at best and has certainly failed to make any discernible improvement in the quality of economic policy.

(b) Negotiating with groups – the corporatist alternative

If the problem lies in the independent power of societal groups, which governments cannot effectively coerce, perhaps these should be drawn into the process of negotiation and consultation instead?

An obvious solution is to treat these as equals and buy or win their support. This would involve mutual concessions, on the part of government as well as of the other participants, but it would be worthwhile in return for effective and workable agreements. Governments were driven to such negotiations in the 1970s. The Labour government's Social Contract with the trade unions in 1974–8, when the government traded legal concessions and price restraint for limits on wage increases, is the major example.

Such mutual recognition is often described as 'tripartism', a form of 'societal corporatism' which emphasizes the need for co-operation between government and the peak associations representing both sides of industry, the TUC and the CBI. This will be brought about by growing recognition of common interests (e.g. the benefits of greater prosperity). While some disagreements will remain, these can be limited to specific policy details. In particular the organizations involved in the negotiations have to set aside fundamental disagreements about ultimate goals in order to arrive at agreed solutions to individual problems. In this process of negotiation all three participants must have influence on the development of policy. The government cannot expect to dominate and coerce, since this would simply mean that the other groups would feel no obligation to recommend acceptance to their members. Such acceptance is of course a crucial part of the arrangements. There is no point in leaders making agreements if their members do not accept the outcomes. It is here that corporatism or tripartism as a description of what is actually going on reveals a fatal flaw. It is only too obvious in the British case that organizations cannot bind all their members, and the 'peak associations' such as the TUC and the CBI are particularly weak in that respect.

To some extent, however, the weakness extends to all the functional groups representing economic interests. Even a powerful individual union such as the Transport and General Workers' finds it difficult to control its individual sections, while these in turn find it difficult to exact compliance from committees of shop stewards in individual factories. (Such committees in many cases were in fact promoted by communists or other left-wingers to strengthen grass-roots representatives against the official union leadership.) On the other side, even the powerful financial interests of the City of London are divided by sharp conflicts of interest. So there is little chance of finding a set of generally supported top-level representatives with whom to do business.

To the extent that corporatism identifies a growing tendency for societal interests to build themselves into organizations with a permanent bureaucracy and some kind of representative leadership, it is undoubtedly right. It is also correct in its recognition of the power of such groups. This is what has driven governments from time to time into seeking some accommodation with them. On the other hand, the diagnosis is surely over-optimistic in assuming that leaders can control their members more effectively than the government itself can, through legislation or other means. (Neither government nor group leaders are *very* effective.) Corporatism also assumes the existence of enough agreement on fundamentals to provide a basis for constructive negotiation, whereas it is the creation of such a consensus that is the root of the problem. If sufficient agreement existed in the first place, negotiation would probably be unnecessary, as what the government did would in any case attract support.

(c) Thatcherism 1979–90

It is against these earlier efforts at improving the ability of governments to direct societal developments, and particularly economic growth, that the policies of the Conservative governments of the 1980s must be seen. These are often summed up in the one word, Thatcherism, reflecting the dominant position and 'conviction politics' of the Prime Minister.

In fact, however, 'Thatcherism' was an evolving body of policies which changed fairly radically in itself over time. At least three major tendencies were involved, which to some extent succeeded each other over the 1980s:

(i) Monetarism and limited intervention: 1979–82

A first reaction to the corporatist and pro-union tendencies of the preceding Labour government was for government to distance itself once more from society. Hence, on coming to power, the Thatcher government rejected incomes policies and made a commitment to withdrawing from direct intervention in the economy. The government could not withdraw rapidly, however. It remained responsible for a range of industries and organizations which could not easily and quickly be returned to the private sector. Moreover union power remained formidable and in its first years the Thatcher government generally avoided confrontation with the more powerful unions – and especially the miners.

Instead, the government pursued a strategy of strict monetary rectitude. Convinced that control of the money supply was the key to reducing inflation, it embarked on a high-interest-rate, tight-money policy – which greatly reduced the level of economic activity in the economy. Part and parcel of this was a fierce commitment to balance the national accounts by reducing government expenditure in relation to income. These policies came to be known as 'monetarism', which offered a philosophical justification for government withdrawing from detailed societal intervention. Instead, government could revert to its traditional general policy role in which manipulating monetary aggregates was all it needed to do in the public sphere.

(ii) Free market, strong state: 1982–6

Because of the fragmented nature of the British polity, however, money and credit were not exclusively under the control of central government. Its non-executant role meant that local government, nationalized industries and the Health Service dispensed a major part of it. Moreover, the unions could disrupt government policies of non-intervention in industrial matters by strikes against closure and redundancy which affected vital services like fuel and water supply.

Accordingly, the central government became increasingly involved in confrontation with unions and local governments, which involved in the former case the use of police powers and coercive legislation on an unprecedented scale. The direct attempts to control local government through rate-capping and abolition have been described in Chapter 7. Coupled with Mrs Thatcher's increasingly autocratic behaviour after her election victories in 1983 and 1987, her intolerance of criticism and manipulation of information to discredit opponents and protect herself, this led to the paradoxical situation in which government disengagement from the economy was being pursued by stronger state intervention in politics and society. Coupled with technocratic changes inherited from earlier periods, this added up to a general impression of increasing state power at odds with other elements in Thatcherite thinking.

(iii) Privatization and internal markets: 1986–90s

Side by side with the assertion of state power other policies were developing which came to greater prominence in the Conservative governments of the 1990s. The desire to restore free competition and autonomous markets led increasingly to sales of nationalized industry from 1983 onwards. Their unexpected popularity with small investors stimulated the government into making them a centrepiece of its policy and into breaking up and selling off even such 'natural monopolies' as electricity, gas, water and rail transport.

Privatization had an impact beyond the purely economic sphere, however, since it provided a solution to several policy dilemmas at the same time:

1. It provided an economic policy for government in keeping with its own preferences for, and administrative traditions of, non-intervention. Essentially, the policy was to free as much of the market as possible, and to provide optimal conditions for competition and private investment (such as low inflation and limited government borrowing). This had political pay-offs too: credit could be taken for the boom of 1984–9 while the government had distanced itself sufficiently from the economy to avoid some of the blame for the severe recession of 1989–93.

2. Privatization also provided an answer to the stand-off between central and local government in controlling expenditures, and the resistance of unions and professional bodies to government policies in education and the Health Service. While these could not be straightforwardly privatized they could be transformed through the creation of internal markets. Either existing entities like council departments, hospitals, general practices and schools could be transformed into suppliers and purchasers of services, with contractual relationships enforcing certain conditions. Or direct privatization could create firms and trusts supplying council, medical and educational services. As we saw in Chapter 2 with 'Next Steps', the same system was applied to central government departments, thus distancing the higher civil servants and their political masters even more from direct intervention in society.

3. A further advantage of privatization and internal markets was that they could be enshrined in general legislation and then left to others – courts, local authorities, Health Service boards – to enforce. This tactic had already been used in the trade union legislation of the mid-1980s, where resistance brought unions up against the ordinary courts and converted their actions into law-breaking rather than defiance of government. Similarly, poll taxes were enforced by local councils, so non-payment hurt them and restricted their activities even if the central government in this case was blamed. General legislation, rather than direct administrative intervention of the kind favoured by governments in the 1960s and 1970s, is more effective in bringing about the desired changes. It is more congenial not only to the free-market, neo-liberal outlook of the new Conservatives but also to the whole British administrative tradition.

Fragmentation: from problem to policy

The Conservative policies of privatization and disengagement do, by definition, leave to a range of societal actors and interests responsibility for the provision of a wide range of goods and services. Will this not reduce the scope of government activity and therefore the potential for coherent and effective policy-making? Possibly, but it also allows government the luxury of avoiding *direct* responsibility for mistakes in these areas. It will, by implication, only play a direct role when 'market failure' occurs or in those areas where market-type solutions are inapplicable.

Policies always carry substantive implications. Three obvious ones following from the 'new conservatism' of the 1990s are:

1. The government has effectively resigned itself to accepting whatever growth rate the British economy is capable of achieving of its own accord. The historical record suggests that this is around 2 to 3 per cent, a level which is generally lower than that of developed economies like Germany and Japan, and which was consequently regarded as failure and decline in the 1960s and 1970s (and even 1980s). By giving up intervention as a general policy (whatever the enlarged Department of Trade, Energy and Industry may try to do) the government has effectively left the British economy in other hands – increasingly those of international capital. With integration into a European economy through economic and monetary union, this may well be a course forced on all national governments within the Community. Perceptions that this may be the case are at the heart of opposition to the Maastricht treaty, from Conservative and Labour members of Parliament alike. Even amid the very serious political problems which faced the Major government on this subject in late 1992, however, a substantial majority of MPs supported further European union.

   As far as the public sector is concerned, the main value underpinning the post-war settlement and the welfare state, *equality*, has been replaced by a striving for *efficiency*. Recent Conservative governments have been convinced that a leaner, more cost-effective public sector will improve both the quality of services and will have indirect benefits for the economy generally. Whatever transpires, one thing is certain: an intellectual revolution has occurred in the way we think about public-sector provision. Opposition parties may complain that the government has gone too far in its quest for efficiency, but the terms of the debate have been all but transformed. No longer does any party argue the case for wholesale nationalization or income security policies based solely on notions of universalism. Instead, all accept the need for efficiency, but argue on the ways in which this might be achieved.

2. A 'hands-off' policy and 'value for money' in local and social services will probably mean that the weaker groups in society have less support. Coupled with a welfare income support policy which is increasingly selectivist and limited, this implies a continuation of the 1980s trends towards a more differentiated and unequal society and greater regional disparities inside Britain. This is likely to stoke discontent among the disadvantaged groups. For the reasons given in Chapter 5 the Labour party is unlikely to be able to convert this into electoral victory, either on its own or in alliance with the Liberal Democrats. While movements for

constitutional change may spread, they are unlikely to carry through significant changes without winning political power.

Deprived of a conventional political outlet, social discontent could express itself in extra-constitutional movements of the kind seen during the 1980s. The most severe political challenge to the existing set-up is likely to come from Scotland, where greater social deprivation is also fuelled by local nationalism. One should note, however, that a Conservative government could buy off regional discontent fairly easily through political devolution. As the example of Northern Ireland shows (with full devolution from 1922 to 1972), such a solution can co-exist with centralized government from Westminster.

3. Fragmentation and a reduced role for central governments do support a certain kind of pluralism. Under the new arrangements in health and education, for example, patients and parents should exercise more control over the delivery of services. Majoritarian democracy, however, may work less well than in the past. For one thing, many of the functions of government, national and local, have passed – or will soon pass – into private hands or into the hands of non-elected boards. While decision-makers in these organizations may be accountable to official watchdogs (such as OFTEL) or to 'consumers' via nominated board members, they are clearly not directly accountable to the electorate. For another thing, opposition parties seem incapable – at least for the foreseeable future – of winning general elections. Without the regular transference of power which was always identified as the very essence of British democracy, opposition to government policies may pass to extra-constitutional activities and movements.

In summary, the new political settlement of the 1990s may produce solutions to some of society's problems and provide short-term political stability. But it may also hold longer-term dangers for social peace and constitutional democracy.

References and bibliography

As each chapter summarises a variety of findings and discussions, and also reports original research, we have not deemed it necessary to clutter the text with detailed references on each point. Generally these have been given only when another author was directly quoted, where a table was based upon particular references, or where a whole section of the discussion was based on one book. The purpose of this note is to give detailed references for the main sources for each chapter. Generally these divide between broad treatments which provide a good overview of a particular topic, and detailed studies on which we have relied for supporting evidence. Books with broader coverage are generally listed first under each heading.

Place of publication is London except where otherwise stated.

Chapter 1   Economic difficulties and government response 1931–1993

C. Barnett (1986), *The Audit of War*, Macmillan.

S.H. Beer (1965), *Modern British Politics*, Faber.

D. Coates and J. Hillar (eds) (1986), *The Economic Decline of Modern Britain: The Debate between Left and Right*, Wheatsheaf.

D. Foley (1963), *Controlling London's Growth*, University of California Press.

A. Gamble (1988), *The Free Economy and the Strong State: The Politics of Thatcherism*, Macmillan.

P. Hall (1986), *Governing the Economy: The Politics of State Intervention in Britain and France*, Cambridge, Polity Press.

P.M. Jackson (1992), 'Economic Policy', in D. Marsh and R.A.W. Rhodes, *Implementing Thatcherite Policies*, Milton Keynes, Open University Press.

J. Leruez (1975), *Economic Planning and Politics in Britain*, Oxford, Martin Robertson.

K. Middlemas (1979), *Politics in Industrial Society*, Deutsch.

M. Shanks (1977), *Planning and Politics*, Allen & Unwin.

Chapter 2   Changing networks

G. Alderman (ed.) (1984), *Pressure Groups and British Government*, Longman.

A.H. Birch (1964), *Representative and Responsible Government*, Allen & Unwin.

W. Grant (1989), *Pressure Groups, Policy and Democracy in Britain*, Philip Allan.

J. Greenaway, S. Smith, J. Street (1992), *Deciding Factors in British Politics*, Routledge.

H. Heclo and A. Wildavsky (1974), *The Private Government of Public Money*, Macmillan.

P. Hennessy (1989), *Whitehall*, Secker & Warburg.

D. Marsh (1992), *The New Politics of British Trade Unions: Union Power and the Thatcher Legacy*, Macmillan.

C. Ponting (1985), *Whitehall: Tragedy and Farce*, Hamish Hamilton.

Chapter 3   Cabinet co-ordination or prime ministerial dominance

B. Donoughue (1987), *Prime Minister*, Cape.

P. Gordon Walker (1970), *The Cabinet*, Cape.

P. Hennessy (1986), *Cabinet*, Blackwell.

S. James (1992), *British Cabinet Government*, Routledge.

A. King (ed.) (1985), *The British Prime Minister*, Macmillan.

J. Mackintosh (1962), *The British Cabinet*, Stevens.

P. Madgwick (1991), *British Government: The Central Executive territory*, Phillip Allan.

R. Skidelsky (ed.) (1989), *Thatcherism*, Blackwell.

Chapter 4   The place of Parliament

A. Adonis (1990), *Parliament Today*, Manchester University Press.

B. Cain, J. Ferejohn and M. Fiorina (1987), *The Personal Vote: Constituency Service and Electoral Independence*, Cambridge, Mass., Harvard University Press.

J.A.G. Griffith and M. Ryle (1989), *Parliament: Functions, Practice and Procedures*, Sweet & Maxwell.

D. Marsh and M. Read (1987), *Private Members' Bills*, Cambridge University Press.

P. Norton (1980), *Dissension in the House of Commons 1974–9*, Oxford University Press.

P. Norton (1981), *The Commons in Perspective*, Oxford, Blackwell.

P. Norton (ed.) (1990), *Parliaments in Western Europe*, Cass.

M. Ryle and P.G. Richards (eds) (1988), *The Commons Under Scrutiny*, Routledge.

Chapter 5   Parties and electors

D. Butler and D. Kavanagh (1988), *The British General Election of 1987*, Macmillan.

D. Denver and G. Hands (1992), *Issues and Controversies in British Voting Behaviour*, Harvester Wheatsheaf.

A. Heath, R. Jowell and J. Curtice (1985), *How Britain Votes*, Oxford, Pergamon Press.

A. Heath *et al.* (1991), *Understanding Political Change*, Oxford, Pergamon Press.

W. Miller *et al.* (1990), *How Voters Change*, Oxford, Clarendon Press.

R. Rose and I. McAllister (1990), *The Loyalties of Voters*, Sage.

R.J. Johnston, C.J. Pattie and J.G. Allsopp (1988), *A Nation Dividing?* Longman.

Chapter 6   Political communications

The most useful general books are J. Tunstall, *The Media in Britain*, Constable, 1985; J. Curran and J. Seaton, *Power without Responsibility: the Press and Broadcasting in Britain*, Routledge, 1988; and R. Negrine, *Politics and the Mass Media in Britain*, Routledge, 1989. For a recent history see C. Seymour-Ure, *The British Press and Broadcasting since 1945*, Oxford, Blackwell, 1991. One general book on the media is D. Barratt, *Media Sociology, Communications Theory*, 2nd edn Sage, 1987.

On the political management of the news, see M. Cockerell, P. Hennessy and D. Walker, *Sources Close to the Prime Minister*, Macmillan, 1984; P. Golding and P. Elliot, *Making the News*, Longman, 1979; and (a general book) T. H. Qualter, *Opinion Control in the Democracies*, Macmillan, 1985. M. Pinto-Duschinsky, 'Trends in British party funding 1983–1987', *Parliamentary Affairs*, April 1989: 197–212, discusses party advertising.

On media bias and news presentation, see M. Hollingsworth, *The Press and Political Dissent*, Pluto Press, 1986, and the Glasgow Media Group Studies: *Bad News*, Routledge & Kegan Paul, 1976; *Really Bad News*, Writers and Readers, 1982; and *War and Peace News*, Milton Keynes, Open University Press, 1985, and the extended criticism of the first book in M. Harrison, *TV News: Whose Bias?*, Hermitage, Berks, Policy Journals, 1985. See also V. Adams, *The Media and the Falklands Campaign*, Macmillan, 1986.

Chapter 7   The other governments of Britain

S. Baine, J. Benington and J. Russell (1991), *Changing Europe: Challenges facing the voluntary and community sectors in the 1990s*, NCVO.

R. Batley and G. Stoker (eds) (1991), *Local Government in Europe*, Macmillan.

J. Bulpitt (1983), *Territory and Power in the United Kingdom*, Manchester University Press.

H. Butcher, I. Law, R. Leach and M. Mullard (1990), *Local Government and Thatcherism*, Routledge.

N. Flynn (1990), *Public Sector Management*, Harvester Wheatsheaf.

J. Gyford, S. Leach and C. Game (1989), *The Changing Politics of Local Government*, Unwin Hyman.

J. Gyford (1991), *Citizens, Consumers and Councils*, Macmillan.

C. Ham (1991), 'Health and Community Care' in F. Terry and H. Roberts (eds), *Public Domain 1991*, Public Finance Foundation.

J. Kellas (1984), *The Scottish Political System*, 3rd edn, Cambridge University Press.

R. Klein (1989), *The Politics of the NHS*, 2nd edn, Longman.

C. Lambert and G. Bramley (1991), 'Local Government' in F. Terry and H. Roberts (eds), *Public Domain 1991*, Public Finance Foundation.

E. Page and M. Goldsmith (eds) (1987), *Central and Local Government Relations: A Comparative Analysis of West European Unitary States*, Sage.

R. Rhodes (1992), 'Local Government' in D. Marsh and R. Rhodes (eds), *Thatcherism: Audit of an Era*, Milton Keynes, Open University Press.

N. Small (1989), *Politics in the NHS*, Milton Keynes, Open University Press.

J. Stewart and G. Stoker (eds) (1989), *The Future of Local Government*, Macmillan.

G. Stoker (1989), *New Management Trends*, Local Government Training Board.

G. Stoker (1990), 'Government Beyond Whitehall' in P. Dunleavy, A. Gamble and G. Peele (eds), *Developments in British Politics 3*, Macmillan.

G. Stoker (1991), *The Politics of Local Government*, 2nd edn, Macmillan.

G. Wistow (1992), 'The National Health Service' in D. Marsh and R. Rhodes (eds), *Thatcherism: Audit of an Era*, Milton Keynes, Open University Press.

D. Wynn (1991), 'Local Services in Scotland', in F. Terry and H. Roberts (eds), *Public Domain 1991*, Public Finance Foundation.

Chapter 8   Preserving order and administering justice

J.A.G. Griffith (1981), *The Politics of the Judiciary*, Fontana.

M. Hough and P. Mayhew (1985), *Taking Account of Crime: Key Findings From the 1984 British Crime Survey*, HMSO.

R. Morgan and D. Smith (eds) (1989), *Coming to Terms with Policing*, Routledge.

T. Morris (1989), *Crime and Criminal Justice Since 1945*, Blackwell.

C.R. Munro (1987), *Studies in Constitutional Law*, Butterworth.

G. Northam (1988), *Shooting in the Dark*, Faber.

P. Norton (1982), *The Constitution in Flux*, Blackwell.

A. Patterson (1982), *The Law Lords*, Macmillan.

R. Reiner (1985), *The Politics of the Police*, Wheatsheaf.

D. Robertson (1982), 'Judicial Ideology in the House of Lords: a Jurimetric Analysis', *British Journal of Political Science*, 12, 1–25.

Lord L. Scarman (1974), *English Law: The New Dimension*, Stevens.

Chapter 9   A third level of government

S. George (1991), *Politics and Policy in the European Community*, 2nd edn, Oxford.

S. George (1990), *An Awkward Partner: Britain in the European Community*, Oxford.

J. Harrop (1989), *The Political Economy of Integration in the European Community*, Edward Elgar.

E. Kirchner (1992), *Decision Making in the European Community: The Council Presidency and European Integration*, Manchester University Press.

W. Nicholl and T. Salmon (1990), *Understanding the European Communities*, Simon & Schuster.

W. Wallace (ed.) (1990), *The Dynamics of European Integration*, Pinter.

Chapter 10   Relations with outside governments

J. Baylis (1984), *Anglo-American Defence Relations*, 2nd edn, Macmillan.

P. Byrd (ed.) (1988), *British Foreign Policy Under Thatcher*, Philip Allan.

J. Burton *et al.* (1984), *Britain Between East and West: A Concerned Independence*, Gower.

L. Freedman (ed.) (1983), *The Troubled Alliance: Atlantic Relations in the 1980s*, Gower.

W.R. Louis and H. Bull (eds), *The Special Relationship: Anglo-American Relations Since 1945*, Oxford, Clarendon.

B. Porter (1984), *The Lion's Share: A Short History of British Imperialism*, Longman.

J. Roper (ed.) (1985), *The Future of British Defence Policy*, Gower.

D. Sanders (1990), *Losing an Empire, Finding a Role: British Foreign Policy since 1945*, Macmillan.

W. Wallace (1991), 'Foreign Policy and the National Identity in the UK', *International Affairs* 67, 65–80.

Notes on contributors

Ian Budge Professor of Government at the University of Essex. He is the author of numerous books and articles including *Parties and Democracy, Coalition and Government Functioning in 20 Countries* (with Hans Keman) (1990).

Ivor Crewe Professor of Government at the University of Essex and Pro-Vice Chancellor, Academic. He is the author and editor of several definitive studies on British elections and has recently published the *British Elections and Parties Yearbook* (1991).

Anthony King Professor of Government at the University of Essex specialising in the study of executives. He is the author of several studies of the British Prime Minister and the editor of *The New American Political System* (1990).

Emil Kirchner Professor of European Studies at the University of Essex and Director of the Centre for European Studies. He is an authority on the EC and the author of *Decision Makin""'g in the European Community: The Council Presidency and European Integration* (1992).

Vivien Lowndes Lecturer in Public Policy and Management at the Institute of Local Government Studies, University of Birmingham. She has worked as a Policy Officer for a London local authority. Her publications include a number of articles on local authority decentralisation.

David McKay Professor of Government at the University of Essex. He is a specialist on American and comparative politics. Recent publications include *American Politics and Society* (Third edition, 1993).

Kenneth Newton Professor of Government at the University of Essex and Executive Director of the European Consortium for Political Research. He has written widely on urban and comparative politics and is presently working on a comparative study of censorship.

Melvyn Read He is Lecturer in Politics at the Queen's University of Belfast. He is a specialist in British politics and is the co-author of *Private Members' Bills* (1988) (with David Marsh).

David Robertson A Fellow of St Hughes College and a Lecturer in the sub-faculties of Politics and Sociology at the University of Oxford. He has published across a wide range of interests including electoral behaviour, the English judicial system and defence policy.

David Sanders Reader in Government at the University of Essex and Head of Department. He has published widely on government popularity and in international relations. He is the author of *Losing an Empire, Finding a Role: British Foreign Policy Since 1945.*

Graham Wilson Professor of Political Science at the University of Wisconsin, Madison. He is one of America's leading authorities on interest group politics and is the author of standard works on American and European interest groups.

Index